# The Life of a Salesman

# The
# LIFE *of a*
# SALESMAN

## A Spellbinding Story by a Modern-Day Horatio Alger

## MARC VAN BUSKIRK

An IMC Publication ☐ La Jolla, California

Editing:  Julie Olfe, La Jolla, CA
Book design:  Sara Patton, Maui, HI
Cover design:  Lightbourne Images, Ashland, OR
Cover art:  Jesse Bilyeu, Santa Rosa, CA

ISBN 0-9646687-0-X
Library of Congress Catalog Card # TXU 662-683

# Dedication

---

In memory of my wife, Jane . . .

For my children, Ann, Marc, Amy, and Pandora . . .

And for salesmen—past, present, and future.

# Contents

# Acknowledgments

I first and foremost want to thank my daughter, Ann, for her insistence that I convert the seemingly endless stories I would relate to her into a book.

To my editor, Julie Olfe, for her excellent work and for encouraging me by her praise, which normally would be reserved only for the very best of writers, I am sincerely appreciative.

# Part One

---

# The Uphill Battles Begin

# Chapter 1

*Liberty Magazine,* five cents a copy—my entrance into the world of marketing. The bag of *Libertys* with its loop around my neck was three feet long, and I was only four feet tall. The sight of me was enough to get a nickel out of almost anyone. Blue-eyed, blond, smiling, adorable, irresistible. I'd sell out my bag of ten magazines and run back to my supplier for more. Although I didn't know it at the time, I was learning self-confidence and discovering that if you could sell something, you would never starve. This was essential knowledge, considering the mean cruel world out there, then and now.

Many order-writing years later, I came to the conclusion that many people are timid about presenting their thoughts and ideas and even convictions on any subject. They are naturally intimidated by presence—impressed by title, age, prestigious names, manners, education, and demeanor, as well as by banks, cars, decor, clothing, and houses. Frightening as all hell. However, no one has ever been killed or even scratched as a salesman; this is a very safe profession.

At the age of seven, I turned to what is today called "creative marketing." This is the evolution from "building a better mouse trap" to "finding a need and filling it." I would look out of my mom and dad's apartment. (Almost everyone in Manhattan lived in apartments, now called condominiums. Condos were an unheard-of concept until someone became creative. You see, it's all so simple to be creative. Why rent when you can sell and pick up a management fee to boot?)

Anyway, as I looked out, I saw storm clouds coming in from the west. Mom asked me to go on an errand, and in doing so I passed the subway station at 191st Street. It was raining cats and dogs, and a large group of people were waiting under the shed of the entrance. What does a brilliant, marketing genius-to-be do? Of course he runs home, finds two umbrellas, and races back to the station, opening them up and crying, "Umbrellas!" I made a fucking fortune!

I'd hand a person the second umbrella and walk him home. I received a reward of ten cents, fifteen cents, sometimes a quarter. The subway ride was only a nickel in those days. I made more money than the subway did, without a capital investment. A beautiful concept for a business—any business.

This was my first introduction to the sensitive law of timing, which is, "A good idea at the wrong time is as unrewarding as a bad idea at the right time." You see, if the morning started out rainy, people would all take their own umbrellas, and my market would be totally ruined. Starting at midday I'd keep an eye on clouds coming over the Hudson River. I became an expert on whether it would rain or shine. The rain could start at 3:00 p.m., but my business would not start then. The beautiful rain had to come around 5:00 p.m. for maximum returns. You have to pay attention to timing. If I had franchised (another unknown word back then) the concept, I'd have made a fee from every kid who worked the station, plus one from all the other kids who worked every other station, over a hundred of them. I might have engaged the services of Brinks! ... Not really. This concept was not patentable, copyrightable, or franchisable. Too many rat fink kids would have opened up their own umbrellas.

This leads one to believe that it's better to continue to create, and let others copy. More people, by far, copy than create. In most cases people just say, "Why didn't I think of that?" and proceed to improve on the idea or product. Japan is a perfect example. We invented the telephone, radio, television, automobile, microwave oven, electric razor, airplane, computer, and put a man on the moon. (Please American Papa-san, create something new. We're reaching saturation levels on our copying production.) Thank goodness for all the laws and royalty arrangements that protect creators. However, a thinly veiled variation of a product can still sneak in to cast doubt on its originality, especially after a patent search comes up with a similar product patented in, say, 1874. I believe marketing ideas should also be patented. If they were, I would, for starters, be known as the originator and CEO of the Umbrella Escort Service Corporation, a listed member of the New York Stock Exchange, which does especially well during the rainy season.

Now let's skip ahead quite a few years. I had grown up in what seemed to be a perpetual depression. It was an era when college graduates were elevator operators. God knows what the less educated did. Among the "weren't anys": there weren't any unemployment benefits, no minimum wage, no welfare checks, no food stamps, no health insurance, and no "help wanted" signs. The technological advances were all in telephones, radios, and airplanes. It was the dark ages of invention, of bringing new products to the market. I'm referring to the 1930s. The ice man still came; the coal man still ran his chute of coal into the cellar. Everyone seemed to be doing what they had always done and living with what they always had lived with. It wasn't only a depression, it was totally depressing, a fight for survival with no mercy shown for losers.

For those with vision and courage and determination, it was the best of times. So at age sixteen, I became a Fuller Brush salesman. I had a vision of knocking on doors to face the unknown with courage, and a determination not to starve to death.

The Fuller Brush Company was well known, the foremost manufacturer of all kinds of cleaning and personal care products. I wonder where it is today? In those days, its salesmen were thought of as easily as the Culligan man and the Avon lady today. The Fuller Brush man came calling at your home. People were trained to expect a call every two months. When the doorbell rang and the man said, "Your Fuller Brush man, I have a new sample for you," he was usually let in . . . usually.

First, I had to attend a training meeting, learn how to use the brushes, what each one would accomplish, etc. About six of us came together for the class. The room had about two dozen chairs, four abreast. Most of us had taken seats in the back rows, when in came the manager. I remember him as a bouncy, totally enthusiastic person, a helluva personality for sales. The first thing he asked us to do was to lift up our simple wooden chairs and turn them over. We wondered why, until he turned over the chairs in the front row. All of them had a dollar bill pasted on the bottom. My God, that was a DOLLAR. That could have been my lunch at Nedick's, a five-cent hot dog and a five-cent orange, for ten days! Oh, my God! Since that day, I've always sat up front in meetings of that nature. Yes, we all have a tendency to sit in the back. We think to ourselves, it's nice and safe. They can't spot me, I'm almost invisible, I'll just blend in with the boys. Using that philosophy, you will advance rapidly as all the others begin to leave the company, get canned, or die of old age.

This sales manager would go through the line of products, tell us how to begin our approach and view a room to determine the need for a certain brush. For example, were there venetian blinds? They are always dusty; use a brush to demonstrate the difference, before and after. She has to buy it, she's embarrassed, write it down, and on to the next one. Take a sofa brush, dip it down between the pillows and lift up. The whole damn room will turn into a dust bowl; another sale. Theoretically, you could sell her a dozen different brushes before you finished or caught a lung disease.

The manager would end the meeting by asking questions about what he had tried to teach us. He'd look around for a raised hand. Finding one, he'd ask for an answer, and receiving it, would put his hand into his pocket, bring out a shiny fifty-cent piece, and flip it to the young man. The next question had six hands raised and another flying fifty-cent piece. We were going utterly mad, flailing our arms to have him choose one of us. We each left with fifty cents and remarked that that was one hell of a good meeting; what a company!

So I was outfitted with a new sample case, ready to go.

They say there is a vast difference between the classroom and the field. I am about to find out as I go into my assigned territory on my first day, for my first call. I walk up six flights of stairs, comb my hair, fix my tie, ring the bell.

A voice with a heavy Irish accent answers.

"Who is it?"

"Good morning," I reply. "It's your Fuller Brush man."

"Be gone or I'll be throwin' a bucket o' shit in your face!"

Maybe the fifth floor will be better. It can't get worse . . . unless they don't give me any warning time.

7

From this somewhat shitty beginning, things began to improve. I knocked on doors, rang those bells and started to write orders. I worked from 9 a.m. to 4:30 p.m. If I was too early, they weren't ready. If I was too late in the day, they were preparing for evening chores. I'd have worked from before they got up until they went to bed if I could. Up and down the stairs I'd go until I was red in the face, gaining precious experience in what is called house-to-house sales. My presentation became polished. My ability to distinguish between what they really needed and what they wanted produced larger and larger orders.

I was having fun, I was making money, the world was beautiful. I became the star of my Fuller Brush graduating class. Here was my manifest destiny, my career as a salesman was taking shape. But then I had to go back to high school for the fall term. My career had been nipped in the bud, perhaps, but the roots had taken hold.

I had no impossible dreams of climbing the ladder of success and entering the unknown world of owning an automobile, having my own one-room apartment, having two suits, having more than one pair of shoes, or having a selection of ties. The dream I dreamed again and again was that I would continue to eat when all about me were selling apples or standing on line waiting for a soup kitchen to open. I would wake up pretty confident that my dream would come true.

England had a deeply rooted caste system based on bloodlines, wealth, accents, and proper schools that emphatically indicated a person's place in society. Our society was clearly divided between the haves and the have-nots—those who had a job and those who were out of work. Absolutely no in-betweens. If you were a banker whose bank had failed or a broker who had resisted jumping out a window, it didn't matter that you were educated with an

M.B.A. or a Ph.D., spoke five languages or were anointed as the second coming; you had no job. And those who had one would walk by you with their eyes straight ahead, determined not to notice you; you might bite, you really might.

The time had come to let the world know I was here, to offer myself as an answer to its sales problems, to move into the big time, into a job that had prestige, class, a bag I could carry with pride. (I don't think those bags were called attaché cases back then. I remember they were called briefcases. As soon as the name changed to attaché cases, sales zoomed. Everyone felt important carrying one, although it might contain only an apple or a homemade sandwich.) My goal was to find a job that met these criteria.

Every morning I would scour the help wanted ads under "Salesman Wanted". NO . . . No . . . no. Many jobs that I would have applied for required an education I did not possess. IBM had openings for a college graduate with a B.S. degree to be a representative (Do they mean salesman?) for its new card-sorting, labeling-machine division, the forerunner of the computer age. That was beyond me. Procter & Gamble needed a college graduate, not necessarily with an M.B.A., someone with sales ability to start as a shelf-filler trainee at grocery stores, a tad before they became supermarkets. Had I but known it, it was a good start-on-the-bottom-and-work-your-way-to-the-top kind of job. I did wonder if I could get by saying "Yes, sir!" as fast and as many times as I could. (Many years later I would tell my son that if he were a gorilla dressed in a blue blazer with a buttoned-down shirt and striped tie and said "Yes, sir," he could last a week as a member of a board of directors before they became aware of who he really was.)

The mirror doesn't lie, even when one wears a disguise. All I had to offer was a pleasant personality, good looks, a neat appearance, enthusiasm, and a willingness to work hard. Sounds pretty good, except there was no substance. It was all folderol, and thousands of others offered the same. I was a white egg, a wild flower in the field, a yearling without a pedigree. At best, I was intensely ordinary in the eyes of the beholders.

But, son of a bitch, the mirror does lie. It can't reflect what is inside all of us.

There is no way to cushion the reaction one would have to my next career move. I should say job, but as future events would unfold, I have to say career. I replied to the following advertisement:

**SALESMAN**
To demonstrate new electrical appliance in department stores.
Salary & Commission.

Salary, oh my, that was attractive, there must be a catch. And a commission too! I followed the directions to heaven's door. It must be heaven, I thought as I trudged up three long flights of single-file stairs in an old building with half-smoked-glass, black-printed office windows. I was met by a frail looking elderly gentleman. He must live in the back of the office, I thought, or the stairs will be the end of him. I gave him about five more hikes and, pow!

I said, "Good morning, sir. I am applying for the sales position advertised in this morning's paper."

He introduced himself and quickly said, "You're very young. Do you have any experience in sales?"

"Yes, sir. I've worked for the Fuller Brush Company."

"What else have you done?"

I wondered if I should or should not bring up my business affiliation with *Liberty Magazine* and my independent sales program with umbrellas. I decided to keep that under wraps, in case I needed an ace in the hole.

"That's about it, sir. However, I was the top salesman in my class during summer vacation."

"Well, I'll show you what we have here, but I think you're too young for the job. What we have is an electric pants presser that will renew the crease in a man's trousers without the need and cost of sending them out to be pressed."

He then showed me a hand-held device that had two metal prongs about three inches wide and three inches deep, slightly separated to form a V. A small handle attached to the prongs with an electrical cord coming out of the back completed the unit. To demonstrate, he showed me the crease in his trouser leg; it was sharp enough to shave with.

"Wow! That's wonderful," I said.

"You have to be able to deliver a spiel on the product."

A spiel, I found, was what you say when you demonstrate. A barker would give a spiel, back in the old days of the circus or county fair.

He handed me a copy of the written spiel, asked me to study it and be prepared to go through it perfectly. I was asked to return for an afternoon performance.

"May I ask, sir, what the job pays?"

"It pays twenty-five dollars a week and a commission of twenty cents on each unit sold after you meet a quota."

"Golly! That's really good. I'll be here!"

I walked out, somewhat confident I might be hired. Settling in on a park bench to study, I began to worry that I wouldn't be able to remember the ten selling points contained in the written spiel plus the answers in the question-and-answer section.

I returned at the appointed time to find five other candidates present. The meeting got under way with the old president giving his rendition of the demonstration. We were then required, one by one, to show him our version.

By the time it was my turn, I was a nervous wreck. I could operate the dumb thing, but my spiel was something else. I got through the first part and then lost my spiel, followed by my mind. I started over, stuttering and making a few other errors, fumbling the sequence, putting the beginning at the end and the end at the beginning or close to it. Good-bye job, good-bye world, it was the end of me. With one more try, I managed a D minus and felt that with six months of practice I could master the three minutes involved.

"Young man," said the president, "you have marginal ability, but I'm going to hire you, give you the opportunity to prove yourself. I'm sending you to the department store in Wilkes-Barre, Pennsylvania. Here is a ticket for your round trip on the Greyhound bus and a check to cover your expenses based on five dollars per diem."

"Wow!"

A big WOW! My first salaried job, my first business trip. I had become a traveling salesman.

Off I went, the bus winding its way down a two-lane highway through the Pocono Mountains. This passenger was one excited kid. My premiere sortie into the wilds west of the Hudson River. We finally arrived after dropping down from the surrounding mountains into the valley that is home to the coal miners of Pennsylvania—almost another world.

I left the dimly lit bus station with its wooden benches divided by armrests, realizing I could not return there for a good night's sleep. I had to find a relatively cheap room. Relatively cheap meant no more than two dollars a night, for the three left over had to go for grub, as they say out west, in eastern Pennsylvania.

By luck I found one. Of course it was a room upstairs, with no bath, no sink, no toilet; I had to go down the hall and wait in line. Okay, no problem. After I washed up, my hunger pains came back, and I was out of there.

Wilkes-Barre was no exception to the classic American town with a main street that was interrupted by a square with a Civil War monument in the center. It was mid-evening and the town was closed except for a small greasy spoon that had a sign in the window, "Hamburgers 10 cents, Yesterday's 2 for 5 cents." Yesterday's didn't look any less appetizing than today's, and I was on a budget, to say the least.

With the craving for food gone, and the aftereffects not yet begun, I strolled around the square and stopped in front of my department store. There it was, my first store, a corner location, all of two stories high and half a block in each direction. No question it was the leading department store of the town. And so, to bed . . . burp, burp.

The next morning I was up early and waiting for the store to open. The store manager or owner was the first to arrive.

"Good morning, sir. I'm the demonstrator for the pants presser appliance."

He was very impressed that I was there before the store opened. I remembered his reaction and followed the same pattern for many years to come. It is especially effective if you are waiting outside in the rain or snow with just a touch of a shiver or a shake.

Of course I received the best location for my demonstration: on the main aisle right up front near the entrance. I was ready, open the doors, let 'em in!

Problem. They came in one at a time in ten-minute intervals, mostly the little old ladies with shopping bags who seem to be the perpetual daily customers of department stores. I wondered if they even made a purchase.

How could I demonstrate a pants presser to ladies who weren't wearing trousers? Well, I did stop them by demonstrating on a pair I had hanging up next to me. They would smile and say, "That's nice."

"It's a wonderful gift for the man in your family," I would say. No sale. I came to the conclusion that it wasn't a family-oriented town or that the men were few and far between.

This became my first business lesson in perceiving or knowing the market. The men of Wilkes-Barre were miners, wearing the clothes of the mine six days a week and then one good suit for church on Sunday. Ye gads! And there I was trying to sell a pants presser. Things picked up around noon as the younger women came in during lunch and again after work for a brief period before the store closed at six.

My spirits went right up after my first sale, started going down, then up again after my second sale. (Where are the customers? Damn, I can't sell to people I can't see.) During the long intervals between customers I would look around, then walk around the store. Merchandise was displayed on long tables with a three-inch vertical border to prevent spilling. It was all so old-fashioned and dreary.

The only thing that was fascinating was a pneumatic cylinder containing cash from a sale. It would shoot up overhead to a cashier's cage, then return with change. I loved watching it.

At the end of the day I had sold only a few pants pressers. I was very disheartened and discouraged. Tomorrow is another day, I thought. But it wasn't. It was the same as yesterday and so were the next two tomorrows. Finally, Saturday; it was shopping day, and the menfolk made their appearance. I was busy, and sold and sold. I sold all the units the store had bought.

On leaving, I said thank you to the store owner for his cooperation. He was very pleased with the results and told me I was "a fine young man and an excellent salesman." What a nice thing to say. I began to understand that man does not live by bread alone.

I suggested he place another order, which I would be happy to take back with me.

"Oh, I can't do that," he said. "The miners are about to go on strike. They will be saving their money and won't buy anything."

"What happens when they are on strike?" I asked.

"Absolutely nothing. We may as well shut the door."

"Well, then, the time to be here is when the strike is over," I said.

"Not really," he said. "Then they're broke and only spend money on food."

"Ah, yes. I understand . . . but after a period of time, surely then?" I asked.

"No, not then, they'll be getting ready to strike again!"

My reflections on the bus ride home were quite elementary. You're wasting your time during the week in small towns. The action comes on Saturday only, and you must have an advertisement to announce the product and the fact it will be demonstrated. In years ahead I would apply this simple formula over and over again.

On a loftier level of thought, years later when I was more mature, it seemed to me that the people of Wilkes-Barre were living under a Damoclean sword of uncertainty. It was clear to me that the life of a coal miner was the pits, figuratively and literally. Hence the expression "That's the pits!" is used to describe a rotten way of life or situation or, in some instances, being a parent.

John L. Lewis was president of the coal miners' union, a king with despotic control over thousands of coal miners' minds and bodies. "Strike!" he'd say, and up and out they went. "It's over!" he'd say, and down into the mines they would go. He easily defied not only management but the United States government time and time again, and he won time and time again. The threat of sending in troops was a joke. He won because his was just about the only fuel available for heating factories and homes. There were no alternatives except to freeze your tail off or shut down a factory. Naturally, the strike threat always occurred in the fall of the year. Now, that's control; that's timing.

The following Monday morning I reported to the office and related my experience to the elderly gentleman. I received some praise, not quite faint, but certainly not warm, and I began to wonder. I'd hit a home run, won the game. Why not "Great! Well done. You really proved to yourself and to me that you can do the job."? Perhaps he felt I might ask for a raise. I subsequently learned this is typical thinking on the part of management. Hell, I just wanted to keep my job. Control . . . mine was zero.

Two more out-of-city assignments yielded similar experiences, but the second one included an encounter that would lead slowly but surely to my second rung on the ladder.

During a demonstration that ended in a sale, a tall, well-dressed man in a navy blue suit, with a vest displaying a chain and a Phi Beta Kappa key, had stopped and watched my performance. I turned to him and offered to start again. He informed me it wasn't necessary and presented his card. "I'd like you to work for my company. Phone my office and make an appointment with my secretary."

"Yes, sir. What does your company do?"

"We have a much improved copy of your product, and we're opening demonstrations in many of the large department stores throughout the country."

"Yes, sir, I'll call your office. Thank you, sir."

Holy Cow! I was in demand, the first time ever! Thrill of thrills!

On the appointed day, I stood in front of the magnificent Rockefeller Center. The outside, as I looked up, was totally awesome. On the inside, I found banks of elevators with operators. An elevator supervisor, wearing a cap and a uniform with two stripes on the sleeve, shuffled people from one elevator to another. I imagined the chief of all the elevators as a four-striper.

Up I went, almost to the top. I found the office and walked in. It was very impressive in comparison to the old three-floor walk-up of my present employer. I was ushered in to the man in the three-piece suit and received a pleasant greeting. After I was seated in front of an imposing desk, he asked me to tell him something about myself. That took about a minute and a half, including the two "Yes, sirs."

"Well, I'm confident you can do the job. I watched you from afar and close up. You're good. As a matter of fact, I'm placing you in R.H. Macy and Company right here in New York City. Your salary is thirty-five dollars per week, plus a monthly bonus if you meet quota."

Holy smoke, ten dollars more per week, and Macy's too! The biggest and best department store in the world. Valhalla, here I come.

He then showed me the pants presser that he claimed was superior to mine. I had to admit it was a bit more eye-appealing, if such a thing could have appeal. But a crease is a crease. I timidly asked how his company came to manufacture the product.

"My father owns a tool and die manufacturing plant upstate. Your unit was easily duplicated with the improvements I've told you about. We're in production. As a matter of fact, we've received orders from all of the large department stores, and they're discounting the pants presser you sell. Actually, that's how I found you. I was visiting the top merchandise manager of the store you were in. Our company is always on the lookout for new products we can improve."

Now I know how the Japanese did it. They copied from Americans who copied from other Americans. Only the Japanese started after World War II, and we started after the Revolution.

One wistful thought lingered in my mind after I said, "Thank you, sir. I'll do my best. And good-bye." Wouldn't it be nice to have a family who owned a factory? One that was still open?

I informed the old gentleman of my departure from his company and wasn't questioned. I assumed he was accustomed to a frequent turnover of people and took my leave. He, in turn, subsequently faded out of the picture of this highly pressed business. Was he too old to meet with and sell to the young buyers of the major department stores, but quite compatible and comfortable with Sleepy Town, U.S.A.? Although the young believe along those lines, and I did, his problem wasn't age. He simply did not have a marketing plan to go along with a new product that was so right for the time of the depression.

In that era, there were very limited forms of marketing outlets: department stores; small household hardware stores and the distributors who served them; and catalog houses like Sears and Montgomery Ward, with relatively few store operations. Among the department stores, only two were considered to be giants of the industry: R.H. Macy and Marshall Field. Sell to them and the rest would fall like timber, in spite of their protests of "Don't tell me what Macy's doing!" However, Macy's was and is today the merchandise mart of the world. Eight stories high, covering an entire city block, dwarfing all competition in size and in assortment of merchandise of every description. In the 1930s coming in to the main floor from the street would knock your eyes out. Massive pillars to the high ceiling, wide aisles, many hundreds of shoppers, a Grand Central Station of people coming and going, all creating an atmosphere of frenzy to shop and buy.

The history of Macy's is fascinating and illuminating, a case study on every facet of retail merchandising and organization of a magnificent company. A retail Goliath, for almost a hundred years it had been impervious to changes in the marketplace, the proliferation of overabundant shopping centers, the large wholesale and discount chains, and home furnishing warehouses. But then it was almost done in by the absolute greed of a few in the company's hierarchy, who submerged it in an ocean of debt.

I've forgotten the number of my asteroid among the small stars in the sky, but it had risen. It was to shine over Macy's housewares basement, the citadel of everything new and exciting from major appliances on down to pots and pans, and below that to a pants presser.

I was instructed to meet Mr. Joe Alexander, the housewares buyer, who, later on, with just a few words, would profoundly affect my future life. His first words, after a warm greeting, were to instruct me on the rules governing nonemployees, regardless of my source of compensation. After that, he led me to my position on the floor and gave orders to have the stock brought out. Soon after, I was under way.

What a wonderful feeling! I made sale after sale. I demonstrated until I lost my voice. This was truly the big tent, a never-ending flow of people going by, a seemingly endless number of demonstrations. The basement was alive with demonstrators. No wonder Macy's was fun to visit!

People would spend hours watching one after another. The demonstrators were real pros in comparison to the sample-givers in today's stores or markets.

There was an art to stopping people, asking a question, doing things with your hands, enticing them with machines in motion. Looking down the aisle, one would see groups collected every ten yards. Of course, I'd visit every one of them and listen and watch. It was a real education in demonstration, a forum of public speaking, a timidity exterminator. After all, as the saying goes, if you don't know about the unknown, keep your mouth shut; if you are somewhat aware, you can say a few words; if you alone possess knowledge, you can talk like hell . . . and those demonstrators did.

Macy's was high on the list of must-see things in New York for the first-time visitors, ranking up there with Rockefeller Center, Radio City Music Hall, the Empire State Building, Broadway, and the Statue of Liberty. The customers, besides New Yorkers and out-of-towners, were the "haves" from South and Central America and Europe who spent freely on whatever they thought they needed. It has to be more fun to have wealth in a depression than in normal times. They were having a ball, a ten-year ball. The recessions of today are more than slightly different; they last all of six to eighteen months—a cup of tea.

I realized over the next month or two that I was doing a pretty good job, but I was still down at the bottom in the pecking order of demonstrators. My product was simply déclassé. After all, the dumb thing sold for only a few dollars in comparison to other high-priced products being demonstrated. And mine was a bit awkward to demonstrate. I'd have to get down on my haunches, hold the pants out from a man's leg and run the presser down to his ankles while I made my spiel.

One rainy day, always good for my business, I was demonstrating away on a man who had just come into the store wearing an upturned fedora. (Men wore hats in those days.) As I looked up while talking, he looked down. The moatful of rainwater collected in his brim splashed down onto my face. It seemed that everyone around had seen this happen. I can still hear the echoes of laughter that ensued. He apologized and purchased the presser out of mutual embarrassment. One day, years later, I experienced a similar situation and drew on my memory of this event to close a sale of major importance. But at the moment, my spirits were not in the "ha ha" mode.

The experience paid off years later when I called on the vice president of sales for General Electric, which had a major distribution center in New York. When I entered his office an informal group of salesmen were seated about. He greeted me warmly and suggested I give my presentation with his salesmen in attendance. Knowing I had a pretty good package, I confidently began my presentation, only to be interrupted by supposedly humorous comments from one salesman after another, changing the concept I presented into a negative. They were having a ball poking fun at every statement I made.

I stopped, put the most injured look on my face, and stared at them, not saying a word. I then bit my lip as I spoke to the VP in a suddenly quiet room.

"I'm trying very hard to do my job as best I can in the circumstances. I would only hope your people will not experience a similar situation when they are making their calls." And I started to pack my bag.

"Hold on, Marc. We're sorry. We apologize. Please continue," said the VP.

Of course I did, to a very subdued and embarrassed group. It was a foregone conclusion that I would write up a major order. Experience is priceless; that time I used em-barrassment to my advantage.

But back to Macy's. One afternoon a few days later, during my break, I strolled down the aisle past the demon-stration of the new Toastmaster pop-up toaster just being introduced, past the tried-and-true rug cleaner man who would put dirt on and wipe it off; on, off; on, off; all day long. From there it was on to a newfangled food blending machine; all the demonstrator had to do was turn it on, and the noise would stop anyone passing by. On to Revere Copper and Brass, who were just getting under way with a new copper-clad stainless steel line of pots and pans. After listening to them for a while, it seemed quite reasonable to assume one could not be a gourmet chef without those pans. It occurred to me that they could offer a chef's hat as a premium with the purchase of a set. I was curious to find out how much more expensive the new pans were than the ordinary aluminum pots and pans, and made a left turn off the main aisle to check the others.

I stopped amid a large display of all shapes and sizes. I picked up two or three and examined the price ticket and was about to walk off. And then, at the end of the counter, my eye caught something different. This pot had a cover with a tubular piece of metal protruding upward. I found I could open the pot by holding the handle at the bottom and moving the cover handle to the right. A breach lock to secure the cover to the bottom . . . but why? What is this? And what is this weight that fits over a stem of metal coming out of the center of the cover?

I looked around for a Macy's salesperson and found one. (Those were the days and years before sales clerks vanished to be replaced by merchandise that had been presold on television, leaving only the need for a checkout counter and an exit sign.)

"Can you tell me about this? It's different and costs more than all the other pots."

"It's called a pressure cooker. It's brand new, and I don't know very much about it."

"Well, what does it do?"

"All I know is that it's supposed to cook faster than a regular pot. Here's the cookbook that comes with it. Perhaps you will find some answers."

"Thank you. I will."

I began to turn the pages. Holy smoke, how exciting! Vegetables cook in three minutes, a pot roast in thirty minutes. The cooking time was incredible. The food would retain vitamins and minerals. I didn't even know that food contained any vitamins or minerals. The food would taste better than if it had been boiled or steamed because it was cooked without air. You could cook onions and string beans together without the flavors mixing. The more I read, the more excited I became. This, if true, was fantastic! The cookbook's cover said that the pot was called a Presto Pressure Cooker made by the National Pressure Cooker Company of Eau Claire, Wisconsin.

My mind was in a whirl. What do I do, who do I turn to? I'm the only person in New York who has seen it! If ever a product begged to be demonstrated, this was the one. Mr. Alexander, the buyer, would know. He knew I'd done a good job; he would help me. And he did.

I found him in his office and explained what I had discovered. He smiled at my excitement and informed me that Macy's had just brought in a few to see if they would sell.

He said, "Actually, they're made by the company that sells pressure canners, very popular in the Midwest for preserving foods. They are large, sixteen-to-twenty-quart vessels with lugs around the side. They don't sell very well in New York because we're hardly a farming community.

"As a matter of fact, Presto's sales manager, Tom Haney, was in to see me yesterday. He's getting ready to open an exhibit at the World's Fair. You might find him out there, in the Home Building."

Those were the words that sent me on the course to whatever success I have achieved in life. At the end of the day I made a dash for the Long Island Railroad, housed in the Pennsylvania Station, and jumped the first train to the Fair.

# Chapter 2

The New York World's Fair of 1939 had barely opened, and construction was still going on. Many exhibits were in the process of receiving the last nail and piece of display equipment. I threaded my way through the maze of exhibit buildings and finally found the Home Building, a cavernous round building void of center displays. Exhibits were all in thirty-foot-long enclosures against the circular walls. I spotted one, all white, with a sign on top for the product and company I was searching for. A white counter with a gas stove in the center ran all along the front of the booth. The exhibit was about six feet deep, and had a similar counter running along the back. There was no one in the exhibit or near it. Oh, my . . . a wild goose chase . . . it's too late, I thought. But just then I saw a man walking toward the booth. When he came closer I said, "Pardon me, sir. I'm looking for a Mr. Haney."

"I'm Tom Haney," he replied. He was to be the first, other than my father, of many mentors in my life, and one of the finest.

"Sir, Mr. Alexander at Macy's told me I might find you here. I'd like to join your company as a demonstrator at the Fair."

"I'm sorry, but we have all the people we need."

My heart sank, but I plunged on. "Mr. Haney, you have a wonderful product, and I know I can sell it, and I'm a hard worker."

It's possible my enthusiasm and sincerity had an impact, for he then asked me questions about my experience. This time I spoke at greater length, and he recognized, I believe, the traits inherent in an experienced demonstrator.

"Well, as I've said, we're full up, and the people I bring in have worked the various state fairs around the country. They really are top men."

"That's another reason I'd like to work here with your company," I replied. And now my last shot before folding my tent: "Mr. Haney, I've got a good job at Macy's. The Fair is open from 10 a.m. to 10 p.m. I'd like to come out here at night and work from 6 o'clock to closing. The other men might be a bit tired after a long day." Damn it, I wouldn't let go.

He thought about that for a long ten seconds.

"Okay, son, you start at 6 p.m. and work until closing. The pay is straight commission. You will earn two, two-fifty, or three dollars, depending on which size you sell. We'll be open tomorrow, and we'll see what you can do. The first night, just stand by and pick up the pitch; then you should be ready."

Pitch? What's a pitch? A pitch is a spiel; a spiel is a sales talk; a sales talk is a presentation; a presentation is what you give to a small or vast number of VIPs. I think a pitch is a tad above a spiel in the rating system of yak-yak levels.

After saying my thank-yous and yes, sirs on leaving, I needed only ten feet of runway to lift off and fly home.

Home was way uptown Manhattan, in Washington Heights. Our pleasant apartment house faced the East River and had an elevator. I mention elevators to make the class distinction between walk-ups and tenements. Our building was definitely middle class. (Downtown, on the river with a doorman out front, you have upper class.)

Home wasn't really defined by the place where I lived,

but by my mother and father, the two lovely people I lived with. As much as I loved and appreciated them, it was after they passed away that I realized, as many of us do, that love of family is a beautiful emotion that is everlasting.

My mother's family arrived from Austria around the turn of the century, eager for the opportunities offered by the new world. My mother became a public school teacher after graduating from Hunter College in New York. Then something happened. At first gradually, and then quickly, she lost her hearing, becoming stone deaf by the age of twenty-eight. The nerves went dead, and there was no cure in those days. I recall, years ago, someone telling me that the human body is like a metal chain with weak links. Under stress or illness, a strain occurs that can break a link. As you become older, the weak links show up one after another. My mother's weak link was her hearing.

She used the time before completely losing the ability to hear to learn about the facilities for teaching deaf children. There were none in the New York school system at the time. How it came about I do not know, but she became the first teacher of deaf children in New York City public schools and received recognition and tributes for her achievements at a very young age. She continued this work, combining the art of lipreading with sign language to teach handicapped children for quite a few years until she met and married my father.

Talk about love stories. My father married a woman who was totally deaf. I cry as I write this, remembering their love for one another. Through lipreading and sign language, they communicated as easily as we do. But my mother always had the advantage; she didn't have to listen to what she didn't want to hear. Another advantage I'm positive she would not have agreed about was that when I was born she couldn't hear me yell and scream. A guy could starve to death, but somehow she overcame this problem.

I had a perfectly normal childhood, learned sign language, and quickly learned to make it easy for her to read my lips. Years later we elevated the art of communication to include telephone calls. Knowing approximately when I would be calling home, she would sit with her hand on the telephone, waiting to feel the vibrations when it rang. When she picked up she would quickly ask "Is that you, Marc . . . ?" I would click the receiver twice for yes, which she could feel. Then we were under way. She would ask questions, and I would give one click for no and two for yes. The code was enlarged to include, among other things, time of arrival when asked (six o'clock was six clicks, etc.). The concept spread to other members of the family and friends who would click in their code numbers. She enjoyed many hours of telephone conversations, just like a teenager. A telephone light button—unavailable in those days—would have negated the need for the hand on the phone, but on the whole it was quite a creative and satisfying system, if you can discount her longing and knowledge that she would never hear the voice of her child.

At no time in all our years together did I see her lament or cry because of her hardship; perhaps she did before my time. She had certainly overcome it. But how she ever crossed the busy streets of New York without hearing the horns of cars, the "Look out!" warnings of people, leads me to believe she must have been escorted by God, as well she should have been.

That evening of my visit to the Fair, I could not go to sleep. My mind kept churning thoughts of tomorrow and my first day on the new job. Wake up feet, legs, shoulders, arms, wake up everybody, mind won't go to sleep. So it was then, and so it is to this day, whenever an important event is about to take place.

28

Finally, in the morning, my body went to Macy's, but everything else was at the Fair. The longest day in my recorded history came to an end at exactly 5:30 p.m. I clocked out and dashed for the Long Island Railroad for the trip to my new job.

I hopped, skipped, and jumped my way through to the Home Building, and as I arrived found a demonstration in progress before a sizable number of people. As I listened my confidence grew by leaps and bounds. The product was so wonderful; the magic of what it would do was amazing. It was an idiot's delight to demonstrate—so simple, so pure, so exciting, and so rewarding!

After being outfitted in a doctor's smock I entered the booth to watch and listen to my peers put on one demonstration after another. I immediately recognized that they were real pros, hucksters from numerous county or state fairs, smooth talking, sophisticated and suave, with an actor's ability to highlight lines for dramatic effect. A conspiratorial lowering of the voice, a pause with the look of a minister who has knowingly mesmerized his flock, a rhetorical question that had people shaking their heads up and down, all combined with the total integrity of the product to make sale after sale a foregone conclusion.

I was going totally nuts, a gladiator bursting to face the lions, and finally my chance came. It was late in the evening, and the crowds were fast disappearing. I didn't care. I would have spoken to shadows and just about did, as one couple left before I finished. A voice behind me said, "Not bad for the first one." How I beamed with praise from the oldest member of the group. We closed down for the night, and I set off for the 10:30 train to the city, transferred to the subway, and made it home by 11:30 or midnight, depending on my luck at catching an express; most of the trains were locals at that late hour.

The next morning, I was up at 6:00 and down to Macy's. Another long day and then off to the Fair. Now it was time to show my colors. I took my regular turn at putting on the demonstrations, made my first sale, and bubbled with excitement. If loving your work was a criterion for success, I was Mr. Success. Wow! I improved with each demonstration until I felt I was as good as any of the others in the booth. And did I ever sell pressure cookers! I made more money in one night than I made at Macy's all week. Within the week it was obvious; "Good-bye Macy's, hello Fair!"

It was also obvious to Tom Haney when I told him I wanted to work from 10:00 a.m. to 10:00 p.m. He simply looked at my orders, heard my demonstration, and said yes. Fortunately Macy's had a replacement for me. I thanked Mr. Alexander and my employer and began my first day-and-night operation at the Fair.

I quickly found out that in spite of all my natural ability, I was a rookie. I could hit and catch the ball with the best of them, but I almost completely lacked experience and understanding of the finer points of the game, and these are not acquired overnight.

For example, the system we followed was that the man giving the demonstration had first crack at the customers of his choice. He would signal his selection to the rest of us. The next man to demonstrate had second choice, and so on until all five of us had chosen a target. When the demonstration was over, we all moved to our targets. Because we all worked on straight commission, choosing the right prospect was damn important. If we selected the wrong one, we would have to go back to the end of the line and wait, perhaps an hour or two, before our turn came up again. In the meantime we would move onto the leftovers from salesmen in front us. These salesmen were pros—very sharp, very experienced—and they rarely made a mistake.

The entire demonstration took about fifteen minutes, although the actual cooking time was only three or four. On average, we spoke before ten, twenty, thirty, or more people, and within that time frame we had to choose our sure-shot customers. It was far from roulette; it was not luck, but almost a science. First of all, one had to bring together a tip. A *tip* in the vernacular is a number of people sufficient to start the demonstration, because once we put the cover on the cooker, it was too late for any late arrivals to know what was going on.

In order to build a tip, we stopped the first couple by some mysterious movements of our hands, holding a long spoon, churning vegetables in small bins, looking into the body of the pressure cooker where a small amount of water was steaming, and telling them we were about to cook vegetables in three minutes. Of course we weren't really about to start; we were about to stop more people to make the sales potential of the demonstration worthwhile. We would ask our audience questions about how long it would take to cook different food items. We would tell them again that we were getting ready to show them cooking in minutes, etc. Depending on the traffic, the crowd would grow, and when we figured we had enough, we would begin. Those people were locked in until we finished. They had seen raw food go in and wanted to see the cooked food three minutes later.

We had approximately four to five minutes, taking into account exhausting the air flow from the pressure cooker (air rises before steam), placing the weight over the stem to contain and regulate the pressure, the actual cooking, an extra minute to reduce the pressure under a water tap, and finally opening the cover. It took about six or seven minutes if we stretched out all the befores and afters.

During the actual cooking, when there was nothing to

see, we would tell them the reasons why they should own this fantastic new method of cooking. There were many reasons, and we made certain we made each one sound important. It was difficult to determine which point would fill the customers' needs or wants.

For example, a pressure cooker saves time. But some people weren't the least interested in saving time; they loved to cook. The more time it took, the better. Others were noncooks who had cooks.

A pressure cooker saves vitamins and minerals and the natural salts and sugars of food. No one was aware of vitamins and minerals; they couldn't be seen or tasted. And saving natural salts and sugars didn't matter; people weren't going to change their cooking habits and methods. We like to add salt and pepper, spices and condiments.

"Just look at all the money you will save," I would say. "I'm cooking four times faster than you do now at home. I'm using only one burner with a low flame, and I'm cooking these vegetables together without the flavors blending.

"Furthermore, my kitchen is cool; there are no steaming pots with four burners going full blast. And when it's over I'll have only one pot to clean.

"This wonderful pressure cooker will cook a pot roast or make a stew in twenty minutes. Vegetable or chicken soup in the same amount of time. It will do just about everything but bake a cake."

Alas, nothing's perfect. Son of a bitch, it isn't a sex machine. What the hell would we have to tell them to make them buy?

There were more reasons; it was perfect for the cabin or the lake or a boat. (We could never tell, one out of a million might own a boat.)

The fact of the matter was that one of the above reasons would hit home, and we had to perceive which one and for whom. This is why I say it was a science, or damn close to one.

To begin with, we were in the Home Building. People were there because they were homemakers or wanting to be, and this included apartment dwellers. The same exciting demonstration in the fashion or architectural buildings or in the hot-dog carnival areas would win little interest or attention. Location is everything.

Assuming our listeners all qualified by visiting the building, we still had to sort them out. Singles were immediately eliminated; they weren't homemakers. Couples, of course, were the "in" people. But, boy, it required careful scrutiny. Did she wear a ring? If she did, then so much the better, solid and straight.

Then I tried to find out if they could afford a pressure cooker. It was much harder to judge by clothes in those days. Blue jeans had not arrived from the farmland. Casual attire as we know it today did not exist. Men wore suits and ties, jackets and slacks, fedoras or straw hats. Women wore dresses, not slacks, T-shirts, shorts, etc. (Today, you can talk to a millionaire who looks like a bum. Then, a bum was a bum.) On the whole, they were average Americans, well dressed and from all appearances wealthy. I carefully chose my prey. But hold on ... were those people South Americans, Central Americans, Europeans? If so, go for Mr. and Mrs. Smith. The foreigners had cooks who worked their kitchens from morning till night, and could not speak or read English, the only language of the cookbook (and all of whom subsequently had a history of destroying dishwashers).

Age was also a factor to consider, on a scale of one to ten. If the listeners were in their early twenties, they were a three on the will-they-buy-scale; in their late twenties or thirties, a five or six. Best by far were the thirty-five to forty-year-olds; they were in their prime. Over fifty, very bad—too set in their ways and on their way out. Sad, but true. There were no miracle drugs, no physical fitness programs for longevity. When people back then said life was short, they knew what they were talking about.

The final strategy was to watch each couple to determine their interest. Did they nod their heads when a question could only be answered with a yes, or shake them for no? Did they comment to one another after I made a profound statement? Did they try to move forward to see better?

Before summing up all these telltale signs and deciding whom to select as a customer, I would open the unit and display the food, offering a taste, all the while comparing the lovely color of the string beans, the whiteness of the cauliflower, and the brilliant orange of the carrots to the original colors of the uncooked food.

I narrowed my prospects down to two or three couples based on their reactions, their facial expressions, or their ooohs and aaahs. I would make my final decision and signal the men behind me. They in turn chose their customers, and the closing of the sale began.

It was utterly simple. Show them the cookbook, briefly go through the various recipes, turn to the instruction and operation page and assure them that the instructions were easy to follow. Ask about how many people were in the family and recommend the appropriate size.

"Which one do you think would be the best, taking into account family gatherings? Very good," I would say, whipping out the order form.

"Would you please give me your name and shipping address. Do you want to pay by cash or check?" No credit cards in those days.

The hard cash for a Presto pressure cooker, twelve to

fifteen dollars, was the equivalent of a day's pay for the above-average worker in a factory or office. An average worker made quite a bit less. Henry Ford had almost broken the back of the capitalistic system a few years earlier by paying the majestic sum of five dollars per day to skilled factory workers.

I don't believe these people had to go to the bank for a loan, but it wasn't a frivolous decision. Overcoming all their reservations was a truly fine product that would last for years, offering all the benefits I've mentioned. As you can easily appreciate, I had intense product knowledge. The gravity of this far outweighed a captivating and charming personality. To the extent a salesman had both, and I did, he was exceptional, and I was.

Seriously, we're a vanishing breed, being replaced by TV commercials to soften people up, and by brochures. Incredibly, we spend many thousands of dollars on an automobile and at the very most receive only a skin-deep presentation. The salespeople will point out the new switches to make the seats go back and forth, up or down; a computer screen for driving data, etc. If you ask, "Tell me about this car," a salesperson will reply by asking, "What would you like to know?"

Ye gads! As Salvador Dali once said, "It's not difficult to be a genius in this world of mediocrity."

The commissions started to come in. I couldn't believe it: a hundred, two hundred dollars a week. I'd struck gold. I mined it twelve hours a day, seven days a week, and acquired experience that I have used over and over again throughout the years of my life as a salesman.

The New York World's Fair of 1939 was one of the most magnificent ever held; few before or since have even come close.

Just about every country of consequence in the world

was represented by huge exhibits in pavilions (the fashionable word for buildings) that captured the flavor and culture of the country. Today's Epcot Center in Florida is vaguely similar. The impact was tremendous on the average American who had never traveled more than a hundred miles from home. New York was awesome, but the Fair was overwhelming.

Giants of American industry were all there in their own pavilions. Among them, futuristic concepts and innovations abounded. RCA was fooling around with a thing called television. Unbelievably, it transmitted a live moving picture from one tiny box to another. IBM had an amazing display of electric (not electronic) business machines. The automobile Big Three were going wild with the automatic gear shift in its embryonic form, to say nothing of Jules Verne's designs of projectiles that nearly twenty years later translated into the elevated fins on the 1959 Cadillac. Again and again, a good idea before its time was held back by the industry. For one thing, they had to bring out a new car every year. If they put in all they knew and could do, they would have lost those twenty years of trade-ins. For another thing, people generally fear what is new and radical; i.e., the Ford Edsel and the Nash Avanti. The Avanti, meaning in Italian "forward," went backward fast. We weren't ready for the future; we had enough trouble with the present.

Noticeably absent were the Japanese. They were still making pâper-maché toys, how very quaint. No Panasonic, Toyota, Mitsubishi. How did we ever survive while they concentrated on more serious manufacturing programs for Pearl Harbor Day?

On the entertainment side, the Fair offered many spectaculars, one of which was Billy Rose's water extravaganza, which he named the Aquacade, the must-see show of the Fair. The name Aquacade continues to this day to be used with shows of this kind. He certainly was the showman of the era, a great impresario.

On the fine dining side, the French Pavilion was the ultimate experience—if you could get a reservation.

But all I've described was based on hearsay. The only part of the World's Fair I was aware of was Presto's booth. I was in it from 10:00 a.m. to 10:00 p.m., seven days a week. If I didn't lunch on the food I'd cooked, I'd grab a quick hamburger in the employees' cafeteria. I was totally immersed—mind, body, heart, and soul—in selling pressure cookers. I spent the long ride back and forth to the Fair reviewing my work. How did I miss that sale? How could I get people to buy the complete set? Maybe I should concentrate on suggesting it as a gift for others in addition to their own purchase. The job was my life, and I lived it morning, noon, and night. I paid the price for this devotion. But I received rewards that have gone far beyond the actual earning, because the dividends of experience were enormous and everlasting.

The party finally came to an end in September when the World's Fair was over. I felt like Charlie Chaplin, who in one of his pictures worked on an assembly line using two wrenches to tighten bolts as they came down the line. After work he would walk down the street with his arms still in the motion of wrenching in bolts, even when he was going after a young lady wearing a tight blouse.

The time had come for me to rejoin and rediscover the world. I had been in voluntary confinement for almost six months. Aside from reading the newspaper on the train, I had been intensely isolated. I did not have a girlfriend; I had not gone to a party, to a dance, to the beach, a movie, or a baseball game; I had not played tennis, worked out, or done one damn thing except work my butt off in a money-making prison without bars.

My recollection is that my bank account had almost three thousand dollars. For a young fella, and for the first time able to make a steady contribution to my parents' household expenses, I was elated and understandably positive in my outlook on life.

# Chapter 3

First things first. I decided it was time to celebrate and vacation. With pride and pleasure, I advised my mother and father that I was taking them on a trip to Florida. Their reaction was an emotional one filled with pride in what I had accomplished. I believe my father recognized I was a chip off the old block. I was indeed.

The Old Block was a kind, loving father. Here again, my memories now encompass so many attributes that I could not fully appreciate during my immature years.

He was a totally self-made man, highly educated, but without a formal education. His speaking voice would lead one to believe he graduated magna cum laude from one of the renowned universities. His knowledge lay in almost every field. He could easily quote Shakespeare, share appropriate lines of poetry, or speak fluently on national and international events, business, politics, and religion. He was a God-fearing man without a strong belief in the church. I was brought up as an Episcopalian, but our churchgoing was pretty much limited to Easter and Christmas, as is mine today.

His sister, my Aunt Anita, in the later years of her life devoted a great deal of time to the genealogy of the Van Buskirk family. She would go from cemetery to cemetery in New York and New Jersey with whatever old letters and memorabilia she had found, to eventually trace our family back to its arrival in New Amsterdam in 1632. Her book on the Van Buskirks is still in the genealogy section of the New York Public Library. Every once in a while when I'm in New York I walk in and visit the old tree.

Dad was a World War I veteran, a captain in the Ordnance Corps. When the war was over, he stayed on for a year or two as sectional chairman of the War Surplus Disposal Board in Philadelphia. The title sounds quite prestigious, and perhaps it really was. All I vaguely remember is that he would wear his uniform quite often, impressing me greatly.

I would like to say that on leaving the service he became extremely successful. He had every right to, but it was not to be. After several ventures into the unknown and unrewarding, he joined the McGraw-Hill Publishing Company as a salesman. Naturally he became one of their best. But the stodgy publishing business did not leave too much room for advancement. I think that he was content with the income he earned, sufficient to keep us in a pleasant, middle-class status, with vacations to Atlantic City, Saratoga, and the mountains of New York every year. He did appreciate the freedom of being a salesman, as well as the higher-class level of his customers, and he really enjoyed his work.

He had time to pursue his avocational activities, primarily politics. Unfortunately, he was an ardent Republican at the beginning of the Great Depression. He had reached a point of becoming president of his Republican Club and, during the Hoover-Roosevelt presidential campaign, ran for nomination to Congress for his district. He lost his bid for nomination. The person who was nominated lost in the landslide for Roosevelt. It simply wasn't meant to be.

A few years later Dad temporarily separated from the Republicans to support the mayoral campaign of Fiorello La Guardia, who was running on an independent ticket.

Dad was a tireless campaigner, making speech after speech in halls, churches, and on the backs of open trucks. He was really dynamic. La Guardia won but did not believe in the patronage system. My father fully expected to be rewarded with a position as a commissioner of one of the many city departments. He was totally ignored, as were others who worked for and admired La Guardia. Much as he tried, Dad could not understand this departure from the norm in politics. Compounding this last hurrah in politics was the loss of all his invested monies in the stock market crash, and the Great Depression that lasted a full ten years.

I don't think he ever recovered from these profound events. From then on, he worked to hold on against a tidal wave of financial depression that was sinking the best of men into a state of despair. He was down but not out. He fought hard to survive in a long period of bank failures that wiped out the savings of thousands when there was no recourse to FDIC protection or other government entitlements. Factories closed all over the country; farms and homes were foreclosed; unemployment reached a high of thirty-five percent; and hundreds of thousands of businesses failed. This crash of our economy has never been equalled before or since and makes the recessions we have experienced only a slight deviation from normalcy.

One contrast among many stands out in my mind when I think of then versus now. There were no major demonstrations, no protest marches, no rioting, no looting, no burning in the streets. Today we are backed by unemployment insurance and manifold benefits of business, union, and government entitlements that make being out of work a time to catch up on the life we missed while employed.

Certainly parents are most involved in molding one's early life, and without question my father deeply influenced me. Aside from all of the fundamentals a father hopes to instill for the future well-being of his son, I had the benefit of a star salesman's experience and philosophies, which I absorbed with a thirsty ear.

If I had to select the three dominating ingredients for success in salesmanship or any endeavor that he instilled in me, first would be the hard work ethic; second would be self-confidence; and last would be an admonition to be innovative and creative lest I become part of the crowd. I can safely say, and all who know me would agree, that these three ingredients, plus or minus my other virtues or faults, define my character.

When my parents and I returned from our much-needed vacation, Tom Haney offered me a promotion as Presto's sales representative to cover the states of Illinois and Missouri, except for Chicago. This was hardly a prime territory in comparison to major markets, but I jumped at the opportunity. After all, I had no experience other than being a demonstrator. I had never made a call on a department store or dealer, and knew nothing about distributors, catalog houses, or chain stores. It was all brand-spanking-new to me and very exciting.

Shortly thereafter I left home, my first departure for a protracted period of time. I arrived by train in Kansas City, Missouri, to meet Bill Walls, a Presto executive who was going to introduce me to the department store accounts in the city. Before I met him, I had to find someone to teach me how to drive a car. Can you believe that? Then I had to buy one.

Somehow I accomplished both in one day. A garage mechanic spent half an hour or so teaching me to drive a Ford tin lizzie. Then I went to a used car lot and purchased my first car. As we all do, I clearly remember that first car. It was a blue Plymouth about five years old and in good running shape; I paid the grand sum of two hundred dollars.

I bought the car in Kansas City, Kansas, and had to drive it across the bridge to Kansas City, Missouri. I did fine until I reached the hill heading up to the old Muehlbach Hotel, which was then the city's leading hotel.

It was a steep hill, so I had to put the damn thing in gear, keeping one foot on the brake, the other foot on the clutch, then lift one foot to the gas pedal and ease up on the clutch without going backward or stalling. But I went backward and I stalled over and over again. It was rush hour; the cars behind me were honking their horns off; and I was going nuts. I'd still be there today if a good citizen hadn't seen my predicament and come to my rescue. I had reached a point of wanting to give the car away to the first pedestrian. Apparently, I needed a few more lessons, but eventually I got the hang of it.

The next day I met Bill, a soft-spoken pipe smoker, who after giving me all the training material, led me around to the department stores to introduce me. I believe there was only one store of consequence. We asked the buyer to place an order, and I arranged to return for a demonstration when the order was delivered. It all went rather well, and at day's end Bill and I said good-bye. I was on my own.

The following morning I drove down a two-lane blacktop toward Joplin, Missouri. A funny thing happened on the way to the forum, as they say. I was thoroughly enjoying the thrill of driving my car when it started to rain and rain. I came to a curve in the road and, having no experience, skidded off into a farmer's field. Fortunately, I landed upright and unhurt on the downside of a four-foot embankment about ten feet into the field.

After the shock had subsided, I looked around and saw the farmer, who was plowing the field, unhitch his horse and approach me from about fifty yards out. It was then I first encountered the really wonderful people of the Midwest.

"Looks like you're in a bit of trouble, son. Are you all right?"

He then proceeded to hitch the horse to the back of the car, gave the horse a command, and within a few minutes I was back on the road.

He said, "You're all set, son, but this road is slippery when wet, and you have to be very careful."

I thanked him profusely and reached into my pocket to offer him money for his kindness. It was a mistake, but I didn't know that—I was from New York. He said he was happy to help me, wished me well, and led his horse back to the plow.

Time after time through the years I met with kindness like this from people in the heartland of the country. One has to love and respect them. As a whole they come from pioneering stock who have contributed through hard work in every field of endeavor to make our country as great as it is. To this day, if I'm interviewing someone from the Midwest, I give them every favorable consideration. I know one thing for sure: they are hardworking people, a breed apart. Here in California, we have mostly a mixed breed from all over the country and the world, and the state's beauty and climate are more conducive to play than to work.

Now for the story of how I made my fortune, for it really began in little Joplin, Missouri. I'm not referring to dollars, but to acquiring the marketing ability that led indeed to my making millions.

When I arrived in Joplin, I went directly to the two-story department store and met with the president and his manager. I told them I was there to put on Missouri's first demonstration of a pressure cooker. No one had ever seen or barely heard of the product in this small town of ten thousand people. It was the county seat, and a good number of people came in on Saturdays from the surrounding towns and villages to shop.

I won the management over by telling them what a pressure cooker could do and how I would demonstrate it the way I had so successfully done at the World's Fair. I asked that they bring all of the employees together before the store opened for a special demonstration and an offer of a special discount.

If ever a product lent itself to word-of-mouth selling or advertising, this was the one. Combined with a small town where everyone knows everyone else, it was sheer dynamite.

The next morning I lit the fuse and produced the bang of bangs. All fifty-two employees were there, including the president and his managers. Every single one of them—no exceptions—bought. What an exhilarating, stupendous happening! Selling to them meant I had fifty-two demonstrators who would show it to their friends and family, who would then march in and buy. And that's just what happened. To this day, I have no doubt that within two months the per capita ownership of the Presto pressure cooker was higher in little Joplin, Missouri, than in any other city or town in the entire country.

Quite a few years ago, Gary Cooper (the movie star) played the part of a millionaire businessman who frequently visited Paris. He would occupy a large suite at probably the George V hotel, order a delectable table of food including caviar and champagne, and a small group of musicians to greet the lovely lady he had invited to make his visit complete. They would dine with background music complementing the champagne, and afterwards begin to dance. Finally Cooper would request the group to play a piece called "Fascination," as the signal for the band to pack up their instruments and quietly leave Gary and his companion to their pursuits. One particular night, his companion looked up at him while they danced to "Fascination" and asked whether he didn't become a bit tired of doing the same thing every time he came to Paris? The same suite, the same champagne, caviar, musicians, and curtain closing? He smiled and replied, "When you find a successful formula, there is no reason to change."

Well, I had found the successful formula, and I applied it over and over again. On to Columbia, St. Louis, up to Wichita, Dodge City, Atchison, Springfield, Peoria, Danville. Bonnie and Clyde had nothing on me for covering the territory. It was really a labor of love, so much fun. Here I was a traveling salesman, totally unencumbered, working for a fine company that appreciated my efforts, with a wonderfully exciting product that would eventually develop a consumer acceptance at saturation levels in the ninetieth percentile.

At the end of 1940, the market penetration was probably only about .001 percent. The simple marketing strategy that was absolutely correct was to demonstrate the unit in all major department stores throughout the country. Once this had been achieved, the plan was to concentrate on general distribution through distributors.

There was no national advertising to speak of, and it would have been a tremendous waste of money to launch a major campaign. First, there was no national distribution. More unfortunately, consumers would not buy until and unless they had seen the product perform. I tend to believe that even if television had existed in those days, consumer apathy would not have been overcome until they actually tasted the food. "The proof of the pudding is in the tasting" was an almost ironclad requirement in those long-ago days, especially as it pertained to a revolutionary new way of cooking.

Time out for some bittersweet recollections. I would now have to say that what I was doing ultimately contributed in many ways to my future progress in climbing the ladder to lofty positions in the business world. But I do have to question the course I had taken. There is no easy road. Here I was, eighteen, living out of a suitcase, from one motel or hotel to another, week in, week out, with no friends, no family. It was a lonely life only fulfilled by my work and a moderate income. The high-paying days of the World's Fair were history.

What would have happened if I had then entered my freshman class at college and gone on to graduate with a B.S., and then an M.B.A.? I could have, should have, would have become rich a hell of a lot faster, for one thing. I would have had the business sense and acumen to recognize that by investing in Presto stock, then selling for about one dollar and thirty-five cents a share, I would be making a sound investment. Sound isn't the word for it. The stock went to a peak of ninety dollars a share, and that was when a dollar was a dollar. Oh my, how sad!

If that's not sad enough, I have gone through life without a degree and all that it has to offer. In spite of the talent and energy I possessed, not having that one damn piece of sheepskin held me back or created unnecessary barriers for me to overcome. I was never part of the old-boy network who could roll so easily along, having been endowed with distinguished names, or by radiating an aura of inherited wealth, or by casually mentioning reunions at the famous prep schools and universities. In effect, I was a nobody trying to be a somebody. That I am a somebody today, relatively speaking, permits me to smile and laugh a bit when I go to the bank, but not without more than a twinge of regret for not having pursued a formal education. Later in life, after having made my mark in business, with all the social trappings of a house on the ocean, Rolls Royce, Mercedes, servants, private schools for my kids, clubs, and extensive world travel, when asked, "Where did you go to school?" I reply by saying, "I graduated from the U of HK, the University of Hard Knocks, magna cum laude. It was a rather tough school, all things considered."

On the road again, back and forth, up and down Illinois and Missouri, visiting the large department stores in St. Louis and Kansas City, and the small stores in towns and villages, carrying the little Bunsen burner that I would fill with kerosene and pump up before each demonstration. Finally, the preliminary work was accomplished. The foundation was in. It was time to call on the distributors who could blanket the territory, calling on every general, hardware, and household store in a four-state radius.

Those distributors have long since died away. But in their day, which lasted a hundred years or more, they were the titans of distribution. Their buildings and warehouses stretched more than two city blocks along the railroad sidings. They all seemed to have Christian names—Smith, Williams, Brown—boldly painted in black letters covering the tops of their buildings.

Their salesmen carried catalogs almost a foot thick, with an endless assortment of merchandise. A salesman would enter a hardware store, greet the owner he must have known for twenty years, open the catalog, start with the one-penny nails, and six hours later complete his order after flipping through hundreds of pages. If Presto was lucky and he was a super salesman, he would say, "Here's that newfangled thing called a pressure cooker. I'm going to put you down for three—one to show, one to go, and one to back it up."

That's the most we could expect, and that's all we wanted. Failing that, perhaps on his next visit, a month or two later, he would mention it again, but it was rather doubtful. He had to pick up from page nine hundred and go on through page twelve hundred.

We would of course try to participate in a distributor's sales meeting and ask for time to put on a live demonstration. Sometimes we would succeed, and then of course that distributor's results were measurably better. But the fact of the matter was, the distributors were flat-out page turners burdened down with thousands of products. If there was a level below order-takers, it was a distributor salesman, pure and simple. All of this was to change in the years ahead. But not because the distributors changed; millions of consumers changed from being completely unaware of what a pressure cooker was, to "I need, I want, I must have it."

# Chapter 4

One day in the early fall of 1941, I received a call from Presto's Tom Haney. He said, "Marc, we're closing down the factory and converting our production lines to make 155-millimeter artillery shells for the military."

If they could stamp out the body of a heavy aluminum pot for a pressure cooker, they could certainly produce shell casings. He went on to say I should fulfill my commitments and plan, in effect, to be out of a job until they could resume production, which, as it turned out, was almost five years later.

He complimented me on the fine work I had done, assured me that my job or a better one would be offered to me just as soon as they were back in civilian production. In those days there was no bonus severance pay, no golden handshake; it was an era of the pure capitalistic system. "You're gone," and so I was.

Shortly thereafter I returned to New York City to a wonderful welcome home by family and friends—and by the United States government, which had a special welcome in the form of my draft number.

I have no recollection of what I did in the brief period before my number came up to join the Army. I guess I presumed it was an any-day-you'll-be-called-up situation and decided to enjoy myself while I could. This was no problem because I had saved enough money to coast for a while.

I was close to being a first-time tourist in New York. I covered the city by car instead of the subway, starving for everything New York had to offer. I enjoyed every sporting event, football at the Polo Grounds, hockey and fights in Madison Square Garden, the museums, concerts, plays, my first nightclub and café. In many cases, it was my first sortie into a world I knew existed but had never seen.

Let me take a minute to describe myself somewhat more fully. Of course I wasn't an immigrant with a card dangling on my coat, nor was I totally innocent or naive. Yes, I was only eighteen years old, and I realized there was a big world out there to explore and experience. Although I had not gone to college, I was educated above high school by osmosis in many ways. First, my parents were well-educated. This of course rubs off and in. My profession, if I could call it that, permitted me to meet and talk with and observe people from all walks of life. To read was to learn, and I was an avid reader of history and especially biographies and autobiographies of successful people. I found it fascinating to discover that the secrets of their achievements were basically hard work, talent, and a bit of luck. The exceptions were those few who had no need of luck because they possessed a mind that was a special gift of God, but even a superior mind did not eliminate the need for hard work.

I am not a rags-to-riches person: to riches, yes, but not from rags. What I have done is climb out of a middle-class upbringing and environment to one somewhat near the top in the "presence" department and in the human relationships in business and society that allow one to "walk with kings, nor lose the common touch."

To sum it up, I would say that I have achieved more than millions of people but certainly less than hundreds of thousands have achieved. This is a fair showing, all considered. However, I know I am not a special person except to those who love me.

With this parenthetical revelation out of the way, we return to what was a change in my lifestyle to say the least: Pearl Harbor and my being drafted shortly thereafter into the Army.

Years later, when my children were to ask, "Daddy, what did you do in the war?" I wished I could say that I went overseas and fought the Germans and Japanese, hit the beaches on D-Day, was with Patton's army running through Germany, was in the Battle of the Bulge, or was in the first wave to land on Iwo Jima.

But all I could say was, "Dad was in the Army." I was never sent overseas. I tried to be a good soldier but made very little contribution to winning the war. My friends did. Several lost their lives. I was fortunate, although I still believe (right or wrong) that it is a serious blemish on my character that I did not make a determined effort to go where the action was in the war. It wasn't and still isn't particularly relieving to know there were hundreds of thousands who also spent the war in stateside billets. When it was finally over over there, I received my honorable discharge papers and returned to New York to begin life anew.

As soon as Presto converted back to civilian production, I was assigned to the territory of Pennsylvania, Washington, D.C., and Maryland. Off I went.

I went to a world of allocation. I wasn't a salesman; I was an order taker. The pent-up demand for all civilian products was tremendous. The waiting list to buy an automobile was three years long. Incredible. The same applied to just about everything and anything. I was informed that R.H. Macy—where my old buyer, Mr. Alexander, had placed his original order for three units—was now ordering ten thousand pressure cookers at a time. The store had set up a booth at the escalator landing on each floor for people to sign up for their opportunity to buy.

Over the long years of the war, the word-of-mouth advertising that I and the original group of Presto salesmen had created with the demonstration program had come to fruition. Never before or since has such a period of demand and undersupply been experienced. To be called a salesman at that time was a joke; the product sold itself. But eventually the bonanza exacted a heavy toll, for when it was over, the salesmen were spoiled rotten and had forgotten how to be salesmen.

Not me. I continued to sell as if my life depended on obtaining maximum orders. I hired and trained demonstrators for all major department stores and did my own demonstrations in the smaller towns, one of which was Wilkes-Barre, where I had gone, it seemed, so many years before with my little pants presser.

While driving into the town, I happened to hear a radio talk show, and the idea came to me to visit the station and meet the woman in charge of the program. Perhaps she would find it interesting to have me as a guest to talk about pressure cooking.

This turned out to be far more than I anticipated. Not only did I find immediate acceptance as a guest on the show, but soon after, as a guest in her home. I guess you could say it comes with the territory.

Our radio interview was a smashing success. She asked the right questions. I smoothly gave the exciting answers and added comments to cover the entire keyboard of what a pressure cooker could do for a family. At the end, I offered all the listeners a small pamphlet with recipes for pressure cooking if they would phone or mail a request. The station was overwhelmed: the phone calls and mail broke all existing records. Wow! I had found a way to promote and advertise that cost us almost nothing!

From there I became a radio personality, going from one city to another as a guest on one talk show after another, with the same outcome as in Wilkes-Barre. I moved on to Pittsburgh, Washington, Baltimore, Philadelphia. This was fun, and I made a lot of friends.

The concrete results were hard to measure because every territory was sending in orders by the thousands. But somehow in the midst of the avalanche, my territory, possibly as a result of my promotional activity, came to the attention of the home office. Within a year I was promoted to New York City, the top territory in the country and, for that matter, the world.

Before this, we all attended a sales meeting on order taking at Presto's headquarters in Eau Claire, Wisconsin. Our sales manager, Tom Haney, the fine person who had hired me at the World's Fair, stood before us and announced, "Gentlemen, we have orders on hand for the next three years with the plant going three shifts a day. However, we have to work harder. We now have competition from Wearever and Mirro, who have come out with their versions of a pressure cooker."

This announcement was met with amusement and complete indifference. The consensus was that we could easily double the orders on hand. We had the country locked up, and the competition might at best get some overflow. It was a time for us to swap stories, drink, and be merry, for we were the best damn sales force in the world. In my book the rest of them were a worthless lot who did their work around swimming pools, on the telephone, or on golf courses, as the guests of allocated customers looking for larger allocations.

And then it happened—so quickly it seemed like an earthquake occurred. I could imagine that people all over the country had phoned one another and decided to stop buying. The party was over.

About two weeks after the meeting, I walked into Strawbridge & Clothier, my major department store account in Philadelphia, and went up to the housewares department on the fifth floor. I found it nearly empty of people.

"What goes on? Where are the hordes of people around my demonstration? Where is everybody?"

"It's been like this the last few days; we can't explain it." Well, I could. Saturation had raised its ugly head, and from then on it was a matter of selling to the remaining twenty or thirty percent of the hard-core population. I quickly checked in on Wanamaker's, the other major department store, and found the same conditions. I jumped for the phone booth and called Tom Haney.

"Tom, something has happened. For the first time in two years, our demonstrators have almost no one around them."

I don't know if I was the first to blow the whistle, but I do know that others followed fast and furiously. Three years of orders fueling three shifts a day disappeared within a month; it was totally amazing. There is an old saying, "The difference between being on allocation and having to sell is one order." We all had to be born-again salesmen. Except for me: I was still hungry as ever to be the best, and— I'll say it again—I was.

Thereafter, things began to change. The original sales force was still pretty much in place, those of us who had pioneered the product the hard way. But the order takers were no longer in the game. Territories were changed and divided. A new boss of sales, soon to replace Tom Haney, came on the scene.

His name was Jules Lederer, and he happened to be the brother-in-law of Morton Phillips, the vice president and heir apparent, whose uncle, Lewis Phillips, was president of

Presto. One of the wealthiest and most successful families in Minneapolis, the Phillipses had bought Presto from its founder, William Hamilton, sometime during the war. A very good purchase indeed.

My first encounter with Jules was in Philadelphia during a housewares convention. He was a rather short, good-looking, very articulate young man with a background in the retail millinery business. Although this seemed quite divorced from housewares, I came to believe that millinery, housewares, major appliances, antibiotics, etc., all have one common denominator—the ability of the person or company behind the product or service. Jules had ability plus, as well as a dynamic, feisty, charming, Napoleonic personality, combined with unbelievable energy and single-minded devotion to work. Throughout his entire life, he never played a round of golf, never played tennis, never worked out or played any sport except the business game, and there he excelled. Julie was my kind of guy.

As I later discovered, his wife, Eppy, had a twin sister by the name of Pauline (nicknamed PoPo), who was the wife of Morton Phillips. They were pleasant, vivacious, gracious ladies with the bright, sharp minds that ran through the entire family. They became famous years later as Ann Landers and Dear Abby, syndicated columnists recognized by the entire country. No rub-a-dub-dub scrub the kitchen floors for them. Talk about independent women; these two are so alive and exceptional.

It was not a little thing in those days, or today, to take over the most important territory of a company's business. New York. As the lyrics of the song go, "If you can make it there, you'll make it anywhere," and was I ever determined to make it. Seven million people at the time, all collected in five boroughs. The state of New Jersey was also part of my territory.

New York is a city that defies description. But to pick out one obvious reality, the per capita brilliance of the people at the top in every field of endeavor was (and is) unmatched. The primary reason was that there were seven million people competing for survival and success, to say nothing of the thousands upon thousands from all over the country pouring into New York to compete for their own place in the sun. It had nothing to do with where you were born, raised, educated. This was the main arena of the world; everyone was welcome to fight the lions. Losers went home with the benefit of a worthwhile experience. Winners could choose from all that the world had to offer. The only thing you had to concentrate on keeping was your health, and the good life was yours to enjoy. You certainly deserved and earned the rewards.

I had a long way to go before I could achieve more than my status as a pretty good salesman who was turning in large orders along with all the other salesmen in a company with a popular product. I made the rounds of all the leading department stores, including, first and foremost, Macy's, where my buyer, Joe Alexander, welcomed me warmly. Why not? Macy's did over a million dollars a year of business with Presto. And in those days, a million was a million.

In addition to the bell ringers that were the various department stores, I worked with half a dozen hardware and houseware distributors, who called on thousands of small dealers throughout New York and New Jersey. Everywhere I went I was greeted as a very important person, not only by the buyers, but by the presidents and top management people who ushered me into their private offices. Again, why not? They were making a fortune on just one product. How dumb could I be? All I had to do was form my own distributing company and hit the dealers with an intensity that the page turners could not offer, bring in a few similar exciting products that were being introduced, use the demonstration formula, and I'd have been rich before my time instead of after my time, twenty-five years later. How dumb could I be? Pretty dumb.

There was no question that Presto's business had fallen off as the supply began to catch up with the demand. There were no lines of people signing up for future deliveries. The groups of people around the various demonstrators had dwindled. This was the beginning of the end of the happy order-taking days. But it was hardly noticed because, over all, the orders kept coming in.

What can you do to stand out in a crowd? Meaning, of course, a sales force. That is if you want to stand out. It's much safer and more peaceful deep in the crowd. Just do your job, go with the flow, follow directions, be anonymously average. Okay, but that's no fun as far as I'm concerned. You have to be innovative and creative. Not every effort in this direction is rewarding, but you learn from failures, as my history proves.

In the innovative department, my record had only one entry—the radio talk shows I had visited. But the sales results couldn't be measured, and unless they could, it was like peeing in a navy blue suit. Nothing showed; all you had was a warm feeling all over.

For a second shot, I had a better idea. If you believe in a new idea or promotion, it absolutely has to be presented with enthusiasm. If you don't have it, you sure as hell are going to find it more difficult to have your idea accepted. Unfortunately, most people reject what is new and unproven. Perfectly normal.

(The early works of a promotionally minded person are similar to those of composers, artists, and writers. They're frail, but show promise of greatness to come. The difference between Beethoven's first and fifth symphonies is an example. I kinda think my progress stopped somewhere between the third and fourth, analogically speaking, but you have to consider how magnificent was Ludwig's fifth!)

I went to see Joe Alexander. "Joe, I have an idea that can fill the store with people." (Further indication of my progress, being on a first-name basis.)

"What I'd like to do is run the first-ever Presto clinic. For one reason or another, I'll bet there are a tremendous number of people out there whose pressure cookers need repair or service. Let's run a clinic. We'll have two or three people in the booth to offer free service, and the customers will only have to pay for parts."

Joe didn't hesitate. "Sounds good to me. Will you pay for the ad?"

That, of course, was a rhetorical question, and I replied with the standard answer. "We'll go fifty-fifty."

Which, in effect, means we'll pay for the whole thing. Macy's had a vendor's advertising rate and of course their own contract rate with the newspapers. If we paid the vendor rate Macy's had a free ad, or close to it. I knew darn well that if I had offered to pay one hundred percent, Macy's would have made money on the ad itself. Actually, one had to have an absolute sure-shot product or promotion to get them to agree to a fifty-fifty deal.

My idea turned out to be a winner far beyond our expectations. Hundreds of people came into Macy's basement, lugging their Presto cookers, some still filled with whatever they had been cooking at the time the problem occurred, including a year-old chicken and other yucky items. It was like old times: huge crowds lined up to be waited on. We satisfied everyone, sold large quantities of the simple parts needed to restore the units to working order, and also sold quite a number of new ones as second units or gifts. And the promotion brought people into the store who, once there, bought other merchandise.

The home office gave me a "well done," sent the advertisement to all salespeople, and told them to duplicate it in their own territory. Within a short time, every major department store in the country held a Presto clinic with the same results. My navy blue suit was becoming a bit more mildewed, but I still had that warm feeling all over. Sooner or later someone would see the stains of my efforts and recognize I was innovative.

# Chapter 5

A few weeks later I had my first confrontation with management—Jules Lederer and Mort Phillips, to be precise. Jules was well on his way to developing his Napoleonic personality. I figured the days of ol' Tom Haney were numbered.

It all came about at a sales meeting held in New York for the East Coast group. Jules had been canvassing the country, meeting the merchandising managers and buyers of all major stores. Of course he received the royal treatment wherever he went. Presto was a major moneymaker in their operations.

Based on what he heard, he was considering making a major change in policy, and had received the approval of Mort Phillips. But Jules was after the consensus and approval of the sales force. Not that it would affect the decision, but it would create unity and set the guidelines for enacting the new policy.

For the fun of it, let's make believe this is a Harvard Business School case study. You decide whether the policy should be changed, remain the same, or be postponed.

The company policy that had been set by Tom Haney as soon as production resumed after the war was that only one pressure cooker demonstration—Presto's—could be in a store. If a store started a competitive demonstration, we would immediately pull out. We didn't say that a store could not buy or sell competitors' models, we simply stood firm on our demonstration policy. Our reasons were crystal clear. All pressure cookers were exactly alike: the instructions, the recipes, the cooking time all produced identical results. There was no difference in taste, in the ease of operation, in the warranty, or even in price.

The advantage we clearly hung onto was that pressure cookers were still mysterious. And the demonstration explained all, even showing the before-and-after results of the cooking. That certain amount of fear in everyone regarding a new product, especially one dealing with pressure, automatically meant that people would buy the one they had seen demonstrated.

There was a much more important reason as far as we were concerned. We weren't selling a bottle of Coca-Cola, a bar of soap, or any product that wears out and is repurchased. We were selling a nonobsolescent product that, once bought, eliminated its buyer from the market for twenty years or more. The pressure cooker was virtually indestructible.

Obviously, if we allowed other pressure cookers to be demonstrated, we would lose sales forever. There was no doubt that we would still be the major force, but every one the competitors sold would be one—or more—less for us. The pressure cooker's owner would have friends and family to show the unit to; this can proliferate at a rapid pace. We knew that not every consumer needed a store demonstration; the home demonstration was very effective with whatever brand was used.

Lastly, we were a one-product factory. Wearever and Mirro, the competition, successfully manufactured all kinds of pots and pans. They were hardly struggling unknowns.

Well, all this certainly makes a case for deciding not to change the policy. But let's examine the other side of the coin.

Jules made two valid and connective points. He found, as he traveled around the country, a great deal of hostility to the policy on the part of the merchandising people. They told him that they deeply resented the status quo as an infringement on their right to do business as they saw fit. They firmly threatened him by saying Presto's days were numbered and that when the end of the demand occurred, they would not only bring in others, but damn well kick us out to boot! And they meant it, I have no doubt.

The other point that probably scared Jules the most was, if and when we brought out a new product, it would be a hard sell in view of our dog-in-the-manger policy on exclusive demonstrations that reminded us "every dog has its day."

When Jules finished presenting his case, he magnanimously asked for our approval of the new policy, one by one. I watched with amazement as one after another of the salesmen raised their hands and voiced approval. Finally, my turn. I said "No," and then went on to give all the "why not" reasons I have just put forth, ending by saying, "If this policy is to be changed, we should wait until the forthcoming Christmas season is over, only two months." I definitely wanted one more Christmas under our belt because I believed that would be the end of the big party.

Jules said something to the effect that my points were well taken, but that everyone disagreed with me, including management, and the new policy would be effective immediately.

They say no one visits the loser's dressing room. Wrong. After the meeting Jules and Mort took me aside and chewed my ass out to a fare-thee-well.

"How dare you blab away at length in front of the group, tearing apart our plan . . ." etc., and "You are as close to being fired as you'll ever come."

I innocently replied, "I don't understand. You asked for our opinions and I gave mine. Perhaps I was a bit too long and forceful; I'm sorry."

Of course I was young and cocky. I knew I was the star of the sales force. It reminds me now of the old salesman's story:

A sales manager was addressing the sales force when he was interrupted by its best salesman, who said,

"What you are saying is a lot of bullshit, and as far as I am concerned, the president of the company can go shit in his hat and you can go fuck yourself."

The sales manager, totally livid, was about to fire him on the spot, until the president got up and went to the sales manager.

"Just a minute. Isn't he the Babe Ruth of our sales force?"

"Yes, but . . ."

"And isn't he the guy who went two hundred percent over quota?"

"Yes, but . . ."

"There is only one but. I have a hat, but you have a problem."

Later on when we all got together for a drink, it was my turn. I asked the other salesmen why they had all said yes when they knew damn well they all felt as I did.

One of them replied, speaking for all: "Marc, you're single. You're not married with children. We can't afford to lose our jobs."

My contempt for their compromising their integrity melted away instantly. Instead, I was filled with admiration for each one of them. The welfare of their families came before whether or not Presto sold a few more damn pressure cookers. The times made it all the more understandable, for even though the depression was over and jobs were opening up, the memory of "No Help Wanted" signs was still very much alive in their minds. I apologized for my brazen, arrogant behavior and told them they had given me a lesson on what life is all about.

Well, all you Harvard Yarders, forgetting the human aspects of the case, how would you decide? Yea, nay, or postpone till after Christmas, two or three months down the road? Actually the answer is moot. For we were reaching the end of the trail for playing monopoly with a product that had achieved almost complete saturation. We undoubtedly lost sales to competitors when they made their entrance into our exclusive domain. But the overall volume was rapidly going down. On the other hand, it's possible we mended some fences in the field.

Please forgive the minor-league play with Harvard case studies. However, that confrontation seemed very important and critical at the time. . . . Don't they all.

It was nigh impossible to lick my wounds. But I applied mental salve that healed me quickly with a feeling that I was beginning to leave, if not rise out of, the crowd.

When I was a boy my father guided me into the pleasant pastime of collecting stamps, as he had been doing since his childhood. I was immediately enraptured and fascinated, and would enjoy the designs and colors that on an inch of paper could partially describe a country. For example, zebras and elephants would be from Africa, gold and silver rims from Persia, pyramids from Egypt, gentle seascapes from Tahiti, Buddhas from Japan, kings and queens from Europe.

I would place the map of the world next to me so I could find the country a stamp came from. The beauty of the stamps would create a desire in me to visit their countries. How exciting, the thought of seeing the world. Those thoughts never died away.

If I had a stamp that reflected my status, worldly knowledge and maturity at the ripe age of twenty-six, it would be bright green. It was important that I begin to play monkey see, monkey do. It was time, before it got too late, to acquire the dressings that make a man indistinguishable from one born and bred to the manor. This I started to do.

If clothes make the man, I was made. Brooks Brothers put me into my chimpanzee suits, blazers, striped ties, button-downs, a Barcelona hat, a Chesterfield coat with velvet collar, and (would you believe?) a derby. The only problem was that I might be mistaken for Tom Watson of IBM, strolling down Madison Avenue. Oh well, that's the risk he takes.

In the car department, I purchased a creamy, white-top Ford convertible with a continental wheel on the back. It was a classic in its own time. Oh my, there I was, driving about town in a polo coat, tan leather gloves, and sunglasses. Look at me, I was a movie star, or—when I wore my pin-striped suit—a stockbroker or an account executive. I was as phoney as a nine-dollar bill. Was it Dumas who wrote something like, "Be concerned about a person that has your appearance, not the tramp"? That's vaguely close.

Next, into the haunts of the social set. I became almost a regular at the Stork Club, Armando's, El Morocco. I made acquaintances, which led to making friends, and invitations to Park Avenue parties and weekends at Southampton and other exclusive spots on Long Island. Very, very illuminating and educational, and of course I was having a ball in my disguise. When asked what I did for a living, I'd reply, "I'm with National Presto Industries. I'm in charge of their New York operations." Ye gads, I was only a salesman.

On top of that, the society columnists began to mention my name in connection with daughters of prominent New York socialites, invariably adding I was the heir to a pressure cooker fortune. This was going a bit too far; if anyone sent those clippings to the office, I could see myself being trans-ferred to Davenport, Iowa, pretty damn fast.

That's not all. I had made a good friend in this circus set by the name of Max de La Gevarra, who was the nephew of the former president of Venezuela, rich as only the elite of South America can be. He invited me to share his aunt's penthouse apartment at Sutton Place overlooking the East River. How could I refuse? And we had the time of our young lives. It was party after party, night clubs, and girls, girls, girls.

With another friend in the circle, we went off to Palm Beach, then popped over to Nassau, when Nassau was really Nassau. We decided to take a cruise ship home, a Holland America ship.

Coming on board, we asked the maître d' for a second sitting table and were told, "Sorry, we have to put you in the first sitting."

"Hold on," I said, "I'm Dutch and this is a Dutch ship and we would prefer the second sitting."

"It is because you are that we are placing you in the first."

We grumbled a bit until we entered the dining room and found ourselves at a table with six pretty girls who had to be solo on the ship for ten days and were delighted to see us. One way or another we didn't see the deck again until we reached New York.

Shortly after our return, Max's aunt came to visit her apartment and found traces of debauchery all over the place. We were thrown out. It had been great while it lasted.

All of this was nonsense under the heading of youth-will-have-its-fling. It certainly wasn't substance toward the making of a self-made man, but it did contribute in a way. I had seen and entered a world within a world. I had tasted the crumbs off the table of what it is like to be up there in a financially secure atmosphere with all its trappings. I was hungry for more.

Through all of this I continued to do my job, and although once in a while I felt a little fatigued after getting home at five in the morning, a nap and a shower would revive me—well, almost—for the day's sales calls. I wonder if among the legions of salesmen before and after me there have been a few who indulged in such atypical behavior. There must be one or two.

The next momentous decision on the part of Presto's management was to go from multiple distributors to one exclusive distributor for all of New York and New Jersey. I've described distributors as we knew them to be for the most part: page turners carrying hundreds of lines of merchandise.

The new concept was to appoint what became known as a major product or major appliance distributor who carried only one line; in this case it was RCA. Television was coming on hard and fast; the whole country wanted it. The demand was fantastic. While there was no synergy between products, there was a positive connection if you wanted your share of TV sets.

My first order of business was to go around to all the distributors and inform them of our change in distributors. This was a rather unpleasant task, but in each case, I told them that the move was clearly a necessity on our part because we were a one-product company that now required the intensity a single-line distributor could offer, for a while. Factories are survivalists. They can change production and change distributors, who have been and always will be at their mercy.

One distributor in particular, not a large one, but an old-guard housewares outfit that had been doing business in the metropolitan area and its outskirts for over fifty years, wanted me to buy them out. I had known the two elderly brothers, who had inherited the business from their father, since I had taken over the territory. We got along so well. They admired my work ethic and—more important—my ability in making successful dealer calls with their salesmen, in addition to my above-average presentation when conducting sales meetings with their group, which was the substance of my qualifications.

They actually believed I could run their business and offered me the opportunity to buy them out for purely the inventory on hand with terms that provided for the cash-flow requirement. The pros and cons flashed through my mind. The one that stood out in the con column was my total lack of experience in having anything to do with running a business except being a salesman. On the pro side, they would stay on until they believed I was ready to take over alone. After expressing my most sincere appreciation of their offer, I informed them I would need time to sort out my thoughts and would let them know.

Not very much time was required. I found Jules and Mort and told them about my opportunity. "Don't touch it with a ten-foot pole" was the essence of their advice. It did no harm to my fledgling career, talking to them as I did. Perhaps in a way it was self-serving, but I wonder to this day what would have happened if I had accepted the opportunity.

One thing I know now and only began to suspect at the time: new creatures in the retail world were emerging . . . the discount houses. At first they were like speakeasies. You probably had to walk upstairs in a nondescript building and say, "Joe sent me" to get in. They offered substantial discounts on all the housewares and electrical products sold at Macy's and in the housewares and hardware stores, in the face of countrywide fair-trade laws that prohibited such practices. It was up to the factories whose products they sold to serve a summons on the discounters and haul them into court. When the case came up, they paid a fine and were told to stop selling that firm's product at less than fair-trade prices. What a laugh. They would stop for a time and then do it again. Some factories pursued and cracked down as hard as they could; others did not but claimed that they did; and some said the hell with it. In the final analysis, they all won except the poor mom-and-pop stores, which didn't have the traffic or sales to make it up on volume, as they say.

I had to admit that the timing wasn't right for taking over a business that sold the same merchandise the proliferating discount houses were carrying. Yes, I could change policy and sell to them. But how in the hell could we face, and sell to, the thousands of more simple little dealers. No way. We would have had to go down like gentlemen. And that the old men did, although I wasn't aboard.

With that decision behind me, it was on to our exclusive distributor, the mighty RCA Distributing Company, headed by the dynamic Irving Sarnoff, the brother of David Sarnoff, the founding giant of RCA. This was a brand-new ball game. This sharp, hard-hitting sales organization made a mockery of the old-time distributors' approach to distribution. Until years later when the Japanese came on the scene, they were the dominant force in the growth of TV.

Their plan for Presto was to hire a separate sales force of approximately twenty men and have them cover New York with an intensity that the multiple-line distributors couldn't possibly match. And so they did, to the tune of several million dollars over about a one-year span. They sucked the product dry, and when the sales finally dropped like a rock, we were understandably dropped and humbly returned to our old distributors.

That's what it's like in the fast lane of marketing and

distribution. One lesson to be learned: never burn bridges behind you. Our old-timers gave us the I-told-you-so's, but were smart enough to take us back.

I'd be remiss if I did not bring up two other additions to my portfolio from this experience. Both had to do with one of the best sales managers I ever knew. His name was Jerry Kaye, and he headed up RCA's sales. He was hardly modest, but not vain. He was personable to the point that you would almost enjoy taking no for an answer.

I never received a no to any proposition, promotion, or program I presented for the factory, our alliance being several million dollars strong. However, nearly every time, he would hear me out, pretend to ponder for a moment or two while I anxiously awaited the decision, and then smile as he told me he would go ahead with the program . . . "but, incidentally, would you do this for us?" How could I say no? The S.O.B. asked for something in return, trivial or not, every time I placed gold on his desk. His quid pro quo was an art in itself.

The second incident of consequence occurred one rainy day. Jerry and I were talking in his office. We were interrupted when the office door was opened by a soaking wet man, dripping water from head to foot, still wearing his soggy hat.

Jerry looked up, but before he could say a word, the man said, "I thought your secretary told me to come in, I didn't understand."

"What can I do for you?" asked Jerry, slightly impatient.

"I want to be a salesman with your company. You advertised, ja?" His German accent was rather heavy, but his English was clear. Jerry hesitated for a moment, then slammed him hard.

"I'm sorry, but I don't think you can fit in or do the job."

The man doffed his hat with a terribly sad face, murmured, slowly turned around, and shut the door behind him.

Jerry and I started to resume our conversation when all of a sudden the door opened and the man walked in again. This time he wasn't bashful or timid. He went right up to Jerry and said, "Sir, who are you to tell me I can't do the job? I was a very good salesman in Germany before the war for many years. I'm a good man and I survived the war."

I think he was trying to say he survived the concentration camps.

This time Jerry didn't hesitate. "You're hired. See my assistant in the next office."

"Danke schön, mein Herr," he said with a wide smile as he left the room.

The happy ending was that he turned out to be one of the best. Who could turn him down in New York when he mentioned he was a "survivor." The moral I learned from the incident was to speak up and don't take "no" for an answer. Try again another way. I always have.

# Chapter 6

A year slipped by. I was turning thirty-three and nowhere close to being a millionaire. As a matter of fact, I was $998,887.15 short.

What is with these entrepreneur, sales, marketing, and business geniuses who have made their fortunes by the age of twenty-six or, at most, twenty-nine? This autobiography is not for them. I'll take into account that this is an age of funny money, but come on . . . who am I kidding? This is a life story of doing it the hard way.

Two major changes in my life occurred as 1953 got under way. The most important, for it endured thirty-five years, was meeting, falling in love with, and marrying my wife, Jane, now dearly departed. She has been gone nearly five years, and the heartache of missing her is still very intense.

So many of us rightfully give credit to our wives for our success in life. This was particularly true for me. She was my closest confidante, advisor, friend, and comforter throughout our years together. She reared our four beautiful children in a manner that has led them, as well as all who know them, to say, "A splendid upbringing, a fine family indeed." I am filled with sadness as I write about her. She was the woman of my life and totally devoted to me. Yes, I've led a salesman's life, and there were times when she would say, "I'll murder him, but I'll never divorce him." We went through thick and thin, and there were lots of both. But nothing and no one could separate us except God. I know that as a human being, I could never hold a candle to her, and now whenever I contemplate my passing on it is with the fervent hope that we will be together again through all eternity.

The second change was that I was promoted to regional sales manager. It was almost as if I had gone to my reward. Forgetting the short sprint before the war, it had taken me almost eight fly-by years for this meteoric ascent to the sub-stratosphere of the corporate ladder. But it was a very long ladder.

The position of regional sales manager was vacant at that time, as it had been for about two years. During the sales boom it had been held by a Harvard graduate, Paul Wilson. Diamond-in-the-rough guys like me had to continue to grind away until their clarity, color, and brilliance became obvious, or so I told myself.

Paul was a handsome man, six foot two, ramrod straight in posture, ethics, and business relationships. He was an absolute model of a high-up corporate executive in dress, manners, and—most of all—presence. Beyond that he was exceedingly charming, with an engaging smile and a lovely sense of humor. He was a person you would enjoy being with and working for.

There was only one problem: he couldn't sell ice cream to kids on a hot day. Perhaps he seemed too stuffy (he looked that way, but he really wasn't). Whatever the reason, he was nowhere close to being a salesman. But on the other hand, he was paid to manage salesmen, and at that he was excellent.

I believe a combination of salesman and manager is ideal, although extremely rare. So once you find one, never let him go. (Reminds me of Henry Ford firing his top sales-man-manager, by the name of Lee Iacocca.) There's plenty of room for argument; super salesmen or athletes do not always make good managers. Babe Ruth—one of the greatest ball players of all time—was never even given the opportunity to be a manager, and many of near-equal caliber in sales, sports, or other fields of endeavor have failed as managers. Conditions are sometimes so severe that no person in charge, even the second coming of Christ, can turn things around.

At the time of Paul's tenure, unfortunately, it was all a downer. Presto was still a one-product company, and all signs pointed to the guillotine. The executioner, Mel Cohen, had walked into our pleasant office in the Empire State Building one morning and announced, "This office is closed." Within forty-eight hours it was closed, and Paul was a goner. (Mel did the same thing over at Presto's office in the Merchandise Mart in Chicago and again on the West Coast, where he took away the umbrella, lounge chair, and suntan cream from the regional manager at the Bel Air Hotel.)

Mel, the legal expert of the company, was another tall, handsome man with a mind sharp as a surgeon's knife. His cutting was swift and efficient. The leases involved were quickly renegotiated; office equipment and furniture was packed and shipped almost overnight. Back then I was out on the street with my attaché case and no office.

But two years later the company was ready to rebuild, and that's when I was chosen to be the leader on the East Coast. Even though that was great, I had mixed emotions, primarily because the promotion meant a drop in salary. I thought it was supposed to be the other way around. When they phoned me with the good news, I was elated. When they added the bad news, I was deflated. What the hell was going on?

I vividly recall the evening of that day. Jane flew in

from one of her trips to South America. She was a stewardess (now called flight attendants) for Línea Aeropostal de Venezuela, an international carrier that flew all over South America and Europe.

Airline travel, especially overseas, was quite different in those days. She flew on Constellations, all first class, for about nine hours between Caracas and New York, serving Dom Perignon, lobster, and Argentinean steaks to distinguished passengers, including Rockefellers and ambassadors of various South American countries. She would refrain from indulging in all of this, for she knew I would be waiting to take her to our favorite restaurant when she arrived and freshened up after the flight, as if you could just "freshen up" after those long flights with frequent low-level turbulence.

The evening was memorable for two reasons. First, she presented me with a magnificent Gubelin watch that I have now worn for almost forty years. Second was my announcement of my promotion, dampened by a reduction in salary. I'm embarrassed to say how little I was earning, but they reduced my salary by two thousand dollars—a lot of money in those days.

We discussed this over dinner, and because I was upset, I decided I'd just as soon bring it to a head right then and there. I left the table, called the plant, and spoke to a guy by the name of Sam Fine, who was just below Jules Lederer on the corporate ladder. Well, Fine wasn't fine. He told me this was the program set up for all new regional managers in the table of organization. He did disclose the mitigating factor that we would have unlimited expense accounts, which should more than make up the difference in salary. I used no expense account at the time, for I was just a subway ride away from all of my buyers. I rarely spent much money in covering the territory.

I replied by telling him flat out that I did *not* understand, nor did I think it was fair to promote me and reduce my salary. I went on to say I did not want to operate a swindle sheet, and that I would put down only the expenses I incurred.

He then said, "It's up to you, Marc. If you don't want the job, let us know. We can bring up Dick Warren, the salesman in Washington, D.C., as an alternative."

Son of a bitch, I was between a rock and a hard place. I told him I would call him back.

I returned to the table and told Jane of our conversation and ended by asking her what I should do. She said, "Take it, it will turn out for the best." I wonder why she said that. Woman's intuition, perhaps. In any event, I went back to the phone and advised the company that I was their new eastern regional manager. They were pleased, even if I was not altogether so.

It took some time, but I believe I figured it out. If they gave me a raise with the promotion, I'd still have an expense account. If the account was used as a swindle sheet, the overall cost of regional managers would be considerably higher. At least with this plan Presto would have a cushion to work on by reducing salaries. Factories and all businesses have to think and act along these lines, lest they end up in the red. I guess it depends on which side of the fence you are on. I was double-whammied, for I had no intention of padding an expense account. I put down what I spent and nothing more. Kind of stupid of me, especially when I had an invitation to do as I pleased.

In the quiet of the evening, a time for reflection on where you are and where you are going, I came to the conclusion, after looking ahead, backwards, up, down, sideways, and inside out, that I'd never make my first million with Presto. But as events and experience came to pass, I was ready when the opportunity finally came.

In the meantime, I'm going to relive my frustration and anger. The company had recently introduced the first new product to be manufactured since the pressure cooker—an electric steam iron. It wasn't the first on the market, but a close second or third, with some improvements over its competitors. We all recognized that a new market was being born, replacing the old hand iron.

My plan for knocking New York on its ass was just about perfect. First to Macy's to get their order. Across the street to Gimbel's to show them Macy's order and get their order. Two down. Ride the subway to A & S, wave the orders, and put number three in the bag. Bloomingdale's, Altmans, and Sterns surrendered without a fight, and I had them all.

On to the distributors. I started with my pigeon, the one I couldn't miss with. I asked them to take a carload of irons. I showed them the department store orders, told them everyone would be running newspaper ads, advised them to join the party and have their dealers benefit from the department store ads. I wrote the order up and moved on to the next best, telling him I wanted the same order because this was one big market. I held onto all the orders, showing them to one distributor after another. Good God, I had maximum orders from every department store and distributor in the city within two weeks.

Back at the farm, Tom Haney was calling every other day. "Marc, where the hell are your orders?"

"I'm getting them, Tom," I would say. "Need a few more days; it's going okay."

I didn't give him a clue as to what I was accomplishing. Finally I placed the whole city in the mail and sat back and waited. The next time he called, just about insane with the lack of information about what was going on in the number one territory in the country, I told him the check was in the mail.

Over eight carloads worth of orders arrived in Eau Claire the next day. If Presto could, it would have held a parade for me throughout the plant. I received congratulatory calls and letters praising the job I turned in, a job that set the tone for the rest of the country. Another warm feeling all over, but no dinero, no cigar. I know I was good; false modesty doesn't become me. Me and King Kong were climbing to the top of the Empire State Building (eventually, I might say, getting popped with the same ending).

This vignette was the frosting on the cake in the minds of management. But they must have had some questions about the inside of that cake, whose ingredients did not include a college degree in business administration. I was being promoted to a semiexecutive position. I may be wrong, but if someone had walked in with an M.B.A. and a good background from a solid company, I think the promotion from within would have been a promotion from without, regardless of my record. Perhaps this is an unfair assessment; after all, I wasn't being elevated to CEO.

I was a bossman in charge of the entire East Coast, as far west as Ohio and Alabama, a pretty big territory, with seven or eight salesmen. I knew them all from having met them at sales meetings, where I had formed friendships and made evaluations; on the whole, it was a pretty good group. I felt it was my job to improve the performance of each of them as much as I could, and this I set out to do. If I was the best salesman, I also wanted to be the best manager. To me, life was a never-ending contest to survive, prosper, and win.

An old reliable DC-3 lifted off the runway at La Guardia, and I was on my way to Boston for my first adventure as regional sales manager. I was met at the airport by the New England salesman, a guy by the name of Ruby Katz, who was well regarded by the accounts in his territory. He was a plodder, following whatever program the company sent out, more like a messenger than a salesman. Oftentimes that's all that's necessary, because a high-powered sales pitch can turn a buyer off, especially in extremely conservative New England. The people there weren't only conservative, they were clannish. They were as class-conscious as their forefathers from Old England. The clan protected its own and viewed all outsiders with suspicion and, yes, hostility.

I'm reminded of when the curtain fell on the last scene in Arthur Miller's magnificent play *Death of a Salesman*. The audience was left crying unashamedly. Poor Willy Loman covered that market all his life. As the playgoers sadly and slowly walk up the aisle, one salesman, as the story goes, turned to another and was heard to say, "That New England territory always was a son of a bitch." It was then, and is probably the same today.

From there it was a matter of covering the entire region, on to Atlanta, where the airport consisted of one rather small building and only one restaurant, more like a coffee shop. Does anyone remember the old black man who sat in front and opened the door with a "Mornin', sir"? They should have put a tablet up in his memory, for he was a touch of the Old South that has long since faded away. There were no four-lane freeways, only two-lane roads surrounded by the red clay of Georgia in and out of town.

Bob White, one of our youngest salesmen, and I would hit the road after calling on Rich's department store and two or three of our distributors. We would travel down toward Savannah and Charleston, passing Negroes walking along the roads as they still do, seeing their small wooden houses that must have been built before the Civil War, and noticing the old barns with faded, red-and-yellow, painted advertisements for Red Dog chewing tobacco, whose maker probably sponsored spittin' contests all over the South.

I'm telling you, this was a far cry from the hurly-burly of New York; the pace was infinitely slower, which I attributed to the languid heat of the day. Decision making was slow, too; no hurry, so peaceful, so lovely and charming, but look out for Yankees carrying attaché cases—they're really carpetbaggers. In an effort to overcome all of this, I pulled out all the "yes, sirs" I could fit in every time I spoke. It helped a little.

Down to Florida, up to Birmingham and Ohio. I'd spend two or three days with each of the salesmen as they called on the stores, distributors, and dealers. Then I'd return to New York. Every territory had a different color in the manner of doing business. Once you understood and adopted, to a certain extent, its style, you were well received.

About every two months, I'd make the long trip through the region, gaining valuable experience in working with and leading men. One advantage I had in leadership was that they knew I could outperform them in every facet of their job—outdemonstrate, outwork, outsell, and out-think them across the board when it came to problem solving or figuring how to increase their business.

Apparently I had the right formulas, because we were number one of the three regions in the country. Two of my men—Jerry Jacques, who covered Ohio, and Dick Warren, who replaced me in New York—subsequently became vice presidents of sales for Presto. I like to believe they acquired some of me to add to their natural ability.

My philosophy regarding salesmen, or for that matter anyone with the company or seeking employment, is quite simple, almost too simple. First, if someone wants the job but can't do it, for whatever reason, don't hire him; if he's already in, fire him. Second, if a man can do the job, but doesn't want to (who cares why), fire him. Third, if someone wants to and can do the job, work with him, encourage him, motivate him to try harder. Finally, if someone wants to do the job and has the potential, but lacks experience and needs training, hire him, train him, work closely with him, bring him along, and you will end up with a new star. It takes time and effort, but that's how everything and everyone is born.

At this point, I suppose I sound like a smart-ass-know-it-all who needs a dose of humility. I've never been certain about the gospel that "the meek shall inherit the earth" and equally uncertain about the survival of the fittest theory. I'm inclined to go along with the same old story that life's a fight for love and glory. I've won a few, lost some, and I'm aware of the fact that no one's perfect. How's that for humility?

The company started to bring out several new electric appliances with the hope and intention of having Presto's well-known name and acceptance carry over to the new products. First was a Presto coffeemaker, beautifully designed and making coffee as good as any other. After this came an electric deep fryer for French fries, etc.; very messy. Then an electric frying pan; I could never figure out why, perhaps for the people who didn't own a stove? The same was true of the new electric pressure cooker. I think it would have been better if we had brought out a line of stoves instead. The coffeemaker did well, but the others did not. No sooner had we introduced the electric frying pan than our arch-rival Sunbeam came out with its version. We were dead in the marketplace overnight. They used two words in their heavy advertising program that killed us: "It's submersible." You could put their frying pan totally into the sink or dishwasher. Ours had to be held by the handle when cleaning to prevent water from going into the socket, unless you didn't mind being electrocuted the next time you plugged it in. The engineers at our plant in those days were about as inventive as those who improved on a buggy whip for a horse and carriage. As I've said, timing is everything, and I was before my time.

We were busy putting together one introduction after another. Jules came up with a great marketing plan for introducing the steam iron, taking a leaf from my book. Instead of having all department stores run their ads on their own schedules, as I had done with earlier products, we had them all run on the same day, a Sunday. It worked. We had to pay the entire cost, but it was worth it. Every store in town came out with its ad—a half page, or more, or less—completely dominating the newspapers. The whole city of New York knew we had launched a new product. It could have been horse manure wrapped in cellophane as a cancer cure. People said, "Look at this, everyone is advertising this thing; it must be good." And they responded. Of course, the sales were divided among stores, but the distributors made out like tall dogs in short grass. Every dealer, discount house, and catalog house immediately placed orders, and the launch was completed. The same concept will work today in any market and would be a hell of a lot less expensive than going the TV route. It would also be far more effective, considering the impact of all major stores banging away on the same day.

There were two other major events: one placed me in doubt with management, and the other completely cleared me . . . well, almost.

First, Bob White, my man in Atlanta, sold our Presto steam iron to the Winn-Dixie chain of supermarkets. They placed the irons on sale as a loss leader, in front of every aisle in every supermarket in the chain—perhaps a hundred stores. They started to sell carload after carload at forty percent below regular retail price. It was absolutely unbelievable. They weren't making any money on the sale (possibly breaking even), but they brought thousands of people into their markets and made the money up on groceries, which was their true business.

Shortly thereafter I received a call from Lew Phillips, our president. "Marc, we're going to have to pull out of Winn-Dixie at once. I've received letters and phone calls from dealers telling me they're going to throw out Presto if we don't stop at once."

"Lew, for crying out loud, Winn-Dixie has sold more Presto irons in three weeks than the dealer organization in the entire South has sold in well over a year. Those damn dealers have told me over and over again that the South is G.E. country. They haven't sold diddlysquat and now they're complaining! They're complaining not about the loss of money on Presto irons, but because their G.E. buyers have gone to Winn-Dixie to buy Presto."

"Marc, that may be, but Winn-Dixie is going to suck you dry. And when this is over, you'll be thrown out for another hot item. The same thing will happen on the next item, and still another. I'm going to write a letter to all of our dealers advising them it is our desire and intent to give them our full cooperation and support, etc., and that we're taking immediate steps to eliminate the cause of the problem." Presidents have their own distinctive style of writing letters to the trade or to the consumer.

"Okay, Lew, but if you can hold out for another two weeks, we will have sold more than the South will buy in the next five years . . ."

"You heard me, Marc. Today. Not tomorrow. Today. Do you understand?"

"Yes sir, Lew, today."

The decision may have been appropriate at that time. Old traditions in merchandising and marketing were beginning to decay, even in the slow-changing South. If Winn-Dixie were to do the same thing today, it would hardly be noticed, because there ain't no such thing as regular retail pricing. As a matter of fact you have to giggle when you see a price list that says "Suggested Retail Price." Let's face it, the only time you pay full retail is when the product is red hot and on allocation. Name one!

The second major event made me a hero. Sometime in the latter part of the year, Jules came out with a biggie, which he presented with great enthusiasm to the regional managers at headquarters in Eau Claire. It was to be the most dramatic and dynamic advertising program in the history of the company. (How many companies have launched a major campaign that leaves the factory as a lion and ends up in the field as a mouse? Thousands. The only place you hear the roar is in the home office.)

The plan was for Presto to run four full-page, four-color advertisements in *Parade Magazine*, the insert in every Sunday newspaper in the country, starting just after Thanksgiving and running every week until Christmas. Jules pointed out that this was a tremendously expensive campaign and that his ass was on the line, for he pushed the idea through with resistance from Mort and Lew Phillips. I'd hate to think of how much those ads would cost today, but back then the price must have been equally appalling.

In the space at the bottom of the ad we listed the dealers. Jules notified the dealers in each market who would be listed, then determined how many units they would have to buy to participate. I think he figured out that it would be a Mexican standoff; the sales and profit would equal the cost of the promotion, but the residuals of this blockbuster would firmly establish the product in the minds of consumers and dealers.

This concept is ho-hum today. It's been done over and

over again. In those days, although not altogether new, it hadn't been done on a scale as notable as this, or during the Christmas season, or with Jules's ass hanging from a tree.

Within two weeks Jules's ass was being measured for a can. We all made our best presentations to the sales force, and they made their best presentations to the distributors and their sales forces. We gave our salesmen copies of the ads and readership statistics by newspaper; explained the timing for the beginning of the Christmas season; and sent them off to make their dealer calls. The results were pitiful.

The dealers said, "Put my store in the ad, but I'm not buying six each of anything."

Jules's baby was in deep trouble as reports came to him from all over the country adding up to the same thing: nothing.

While Jules was eating his last supper before being led away, I phoned him with my idea to save his entire plan. I told him, "If we can't get to the mountain, we'll bring the mountain to us."

"What's that mean?" he asked.

"It means I'm going to hold a dinner meeting for two hundred of the best dealers in New York and New Jersey at the famous Toots Shor's restaurant in Manhattan. I'm going to bring in Toots and Joe DiMaggio to say hello to them. After dinner, I'm going to give them a story on each of the models, and then I'll set up a big screen to show them the advertisements and tell them about the program. Finally, damn it, I'm going to sign them up for orders right then and there. That's what I'm going to do, you can bet your ass on it." And he did.

Again the old expression is, "An idea is two percent, execution is ninety-eight percent." I tackled the execution with a plan thought out to a point that made me weep with its beauty and potential results.

I first decided to go to our best distributors in New York and New Jersey. The "best" meant that they had been breathing when I had last seen them. If the other two did not meet the criteria I established, I'd dig them up and give them the leftovers, the dead-ass sons of bitches.

I told them we were inviting their fifty top dealers to a gala dinner party at Toots Shor's. The reaction was nothing less than terrific. Toots ran the most well-known restaurant in New York, primarily because it was the watering hole for all the stars of the sporting world. The place was routinely written up in the daily papers, as one who's who was reported having dinner or being seen with another who's who. The dealers would give their eye teeth to be there. In absolutely no time, each distributor sent out invitations, had its men follow up with a personal call, and obtained enthusiastic acceptance of the invitation.

I informed the distributors that certain requirements applied. Number one, only the best fifty dealers. Two, I wanted each salesman to prewrite dealer orders covering all the models in the quantities originally requested, and have those orders in their coat pockets the night of the affair. Three, each salesman would sit at a table with his dealers. Four, at the given signal, they would take their orders out and pass them to the appropriate dealers. Five, leave the rest to me.

I had met with Toots to set up the reservation for two hundred dealers, distributor personnel, and our Presto gang, including Jules and Mort, who were flying in from Wisconsin for the event. Toots had a big room on the second floor for meetings of this kind. The atmosphere was great, the walls lined with baseball, football, and prizefighting memorabilia going back to the turn of the century. I told Toots I needed him to show up and say a few words, and bring along one of the sports luminaries. Can you bring up

Joe DiMaggio, Yogi Berra, the bat boy, anybody? He assured me he would. We were all set.

It was a wonderful night. In they came, all dressed in their Sunday best. They gathered around the bars for a splash or two, all in an excellent mood. Shortly after they had sat down at their tables for dinner, talking away, in came Toots with a celebrity they all recognized. It wasn't Joe, but no matter. A hush fell across the room for a moment, and then, "There's Toots, it's Toots!" came from all over the room. Toots walked down the aisle between the tables with a big smile, "Hi there! Hi fellas!" he turned around, waved to all and said his piece.

"I want to welcome youse to my joint. I understand you're the best dealers in New York. If I can do anything for youse guys, just let me know. I hope youse have a good time." Excellent speech, excellent.

After dinner was served, it was time to get down to business. I walked to the podium, introduced myself, expressed our appreciation for their coming, etc.

They were having such a good time it seemed hardly right to talk cold turkey business, but I wasn't there on a goodwill mission. I plunged ahead by telling them we were all there to increase their business, first, by the simple and very effective tool of product knowledge. Then I asked, "Can you or your sales clerks tell your customers the selling features or the differences between the six or seven irons you have on display, other than the brand name? Probably not. Here's an example of what I mean."

I held up our Presto iron and said, "The Presto's cord comes out of the back, not out the side like all the others. This means a left-handed person can use the iron without the cord getting in the way. In addition, we have a small niche in front to fit under the buttons when shirts are ironed."

Hell, I'd settle for an exclusive on the left-handed market.

From there, I picked up one appliance after another and quickly highlighted our products' advantages. It was our nickel, so I let them have it; it was good medicine for them.

I closed by telling them to build their business through product knowledge and that both their distributors' salesmen and our salesmen would be visiting their stores to make the same presentations to their salespeople. Well, at least I could dream that this would happen.

Now it was time to start the fireworks.

"Gentlemen, you have been carefully selected by your distributors as the finest and best dealers in New York and New Jersey to participate in the most spectacular Christmas promotion ever offered in the housewares industry.

"Starting the Sunday after Thanksgiving, your store's name will be advertised by location in four full-page, four-color advertisements in *Parade Magazine,* the widely read supplement of your Sunday paper."

We then flashed the advertisements on the screen, all the same, one after another, with the Sunday date superimposed. It was pretty impressive because I had a large screen. I then told them the number of readers, which of course far exceeded the circulation, for there was more than one per family.

"Just imagine the impact this will have week after week after week. The campaign will be backed up with in-store and window displays."

Then we came to the crucial point.

"Gentlemen, you are the outstanding dealers in New York and New Jersey." (It didn't hurt to tell them again.) "You have been selected out of a thousand or more dealers in the metropolitan area to join Presto's exclusive dealer club and have your store's name in front of millions of people week after week during the Presto season of the year."

(Wow, that was pretty good.) "At this time, your salesman will present you with the membership dues for the exclusive Presto club."

That was the signal for the distributor salesmen. Out of their pockets came their orders for the dealers, amid good-natured laughter. It was the moment of truth.

My instructions to the salesmen had been to turn to their sure-shot, their "he's in my hip pocket" dealer and have him sign the first order, then turn to their second best and say, "Come on, Joe, I need yours," and the rest at the table would follow suit. They would almost be embarrassed to hesitate. After all, weren't they the best?

Everyone was busy as hell having the dealers sign the orders when I announced that we were going to have a drawing; someone would win all the Presto merchandise on display.

"Just bring the orders up and place them in the box."

I waited a few minutes.

"Are we ready for the drawing?" I asked devilishly prematurely.

"Hold on, Marc, more coming!"

No problem. I was trying to keep a poker face, but my insides were smashing from suppressed laughter. I had 'em, I had them all. I'd made the sale of sales of my lifetime. Nothing before or since has ever given me the thrill of that one evening in salesmanship. We had sold them all; all of, no question in my mind, the best damn dealers in the world.

I wish I could have bottled the aftermath and, in later years, sipped it like fine old wine. The accolades came in many forms: Jules and Mort's sincere congratulations; the distributors and their salesmen beside themselves with admiration of me for the concept, the presentation, and the orders they received; most of all, the salutes I received from our own salesmen. The only dampener was when

President Lew Phillips subsequently asked, "How much did the party cost?" Can you believe that? Yes, I'm sure you can.

Blessed are those who believe and have not seen, say the scriptures. I had advised Jules to prepare to duplicate the program in many of the key cities at the time I originally presented the program, but, as a handicapper of horses would say, "Let's see one first," was his answer.

As it turned out, it was too late to proceed into the other markets in time for the Christmas deadline. Too bad for the overall program, but not for me. My asteroid had turned into one hell of a bright shining star, at last.

Down on earth, I rather anticipated I would receive a letter from the home office confirming their praise for my work, along with perhaps a bonus check or a raise. The postman never rang once, let alone twice. No envelope to shake out, no letter, nothing except the ringing in my ears of the memories and then a separate ring I usually interpreted as "practical appreciation would be coming to me in the hereafter."

Seriously, this is not to say every time you achieve a measure of success beyond the norm you should receive an immediate field commission and have the band pass in review. Hard work, however, over a period of time is accumulative and eventually recognized.

One of my problems was being too close to the management tree. We would work, carouse, and have fun together, sit and talk for hours on rainy Sundays in our New York duplex, or meet in Palm Springs or Las Vegas for good-time get-togethers. They knew me inside and out, as I did them, and we enjoyed each other's company. However, from a business standpoint, it was a bad thing to do. I was thoroughly transparent. Totally. A Rorschach test, psychiatric evaluation, an x-ray, and a CAT scan could not reveal more. This worked for and against me, as you can easily understand. I had my virtues and faults, as we all do, except there is a normal tendency for management to accentuate the faults when they pass judgement and make decisions regarding your position or future position with the company.

Contrast this to the unknown man in the grey flannel suit with an M.B.A. and a solid resume with supportive recommendations. He can be intensely investigated, interviewed several times by three or four executives, taken to dinner to pass the knife-and-fork test with his wife, carry on with the right answers, philosophize generally on the fundamentals, and end up a prime candidate for an executive position. That's the way it is in the fortieth-floor suites. The old expression about fooling around with the girls in the office also applies to top executives, especially when you're not one of them.

Well, lo and behold, just such a man was brought in as national sales manager, as Jules's assistant. For some time Jules had been vice president of sales. Tom Haney, my original boss, had been retired, shall we say, and not too long afterward went to the big state-fair tent in the sky.

I can't remember the new man's name. On the whole he wasn't very memorable. He had all the credentials I've mentioned, but somehow he was a merry-go-round man never catching the ring, either in sales rapport with customers or with our crew. It always takes longer for management to recognize a personnel mistake, especially when they made the selection. They usually back the person up, support him until it is finally too obvious, even to them, that a mistake has been made. He lasted less than six months and disappeared. Not me; I was still the turtle crawling along toward the finish line on an unimproved road.

# Chapter 7

My wedding day came along at a much faster pace. That was the beginning of the best thirty-five years of my life, although back then I had no idea of what was to be. But I was in love. Jane had a terrific sense of humor. We never stopped laughing together, and that was more than sufficient reason to make the transition from being a perpetual bachelor. No question, I was an eyetooth type who required a pretty hard yank to bring me into a new life in my thirty-third year.

The wedding was a lovely affair performed by the pastor of St. Bartholomew's, with the reception at the Waldorf Astoria. The turnout was a testimony to the fun of going to a wedding and possibly to my popularity. Present were many of my distributor principals and their wives, all our sales force, department store buyers, and the sales personnel we had stroked over the years. Jules was my best man; Mort Phillips was second, if there is such a designation in a knot-tying ceremony. It was so much a company wedding that I almost felt compelled to make a speech, give them a product story, offer them a deal, and have our guys write orders. Damned if I wasn't tempted.

I understand that the party rolled on until the wee hours—a memorable event, reminisced about for years whenever I visited the people who were there. I'd be remiss if I did not mention that the company picked up the tab for the gala. I sure as hell wasn't able to, nor were Jane's family in a position to do so. This somewhat evened the scale for my drop in earnings after my promotion and for the fact that I ran an honest expense account. It was all happy-ever-after from that point forward.

A day or two after the wedding (because of a couple of "must do" business calls), we left for a honeymoon in Sea Island, Georgia, where I really found out about my woman. I caught her leaving the room in the early morning for breakfast while she thought I was still sacked out. What a rotten trick! You certainly have to marry them to know them. Before that, it's all la dee dah. I adored her.

On our return, we moved temporarily into my mother's apartment. Jane was still flying back and forth to South America. I was doing the same thing up and down the East Coast. Ours was a catch-as-catch-can marriage for the first three months, until without too much persuasion, I grounded her.

My mother thoroughly enjoyed the living arrangement; she and Jane got along beautifully. As a matter of fact, it was the smartest move I could have made. Jane couldn't make toast, let alone cook. I considered sending her to a cordon bleu school in Paris, but then decided she wasn't ready for a high-tech culinary education and sent her instead to my mother's kitchen for basic training.

They would go to the market together, for I doubt Jane had ever been to one. There she learned how to choose the vittles for my most preferred breakfast, lunch, and dinner courses. More important, she would watch carefully as my mother prepared them. Within a relatively short time, Jane graduated to doing it on her own. This act of love absolutely bound our marriage forever, considering my long-time fear of starvation.

A few months later, Jane advised me we were going to

be a mom and pop. We were all delighted. I was no longer the carefree, fun-loving boulevardier of old. Now I had responsibility, and with that a concern for where I was and where I was going. It seemed like nowhere.

The company was stagnating. No new products were introduced, nor were there any on the drawing board. We continued with the fundamentals of distribution, would launch a promotion now and then with moderate success, but the days of fiercely paid allocation or explosive new products were long gone. I continued to do the job, flying all over the place, subsequently being awarded one of the first brass cards from United Airlines, as a member of its 100,000 mile club, all of those miles acquired on old DC-3s and -4s and -6s on seemingly endless flights. My record today probably exceeds eight million miles.

I recall Jane keeping track over the years of the time I was at home and away. One year, she informed me, it was eight months away and four at home. I think this was later on, after I went international. I used to facetiously tell her, "I'm away long enough to know I want to come home, and home long enough to know I've gotta go away." After all, I was a traveling salesman.

The months rattled by. Jane had a beautiful baby girl we named Ann, after my mother. This wonderful event was followed by another, the birth of a new opportunity for all of us.

There was trouble in River City, big trouble. Jules and Mort were in a kitchen fight with Lew Phillips, our president, regarding policy. I'm not certain what it was all about, but I believe one could say new directions versus old. The trouble continued to brew until it boiled over on both of them.

One day out of the blue, my ship came in. I received a call from Jules telling me that both he and Mort were leaving the company. I was to be the new national sales manager of National Presto Industries. It had been eight years since I rejoined the company in 1946 as a salesman. If you add up the fast risers, the slow runners, and the no risers, and then divide by three, I guess this would be about average.

One has to decide early on about one's contentment level. In business, I'm very much like a golfer. First I want to break 100, next the low 90s, then the hell with the 80s— I want to drive on to becoming a scratch player. What's next? I'll turn pro. I've never been content; my mountain has never had a top.

We pay our dues, that's a fix for all members of the sales fraternity. Then we pay the monthly fees, and they are heavy duty. We're on twenty-four hours a day, working and thinking the job. The damn road trips in all kinds of weather, driving and flying through shit, the nights alone away from home, except for one in a hundred, when by chance you meet a meaningless stranger in the night. You will have to use your own calculator to determine the odds of making it. Then there is the minor matter of getting orders, calling on dealers with distribution salesmen, waiting for dealers to break free from a two-dollar customer, waiting in an outside office with five other peddlers, waiting for every idiotic thing you could wait for—all under the heading of "It comes with the territory." That's the job. Well, it sucks.

Now, let's take a look at Mr. Average. He's a nice guy, has a skilled job at the factory in an office or on the assembly line. He arrives at eight in the morning, goes to his steel desk or assembly line position. The whistle blows and he's off, doing the same thing he does day after day. He gets two twenty-minute breaks during the day for coffee and a quick hand of gin rummy, plus a forty-five minute lunch period. All is governed by factory bells and whistles. The final toot comes at four, when his day's work is done.

Now here's the difference, need I tell you? Home he goes to wife and kids; he's got time to play with them, to listen, to have a beer, work in the garden, have dinner, watch TV, go bowling, or just plain go to bed. The S.O.B. probably snores like hell.

I once met a man who told me God was very chary with His endowments. He would give a girl a beautiful face and a dowdy figure. Or He might break it down further— give her lovely legs and neglect her bosom, etc. The same for men: ugly but rich, handsome but stupid, or just plain average.

Because he has no business problems to solve, no quotas to meet or commissions to earn, Mr. Average sleeps the peaceful sleep of a baby. He has forgotten his job since four o'clock. That, together with weekends entirely free for playing and puttering around the house, means this guy is almost on perpetual vacation. For God's sake, he doesn't even have to go in to the factory or an office on Saturday mornings, when he might have the privilege of wearing blue jeans and a sport shirt instead of the everyday monkey suit. This guy has it made. Or does he? It's your choice.

There's a lot to be said for the backbone of America. Without them, what would little salesmen do? We'd have nothing to sell. I'd starve to death, and so would you. On the other hand, they need us as much as we need them, lest the inventory build-up begins to come out their yin-yang. A good salesman never slips off the raft into a sea of the unemployed. He's always wanted. Best of all, he has a freedom unmatched by any other profession. His only slavery is to the road and the sky, as only a salesman will appreciate and understand.

I put on my epaulets, packed my bag, and flew off to

Eau Claire, Wisconsin. En route, I looked down on the countryside I had come to know so well over the years. I could see close up, since planes flew at about ten thousand feet in those days. There was Wilkes-Barre. I could almost see my first department store, a few pedestrians. Most of the people must have been down in the pits.

That triggered a series of kaleidoscope images of my history as we passed over the cities and towns of my old territory. I was no longer the kid on the bus looking out on a sparkling night, with stars in his eyes. This time I was the star, and I smiled, shaking my head up and down when I asked myself whether or not I had earned the job. Hell, yes!

Arriving in Chicago, I transferred to the famous Four Hundred, a crack train that went to Eau Claire and on to Minneapolis. That marvelous train had the best lounge and dining car in railroading, all now faded away. Taking the train was fun in those days, especially when you boarded an old Pullman car on a rainy night, met the fraternity of the road in the lounge, joined up for a drink or two, exchanged sales stories, had an excellent dinner, went to your compartment, and read for a while until the click-clack of the rails put you to sleep. Those were the days, my friends.

Strangely, there was no welcoming committee or committeeman to greet me when I pulled into Eau Claire. They must still have been throwing things at each other in the kitchen. So I went directly to my home away from home, the Eau Claire Hotel, the one and only hostel of the town.

Eau Claire had a population of about fifteen thousand. Main Street ran about four blocks, then petered out to front-porch houses at either end. The town had one movie house, a nice but small country club, and was well known for two exciting parades each year. One, on the Fourth of July, featured the high school marching band, followed by the fire department's three wagons and a police car. The other, somewhat less formal, took place during the hunting season and consisted of cars going up and down Main Street with deer on the hoods, and honking horns.

It was moving day at the factory; Jules and Mort were moving out. Mel Cohen, the young eager beaver of the legal department who had married the boss's daughter (a lovely girl by the name of Ilene), was the new president. Lew Phillips was now chairman of the board and father-in-law to Mel. Last, but not least, according to my view, was my moving into Jules's office as national sales manager.

No sooner had I seated myself in his office, behind his extravagantly large desk, than Jules walked in. Feeling rather awkward, I jumped up and mentioned that I may have been a bit premature. He assured me I wasn't. He was there to see me and pick up a few items left behind. The bruises of his fight were still evident in his attitude, and although he was warm and cordial as far as I was concerned, that attitude did not carry over to supreme management.

I don't recall a long discussion about business matters or my duties and responsibilities. Our talk centered mainly around what he was going to do. He told me he was going to take over as marketing chief or president of a ballpoint pen manufacturer in Chicago. It was all rather hazy and not too inspiring, but he seemed confident and happy about the prospect of a new challenge.

The main subject of our meeting was his offer to me to take over his and Eppy's modest apartment, furniture and all. I told him I would be delighted to do so, all the more since Jane and I had no furniture. Within a day or so he left town and I moved in. That was easy. But the suddenness of his departure from the office prevented my easing into my new job. I would have dearly appreciated his staying around so I could shadow him at the various meetings, day-to-day activities, and catch a sampling of his administrative acumen.

But that was not to be; I was left on my own. I told myself that being a sales manager was no problem. If I had handled a region full of men, I could handle a country full of them. But there was a lot more to it than that. For example, what the hell did I know about preparing sales estimates and production requirements, sales and advertising budgets, etc. Not very much, either by education or on-the-job training.

Fortunately, most companies have an administrative assistant who has worked himself up from a lowly clerk in the sales department to a point where he is the right hand of the man in charge. In my case—and going back before Jules to Tom Haney and the unknown predecessor, all of whom he had served—was a bright, sharp, young person by the name of Walt Ryberg. He had started out as a sales correspondent, answering consumer complaints and inquiries. This led to one thing after another, and after a while he knew the management requirements of every executive in the plant. All he needed was some heavy field experience to be capable of running the whole show, which he subsequently did.

I don't know if I was a born leader of men. Most unlikely. But I was sure as hell unborn when it came to executive administration. I didn't know my ass from my elbow when I came in. However, within three months of total immersion and on-the-job training from Walt, I could speak the language, act the part, and make the executive decisions with confidence. I may not always have made the right ones, but who can?

Back on the home front, Jane informed me that all our worldly possessions were packed and ready to go . . . Jane, our daughter, Ann, our dog, Patches, and four suitcases.

They all arrived one bitterly cold night on the Four Hundred. "Bitterly cold" to me was twenty below; to Eau Clairians that was just a pleasant, nippy night for ice fishing. There was definitely an adjustment to be made—entirely ours.

Jane was not a newcomer to Eau Claire; I had taken her there during our engagement. Just a few years before that, you practically had to show your marriage certificate to sign into a hotel, or the house detective would be knocking on the door. Even though the rule had been relaxed, everyone in town knew we were sharing the same room, and that was a juicy topic of conversation at the breakfast tables along executive row. Now that we were married, Jane could shed her scarlet dress and become a member of the society of the town, one of whose members was the druggist on Main Street whose family had lived in Eau Claire before the Civil War, and probably as far back as the Roman Empire.

All of you knights of the road know there is a vast difference between visiting a town on business and living there. The visiting includes checking into the hotel, having a drink or two, eating dinner there or close by, going back to the room for TV, and going to bed. Once upon a time, there was a hotel chain called Statler. Its hotels were all over and all the same, with identical carpeting, room furniture, etc. When you stayed at one, you could open, or shut, your eyes and wonder where the hell you were. Was it Cleveland . . . Pittsburgh . . . Buffalo? Or was it Tuesday? Must be St. Louis. The only identification you had with a town or city was the name of the customer you were calling on.

If, however, you actually lived in a town such as Eau Claire, there was much to do. Fall and winter brought in the bow-and-arrow hunting season, the local high school football games, ice fishing and sailing, and cross-country skiing. In the summer, the sports changed, and added to the list were visits to the A & W for root beer.

We settled in and participated in many of the afore-mentioned activities, including entering Patches in the annual field trials for hunting dogs. I would come home at night and train him as best I could by the light of the northern lights, a phenomenon of the skies in that part of the country during winter and early spring. Patches was an English springer spaniel and, being a hunting dog, suppos-edly inbred.

The day of the trials came. I felt he was ready; his work-outs had been pretty good. On arriving, he had his number strapped around him, and my corresponding number was attached to my chest. Twenty-five yards away a man stood with a rifle. A dead pigeon was thrown high in the air, the gun went off, and I said "Fetch!" Patches leaped away, just as I had trained him to do. He ran to the bird, stopped, sniffed, lifted his hind leg, made a pee, and turned back, running to me wagging his tail.

The second heat arrived with the crowd still laughing. The bird went up, the gun went off, and so did Patches. This time he picked the bird up in his mouth and started to chew on it as he trotted back to me with feathers flying all over the place.

That S.O.B. set us back twenty years. We added another ten to that when our landlady found Jane planting vege-tables upside down. All echelons of the town's society decided we were city slickers who couldn't tie shoes. One thing we could do, however, was make babies. In August of 1956 our son, Marc Arthur II, was born.

Factory life starts at 8:00 a.m. During the long winter months, it's still pitch dark outside when you arrive. If you stay in the plant cafeteria for lunch and leave after all the clerical staff (very good form), it's night again. One could work all during the week and never see the sun. Ah, but Saturdays were different . . . 9:00 a.m. was an acceptable time to arrive at work, and of course you could wear casual clothes. Saturdays would not have been mandatory except that Lew Phillips was always there; that made working on Saturdays mandatory. As soon as he would leave, around lunchtime, the rest of the execs would count to a hundred and get our asses out of there.

Just a fleeting glance at the plant's parking lot revealed the pecking order. Lew Phillips, of course, had the only Cadillac. Next in line were the Oldsmobiles and Chryslers (small ones), then, in rapid order, Buicks, Mercuries, Pontiacs, and finally the nobodies—Chevrolets and Fords. We had a Ford, but it was a convertible, a smooth tan with a cream top plus a continental wheel on the back. A touch of class, but I should have ordered cars in assorted colors; everyone in town knew where we were.

Well, you may ask, what did I do all day? The answer is that I worked pretty hard. The sales force consisted of about thirty men who had to be tracked and supervised. Their weekly reports had to be scrutinized and responded to, along with numerous telephone calls to and from all over the country. Department store chains, mail-order houses, and distributors all had occasion to call or write. Then there were the usual endless meetings with the people involved in production, advertising, and credit. Sales projections had to be made so procurement and production schedules would mesh with sales. New salesmen had to be interviewed, training programs prepared, and on and on.

Talk about training, I was the guy who was getting trained. I was acquiring an education in business on the line that was anything and everything but theoretical. I'd battle with the credit department for larger credit lines on accounts I believed were about to become big. I'd work with the advertising department and agency on layouts for ads, copy, media, and scheduling. Our budget wasn't small;

it was tiny. We had no new products. It was more reminder advertising than innovative. We were, for economy's sake, forced to bunch all our products into one ad with as little copy as possible. Our layouts were so dull and boring that we might as well have been advertising one-penny nails.

When Jules was running the show, one of the outstanding public relations firms in New York handled our account. PR is a vital ingredient in the launching of a new product. Being in New York at the time, I had an extremely close relationship with Lynn Farnell, who was the head of his firm. As a matter of fact, I was responsible for bringing Lynn and Jules together. I had received a call from Farnell's office asking that we supply a person who knew pressure cooking to advise and consult on a movie being filmed in New York. The star was a house-to-house salesman selling a pressure cooker. Now who could advise about that better than I? No one. So there I was on the set for the shooting of the scene. As I remember, I asked them to mention the brand name in the script, but if that was not possible, at least show the unit with the wrap-around band displaying Presto's name. (C'mon, there's no free lunch.)

One thing led to another, and I introduced Jules to Lynn Farnell. Jules was immediately impressed and hired him to launch the new Presto products we were shortly to introduce.

Lynn's style was flamboyant but without push or shove. He was well known by every editor and journalist throughout the newspaper and magazine business, as well as by TV and radio personalities. An invitation from Lynn to attend a media event just about assured perfect attendance, a victory in itself. That he would hold his events at the 21 Club or on the St. Regis roof did not hurt his cause.

Once in a while, he would depart from the luxurious settings and hire a bistro. I remember that when we introduced a new Presto deep fryer he chose a rather small French restaurant over on Tenth Avenue. It catered to the locals rather than tourists, and we filled it to capacity. As everyone was enjoying the champagne and wine, they began noticing two men wearing berets and conversing in French. Naturally, luncheon was served with quantities of crisp French fries as part of the menu. The conversational level of the two Frenchmen became a bit louder, and the guests began to wonder why they were there. Just as the deep-fried banana fritters were being placed on the tables, the Frenchmen became embroiled in a fierce argument that reached a pitch to stop all conversation in the room. Suddenly one of them got up, pulled out a long dagger, and waved it at his companion, who jumped up and ran for the kitchen with the knife wielder yelling and chasing after him. Wow! That created a stir of sizable proportions until one minute later they both came out of the kitchen with big smiles on their faces.

"Voila! Mesdames et messieurs, zee new Presto deep fryer! C'est si bon! C'est magnifique!" They held the new product between them.

The crowd went nuts with laughter and applause. No question that this product would receive the royal treatment in their respective publications.

Not too long afterward, reams of newspaper clippings with the story and pictures of the product began to flood the office from all over the country. Not only the major cities, but also every town and hamlet that had a daily or weekly newspaper used the story. Within two or three months the same thing happened in all the monthly magazines. So great is the power of public relations if conceived and executed by professionals.

After this ground-softening approach, the plan to follow was almost academic. We had every major department store or chain introduce the product with a large advertisement, and we placed live demonstrations in the stores. We had our distributors and salesmen cover every dealer in existence with point-of-sale displays. Then, and only then, did we kick off our national advertising campaign. If we had done so before we would have wasted good money.

A year went by rather quickly. My travels had expanded to cover the entire United States. The heavy migration to the West had not begun. Cities such as Phoenix, Denver, and Las Vegas were small towns in comparison to their size today. Phoenix had a business district four blocks square; after that you hit the desert. I enjoyed the variety of people and geography. What a fantastic country we have, unequalled in the world.

On one such trip I met with our West Coast manager, Paul Seaman. (How I remember all those names of thirty-five years ago amazes me. Somehow they just pop up as I put my mind to it; it's not all that unusual, I guess.) We came down the coast from Los Angeles on a two-lane road, Route 101, passing one small coastal town after another en route to San Diego. As we neared San Diego, a sign that said "La Jolla" came into view.

"Let's drive through; I've always wanted to see it," I said.

"It's just a sleepy little retirement village, not much to see," Paul replied.

It was indeed sleepy. So much so that I wanted to go to sleep and have sweet dreams of living in that charming and heavenly place. Subsequent events have made me a firm believer that dreams can come true if you dream and work hard enough.

Throughout the entire country there were no hotshot chains like today's Circuit City, Target, Price Clubs, etc. Just old-fashioned department stores, distributors, and thousands of independent dealers for every category of merchandise. Mail-order firms beyond Sears and Montgomery Ward were few and far between, so the overall market was clearly defined. The pace of business seemed infinitely slower than today. No fax machines, copiers, computers, 800 telephone numbers, jets, freeways, or info highway. We were barely advanced from stagecoach days. Christ, we didn't even have power lunches!

One day when I returned home, Jane advised me that our landlady was going to sell her house—our house. Hers was the bottom of the duplex, ours the top. Of course, we decided to buy it for what she was asking—$15,500 American dollars—providing we could obtain a mortgage. We quickly calculated that if we rented out the bottom we would have a Mexican standoff in our favor. We were able, but not by a wide margin, to come up with the ten percent down. But getting the mortgage was not so simple. I applied to one of the life insurance companies who aggressively offered a mortgage program. The asshole of an agent put us through a wringer of questions, detailing our life history, financial position (What's that? I didn't have a position), plus a heavy-duty medical exam, and a wait of one month. But they gave us a mortgage in the amount of $14,000 dollars. I think I had to buy a life insurance policy in that amount before they approved the loan. And you can damn well believe the loan would have been paid out of the policy if anything happened to me before the mortgage was paid off.

I realize I'm being unfair to an industry whose noble purpose is to make homes available to American families, but I resent the depth of their investigation of every crack and crevice of your life. For chrissake, they have collateral; if you don't pay the money they have your house. They factor into their gracious decision to make the loan additional interest called "points" that more than covers any expense they have for one-in-a-thousand foreclosure costs. And they also have the balls to charge you a fee to have the (their) loan appraised. We are all at such a feverish temperature to own our own dream home. Here is one time where we're ready to do a Daniel Webster, soul and all. I think I'd rather do business with the Merchant of Venice before he gave his explanation, even more so after.

Along this vein I might mention, "Neither a borrower nor a lender be." I've always had an abhorrence of being either, and only in the most dire circumstances have I committed myself. There is one exception: I would willingly borrow money to make money. But for pleasurable needs, damn it, I'd rather do without.

I'm not holier than thou; actually I'm full of it. There was a time, as I'll recount, where everything was on the line—everything. I called on friends, third cousins four times removed, and contemplated an advance from the church against future tithings. When I'm about to be tied to the stake, pride and image can take a flying leap. Survival takes precedence over going to the poorhouse or debtor's prison with dignity.

Later still, there's a wonderful story of how I borrowed three quarters of a million dollars from a bank with a statement showing a capitalization of ten thousand dollars. I'm quite certain a business could do the same thing today in similar circumstances.

There is a special feeling in owning your first home. You own a piece of the good earth with a house and a yard. Now you can mow the lawn with pleasure, plant upside down vegetables, and play fix-it-up. For example, I decided the front door was a bit scrubby and needed painting. So I painted it. Once done, it looked gorgeous, but the rest of the house looked like hell. So in came the painter man, and we were out a few hundred bucks. That was a clear case of any action creates a reaction, covered by the rationale that you're investing in your investment.

Within a year we sold the house for about what we had paid for it, which was par for the course in those days. People were happy to make sales like that, for they concluded they had lived in their houses for free. The idea of making a profit didn't occur to them, especially in places like Eau Claire.

We had found a lovely house with three bedrooms instead of two. We needed them because Jane was pregnant with our soon-to-be-born third child. I tell you, it was getting to the point where if I shook hands with Jane there was a fifty-fifty chance she would become pregnant.

The new house was charming, with a long lawn rolling down to a clear-water creek. We could not have been more excited. This was a step up to the $17,000 range—progress, no question about that. Jane pulled a "front door job" on me by bringing in a man to turn a small area, conveniently located, into a wet bar. A couple of thousand dollars later the whole house was redone on the inside: pantry, wallpaper, furniture, curtains, etc. It turned out to be so beautiful that we held a grand opening party. Everyone came and walked through as if it were the palace of Versailles. (Here is another chance to point out that what we did in the 1950s for $2,000 would cost more than $20,000 today.)

A few months slipped by, and Jane gave birth to our third child, Amy Lynn. It was almost as if her name was printed on her forehead when she was born. She was so petite, a real lightweight. I assumed I was losing steam. Now we had three babies, ages one, two, and three. I remember a matron remarking we were either very Catholic or very careless. It had to be the latter, as I've never been very religious.

The winds of change began to blow. At first it was only

a slight breeze. The company was pretty much in a dead calm. We had sold the same five appliances for over two years. We were holding our own, replacing customer inventory, preaching the product story (if not advertising it), running a mild promotion once in a while; on the whole, neither going ahead nor falling behind. Time was running out. We couldn't even say "New and Improved." The soap makers say that every six months. The auto industry changes models every year with a dynamic introduction to try to make you believe your old car without automatic this and electronic that or fluid whatdoyoucallit will barely get out of the garage. They have been getting away with this for over eighty years. They have been the greatest and best marketing people in the world.

Traffic appliances, such as those Presto manufactured, are somewhat of a hybrid. Unlike Coca-Cola—a product that frequently costs a dime, sells for a dollar, and is habit-forming—or a car with built-in obsolescence, a coffeemaker, hand iron, or pressure cooker will last for years and years, after being purchased at a modest price and offering the manufacturer a profit of only a few dollars. The problem obviously is that such appliances don't sell as fast as Coke, or as often, nor do they have millions of outlets throughout the United States and the world. They are not automobiles that sell for thousands of dollars and are traded in every two years or so for a new model. No wonder TV commercials for cars dominate the networks, paying more than $500,000 per minute for the Super Bowls of various sports. The automobile industry spends well over a billion dollars every year for advertising.

Equally obvious is the saturation in the traffic appliance industry. Manufacturers have to come out with an innovative, fill-a-need, want-to-own product almost every year, or they'll stagnate and slowly die.

Realizing we were in this unfortunate position, with nothing new coming out or even being planned, I pressed my creativity button, and out came the Dietmaster by Presto. This was the nearest thing to a shell game at the carnival (now you see it, now you don't) and almost required a firm belief in the possibilities of the hereafter. The "hereafter" was, first you're fat, then you're skinny.

I took the same old two-quart pressure cooker we had been selling for years, dressed it up with a green band to denote that it was a Dietmaster, added the same color design to the carton, and enclosed a new dietary cookbook containing all kinds of recipes for losing weight.

The concept was quite simple. It was created for the one person in a family who wanted to lose weight without interfering with the family's regular meals. For example, a person on a diet could use the pressure cooker to bake an apple for breakfast in three minutes, then eat a salad of greens with a dash of dressing and cottage cheese for lunch, and for dinner, put three vegetables in the pressure cooker, without seasoning, and cook them in three minutes.

I can guarantee you, then and today, this simple diet melts off pounds. Of course you can vary the vegetables, or, for example, cook a skinless piece of chicken without butter. Knock off the bread, butter, and booze and you're in business. The pure fact of the matter is that all foods carry natural salts, sugars, and vitamins, and pressure cooking retains them, so no additional condiments are necessary. When you boil or steam for twenty minutes or more, those nutrients disappear, along with the food's original color.

Just like the old days: step a little closer folks, and I'm gonna show you a small miracle in the making.

Putting this promotion together wasn't easy. I had to obtain the approval of everyone in the plant, from Lew Phillips on down, even though there was no capital investment involved, except for a newly printed cookbook and a redecorated carton. Nothing to tool up for, nothing to engineer; the cost was practically zero. We could even use the present inventory in the warehouse, and there was plenty of that, because the two-quart model was our slowest-selling unit.

Those were the days before Jenny Craig, NutriSystems, and Weight Watchers; before spas, the Golden Door, and health clubs; before the hundreds of dietary supplements and low-calorie frozen dinners sold in supermarkets; and before drugstores full of quick-weight-loss pills; all of which today represent a multimillion-dollar market. All we had then was a cheap looking ad in a third-class magazine headlined LOSE UGLY FAT and showing a fat person before and after, without mentioning side effects, doctor's approval, or consequences. We did have health food stores, as we have today, pounding out the value of organic foods that might have been appealing to Alpo customers but were "ugh" to humans.

As I mentioned in the beginning of my story, timing is important. In this case, I was certainly before my time. Nevertheless, I plowed ahead and put the product, program, and promotion together.

I decided to blow my entire advertising budget, and I mean budget, on one full-page editorial ad in Reader's Digest. I chose this route for two reasons. One, I was using an intellectual approach to a compatible audience in a magazine that had over five million readers. Reader's Digest in those days competed only with Life magazine as the most widely read publication in the country.

Two, I had a clear-cut, absolutely factual method for losing weight, and I wanted to spell it out in detail, using the entire page for copy, with only a small picture of the Dietmaster. I ran into strong opposition from our advertising agency, which insisted we use the LOSE UGLY FAT layout, complete with the before-and-after pictures as the only tried-and-true ad. It had proven successful in the past and, I might add, is still used today. I heard them out and told them that we did not have the budget for a multiple-ad campaign, which their concept required.

I have to honestly say that the best of execution in what we were trying to accomplish—including the I shoulda, woulda, coulda's—was all to no avail. The idea was too abstract for a budget of twenty thousand dollars. I applied every no-cost band-aid I could think of. I flew to Miami to set up a booth at the annual health food convention, which offered an opportunity for brand-new distribution to thousands of health food stores around the country. The concept of the Dietmaster would certainly mesh with their preaching, "Eat health-food-store produce and you'll live to be a hundred." If anyone could understand the concept these people should. The Dietmaster would preserve the very purity of their untainted-by-chemicals foods.

I demonstrated my heart out at the convention to mixed reaction. The mix was divided between those who said they weren't interested in the business and those who saw some unfounded interference with their food sales. Quite ridiculous, but on the whole they are slightly tilted. Nevertheless we sold a fairly good number, which amounted to my peeing in the Atlantic Ocean and measuring the results before and after. Of course we sold minimum quantities to our normal distributors and to their dealers. I'm inclined to believe you can still find one of their original inventory in your local hardware store today.

There was no joy in Mudville; the Mighty Van Buskirk had struck out. I went down swinging, after hitting a few fouls that turned out to be an avalanche of requests for the Dietmaster cookbook, the flimsy, thirty-page recipe guide that was included in the carton. The saturation index of pressure cooker owners in those long-ago days must have exceeded ninety percent, and those smart-ass owners decided they could do the same thing in their own three- or four-quart pressure cookers. And so they did.

I can't help it; I've got to speculate on what might happen in today's world, where pressure cooker use is minimal, but everyone is a physical fitness nut and diet conscious almost to the point of paranoia. What would happen if I had a million-dollar budget (low by today's standards) and blasted away on all TV stations, showing a fat person before and after, exclaiming it was all due to the wonderfully delicious, low-calorie foods she prepared in her new Dietmaster?

All of this would come under the criteria of A Good Idea At The Right Time Spells Success—except for one thing. It was also similar to the dog food manufacturer who had everything going for him, except the dogs: they didn't like it. So it would be today. We're inundated with diet pills and low-calorie drinks and Weight Watchers dinners. Doing more than opening your mouth is considered too much of an effort. No, I'll keep it in my mind as one of those magnificent failures that wasn't meant to be. Yes, I've had a few.

The wind started to pick up shortly thereafter. Because I had been a meteorologist since way back in my umbrella days, I could easily forecast gale-force winds ahead.

Mel Cohen informed me that I would henceforth be reporting to a new vice president of sales. This was based on the need, as the old cliché has it, of "going in new directions." I had trouble figuring that out, considering we'd been going around and around to nowhere for over two years. I don't think I missed any directions, old or new, but this apparently was only my opinion.

The guy's name was Bob Draper, and he had all the credentials to satisfy Mel and Lew Phillips (you know what I'm talking about). Not being entirely stupid, I figured my days were numbered, even more so because Bob and I got on extremely well. I felt no hesitancy in offering my complete support in whatever direction he wanted to take. It wasn't too long before he had his bingo card filled and announced his decision to bring in my former salesman and then regional manager on the East Coast, Dick Warren, to become the new national sales manager. In other words, I was canned, fired, and blown out of the water.

Now this is a typical situation in normal business, and also, for that matter, in the sports industry, when a new manager wants to bring in new blood, his kind of right-hand man and coach. Dick filled the bill quite well across the board. He had been my number one salesman when I was in charge of the East Coast and my best regional manager when I moved up. He is still one of my closest friends after all the many years we have known each other. I was very pleased it was he who was chosen to succeed me.

But when I went home, shut the door, and took off my mask, the pain was extremely intense. Have you ever been fired? It's different from being laid off. Laid off is when it's vital to a company to cut costs—not at all uncommon when the economy pitches downward and sales volume shrinks, etc. Fired is when management believes you are not capable of doing the job. There is no Novocaine; it hurts.

There was also no golden handshake or parachute. I was given a month or two on the payroll to hold the fort while Dick tidied up on the East Coast, but primarily giving me the opportunity to look for another job while I could still say I had one.

Now it gets kind of interesting. One, here we were in the wilds of Wisconsin a few hundred miles from the hub of Chicago and farther still from New York. Two, I had to start from scratch, because I was not quite prepared for this event. Three, I had to prepare a resume and figure out what I would say about my education. (I thought I'd leave that space blank or indicate private tutoring combined with field trips.) Four, I had a house to sell if I wanted to leave town with some cash. And, oh yes, five; Jane was pregnant again, and the first three were chow hounds of the worst kind. Other than that, everything was fine and dandy.

Okay. First I put the house on the market via an ad in the local paper. I don't recall real estate offices in Eau Claire. I am sure if there had been realtors, sales would have been few and far between. Also Jane and I had purchased some land on the west end, believing the town would grow in that direction. It did—about twenty years later when the University of Wisconsin opened a campus. In the interval, it was open range.

Of course the whole town knew the house was for sale about twenty-eight minutes after the first word went out. I believe there was a smoke signal system handed down from the Chippewa tribe that had inhabited the area in the early days. Within an hour our first looky-lou called and came over. As I remember, he was the well-known proprietor of a large retail establishment in town and a bachelor. He walked through and said, "I'll buy it." He then sat down and wrote out a check for five hundred dollars as a deposit, and told me the balance of the down-payment would be forthcoming in two or three days. Knowing his stature in Eau Claire, I accepted this without reservation.

Holy smoke went up next and broke the existing record for communication. In twenty minutes it was all over town; So-and-so, who had never bought a house, had purchased the Van Buskirks'. If you think that was fast and exciting, the next event blew all records before and since.

"I can't go through with the deal, my furniture won't fit in."

I replied by saying, "Very well, I'll hold your deposit, and if we sell it at the same price, I'll return it to you."

Really high-power negotiations. Now the town was in a frenzy of excitement—What was the real reason he decided not to buy?—and rumors started to fly. The worst rumor was that the house was a prefab put together like an erector set. That was bad, real bad.

I phoned Heidrick and Struggles in Chicago. (How come they always have names like that?) They were and are a highly reputable and successful executive recruiting organization. Whomever I spoke to certainly knew about Presto and my position in the company. I was treated with respect. We set an appointment to meet the following week.

Now this is funny. You know you're canned, and chances are the recruiters know it too. Not always, but it's among their top thoughts. The first interview is a dance without holding your partner too close. If you like each other it becomes belly to belly.

I hadn't been interviewed for a job in over ten years, so I was a bit out of practice. I had had the murky feeling I was married to Presto for life, à la the Japanese system. My devotion had included wearing blinkers that precluded my looking into other opportunities. I brushed up on my "Yes, sirs" until I could do them three times in a row, put on my chimpanzee suit, and set off for Chicago.

Actually I had no trepidation. At thirty-eight, I was quite self-assured. First of all, I had a wealth of experience in almost every facet of marketing. I came from a highly respected company where I had sufficient tenure in management to know I'd be supported by excellent recommendations if and when they were required. I can tell you, if your demeanor gives the slightest sign of being hungry for a job, you will most likely starve to skin and bones. But I exuded an aura of confidence along the lines of I-might-be-available-if-the-right-proposal-is-forthcoming.

When the subject of education came up, as it always does, I decided to handle it in a positive, forceful manner by saying, "My record of achievement speaks for itself and unquestionably includes a hands-on education. I am sure you will agree there are a few exceptions to the norm, and I happen to be one of them." On the whole, the interview went rather well.

A week or two slipped by and I became a bit anxious. Two offers resulted from my following up on advertisements. One came from a young company that made the Papoose Pack, a harness for carrying infants, still being made today. Another from a mushroom bottler in Moundsville, West Virginia. Although I was partial to mushrooms, come on! Moundsville? Mushrooms? Give me a break!

The phone rang. Heidrick and Struggles. "We believe we have found an excellent position for you to consider, and we'd best get together again."

"Sounds good," I replied, and we made an appointment.

Within a few days, I appeared at the appointed hour and was greeted in a manner befitting a gathering before a board of directors meeting, all jovial with the light, dry humor of those whose station in life has been polished over time to a satinlike finish.

Once we settled down, he (Heidrick or Struggles) informed me that a client, Cornell Paperboard, was interested in meeting me to discuss a position as vice president of marketing. They had a subsidiary, Superior Paper Products Company, which manufactured paper plates from the parent company's paperboard. He went on to say that my overall marketing experience combined with my familiarity with the supermarket industry appealed to them. He then gave me a rough outline of the parent and child, and I began to find it quite appealing.

Cornell Paperboard was a strong but relatively small entity in the paperboard industry, compared to International Paper, Continental Can, etc., who had forests in several sections of the country. Cornell was primarily located in northern Wisconsin.

Paperboard weighs a lot. When it has been converted into all types and sizes of cartons, the freight rate for shipping it to manufacturing plants all over the country is a killer. Therefore the manufacturers market it within the geographical areas of acceptable freight rates. Paperboard plants in several locations of the country owned by one company, of course, have dominance. This applies to a lesser degree to the paper plate industry. But Cornell believed there was potential for expanding its business within the range of its central location in Marion, Indiana. This was the broad outline of the information I received. I responded by saying I would be interested . . . as if I had a desk piled with other offers.

Hiedrick and Struggles arranged for me to meet Cornell's president and CEO the following day.

Headquarters was in the Kemper Building, an attractive suite of offices overlooking the Chicago River. I saw at first glance that this was an old-guard business, and my perception was solidly confirmed when I met the president, June Osborn. If the Cabots and Lodges typify this in New England's old guard, the Osborns, Swifts, Careys, and Armours are "it" in Chicago; they go back to before Mrs. O'Leary's cow kicked over the lantern.

June was a classic example of a blue blood: breeding, education, charm, family, society, given and earned leadership all came together. He was indeed a gentleman and easy to recognize as a general, in or out of uniform.

We hit it off from the very start of our discussion. Being very relaxed, I related my background in business, my family status, and my aspirations, leaving out the bottom line of not wanting to starve along with my wife and kids. He, in turn, told me his company had recently agreed to manufacture paper plates as an end-source outlet for its paperboard, which mainly went into the manufacture of cardboard cartons.

He went on to tell me that the paper plate industry was unique in having little or no brand recognition. A supermarket might carry eight lines of coffee and six lines of beer, bread, and beans, but only one line of paper plates. Furthermore, he pointed out that each manufacturer had its own lock on a supermarket chain. For example, Superior had A & P in the central region of the country, including the Chicago area, and also two major companies plus two or three smaller, inconsequential chains. Competitors had other markets. It was pretty much as if there was a sacred understanding: these are my accounts, those are yours, and let's not have a gang war.

If there was anything generic, it was a paper plate. Yes, it came plain or coated, but a paper plate was a paper plate, no need to carry more than one line. If a manufacturer tinkered around with price or quantity per package to steal a competitor's account, the move would instantly be matched, so nothing would be gained. (Now, there might be a really powerful Harvard case study.) June Osborn did feel that an experienced sales and marketing guy could improve the business. But he could not give me any clues as to how, except for acquiring business from fringe and new accounts. Not very encouraging.

In conclusion, he told me that the person hired would become a vice president of Superior and would work out of an office adjacent to his there in Chicago; he didn't believe it was necessary to locate at the plant in Marion, Indiana.

My mind began to lather. Chicago, an office next to June, a rock solid company, out of the wilderness of Eau Claire, out of the rat race of the appliance industry, an escape, a sanctuary, and an interesting challenge to increase business without worrying about losing some because of the crazy status quo rules of the industry.

"Yes, sir. I believe the position is indeed extremely interesting, attractive, and challenging. I am confident I can improve the business. I don't know how, any more than you do, but I'll certainly give it my best."

We both laughed, and I was ready to light up a cigar. He then took me into the office of his brother, Frank Osborn, made the introductions, and left us to chat (so they could compare notes later on). I left feeling quite confident and returned to Eau Claire, where I told Jane I thought I had scored a hit. I had.

The following week June called me at home. "Marc, we've decided you're the man for the job. The starting compensation is somewhat above what you are making now. If you agree, we'd like to have you get under way as soon as possible."

"I'm elated," I replied. "The answer is yes, and I am most appreciative of your confidence in me."

"I'm sure it's not misplaced," June said. "We look forward to having you with us."

I told him I would be ready to join up within the month, possibly less. (Less was more likely because Presto had a stopwatch on me for clearing out the ol' desk.) I turned to Jane and hugged her tight. I wouldn't have to float the girls down the river after all.

Luck sometimes runs in streaks. We sold the house within a few days of the good news to a lovely couple, both doctors who had returned from missionary work in South

America. No problem. They were ready to move in, and we were ready to move out. Our peaceful location with the lawn running down to the creek was as appealing to them as it had been to us. There is something magical about a house on a stream, lake, river, or ocean. The magic is that it's easy to sell. Actually, you're selling the water and throwing the house in.

The world looked pretty good to us that summer of 1958. Everyone was healthy. I had a promising new job with a VP title that placed me in line of succession for the presidency, albeit a long line. No matter. We were born again, happy and gay, as we boarded the Four Hundred to Chicago to find a new house. Having heard about Barrington Hills, a suburb northeast of the city, we decided to investigate. It was like finding gold on the first dip of the pan.

Barrington was and is absolutely lovely, and Barrington Hills was even more so, a charming enclave with slightly rising hills contrasting with the flat terrain of most of Illinois. It was also designated as the Tuxedo Park, Bloomfield Hills, Sea Island, or Palm Beach of Chicago, competing only with old Evanston as a prestigious location. That is to say, très enchanté. Translated, that means expensive.

We fell instantly in love with the first house we were shown, on the old county line road about three miles straight out from the Barrington station, past one of the gems of the country clubs in the Chicago area or, for that matter, in the entire country. The house could best be described as a French country home, situated on five acres (the minimum for Barrington Hills). A half-moon, hard sand driveway led to the front door. Tall windows with grey shutters ran almost up to the grey roof shingles. The inside was equally attractive, with a dark slate floor leading from the door past the bedrooms to a spacious living room flanked by east-west windows. Outside, the house was surrounded by a hedge of wild roses growing against a split-log fence; lovely old elm trees bordered the driveway.

The owner of the property was Harold Byron Smith, a prominent banker and industrialist. He was asking fifty thousand dollars, which was well beyond our limit, but when you fall in love there is no limit.

We had no idea of the who's who of Chicago, but we learned very quickly. As soon as Smith heard I was joining June Osborn as a vice president, I was immediately accepted as a most satisfactory buyer. Not only that, but when we had the pleasure of meeting him, he mentioned, somewhat rhetorically, that if we wanted to belong to the Barrington Hills Country Club, he would be delighted to sponsor us. His doing so made our acceptance at the club purely automatic.

How happy were we? Ecstatically so! You know there are only a few times in a lifetime one feels that way—very few—and I would only hope all of you have had your share.

There was one minor problem. I could scrape the money together for the down payment on the mortgage (with interest at three and one-half percent), but that would leave us with only grocery money, providing the kids cut down a bit.

Shortly afterward we said farewell to Eau Claire. I had acquired immense experience there; without it I'd still be just a salesman. Now I had epaulets, ranking insignia, and campaign ribbons, but underneath I was still a salesman.

As has been written, "Parting is such sweet sorrow." We had made many lifetime friends—good people one and all—but departed a lovely little house, pulled up the just-hardening roots of a pleasant lifestyle, and headed into the unknown. One small item was known, however; as we left, I was still $970,000 short of my first million. I actually thought I was closer than that, but the milk bill came in, and down we went.

We left on the hottest day of the summer—a short season in Eau Claire. There may be one, two, possibly three such days, and then the police put on fur-lined jackets and snow boots. All five of us were sandwiched together in a small car, but happy as we could be, off to the big city. We finally arrived, probably looking like Coxey's army. But we had beautiful, smiling faces as we drove up the elm-shaded driveway to our lovely new home and new way of life.

# Part Two

———•◦•———

# Brilliant,
# Magnificent, and
# Unbelievable Failures

# Chapter 8

The new life was all rather civilized; no more would I have to be at work before the morning sunrise. For my first day on the job Jane drove me to the Barrington station to catch the 8:05, which arrived downtown about 8:45. Then I walked for about five minutes to get to the office. I was warmly greeted and found my office just where June had said it would be, right next to his. We soon got together, and he outlined the introductory program. He had scheduled me to fly up to the Cornell Paperboard plant in northern Wisconsin. After that I would go on to the converting plant in Milwaukee and lastly to the Superior paper plant in Indiana. From the falling tree to logs, meshing machines, mixing machines, pulp tanks, drying and forming equipment, cutting and sizing equipment, automatic folding assembly, and lastly a mold-stamping machine, out popped the paper plate—my new baby. And I had its first formula ready to shove into its mouth.

While flying up to the paperboard plant on an old DC-3 of North Central Airlines, I was served some tidbits on a plain paper plate. Hmmm. Wouldn't it be a good idea to have their logo imprinted on the plate? It would give everyone a warm feeling all over and cost so little. Yes, it would. On my return to Chicago I went out to the airline's purchasing department with a hand-painted logo on the center of the plate. I remember receiving an order on the spot for several thousand plates.

The quantity was small, as paper plate orders go, but the impact made me an instant hero. June Osborn thought it was great. He and all the other executives of the company flew frequently on North Central, and soon they were eating their peanuts off their very own plates.

I flew over to Marion, Indiana, to visit our paper plate plant. The other vice president (we were the only two) was the former owner, who had sold out to Cornell. He was a nice guy who knew how to manufacture paper plates and that's about all. I quickly realized that Marion was no Barrington Hills, and if it ever came to my living in Marion and headquartering at the plant, my tenure would be quite brief. Fortunately we came to a happy arrangement: he would make 'em and I would sell 'em. My tour and training were now reasonably complete, and I returned to Chicago to get down to business.

I was somewhat like the king on the asteroid in Saint Exupéry's story *The Little Prince*. I was a king without subjects. I didn't have a company salesman to my name. My realm covered the entire United States and I was the chief cook and bottlewasher. At least no salesman could complain that I had been seen in his territory.

What we did have was an army of food brokers—ninety-five percent in name only, because sales outside the geographical area of the upper Midwest were quite isolated. My job was beginning to shape up as a pretty tough proposition. Competitively, it appeared to be a status quo situation.

I began to think about it. What could we come up with to give markets a reason to carry a second line of paper plates? What if we came up with an exclusive design imprinted on the plate; for example, Mickey Mouse (too late—already taken). Okay, how about Winnie-the-Pooh? (No, not as well known.) What would be a sure shot? I couldn't think of one. If I did, it would entail a royalty arrangement. I decided to concentrate on the accounts we had until I knew what the hell I was doing. And a month or two slipped by.

Life in Barrington Hills was so pleasant. I'd take the 5:15 home. Jane would meet me at the station and we would stop off at the country club for nine holes before it got too dark, which it did after the third hole. If I shanked one into the trees and high growth bordering the fairway, to hell with it. I didn't have time to look for it. I'd drop another ball, get on with it. On average it took four drop-a-new-ones to cover the four or five holes we managed to get in before we needed a searchlight to find our way back.

We were introduced to just about everyone by our patron, Harold Bryan Smith, and enjoyed the pleasure of meeting them. If ever the expression "birds of a feather flock together" was applicable, it was to Barrington Hills and the club. They were old-guard families of inherited wealth, the very top executives or the principals of Chicago's major companies—a tribe of beautiful, dynamic people. Little did they know I was a chimpanzee, although the costume was getting a bit frayed around the edges. We would reciprocate invitations in the early days after moving in, but how long could we do this without curtains or drapes? We didn't have a plugged nickel to spend on the house.

During one of the last lovely days of autumn—calm, peaceful, with a still-warm sun—an explosion of excitement occurred.

We found a delightful spot for a picnic, spread out a blanket, and pulled out all the picnic paraphernalia, including our paper plates. We were just about set up when a sudden wind came along, cartwheeling our paper plates down the lawn as we laughingly gave chase. After the kids had retrieved them, we put something on each plate to hold it down.

You have all heard or read about memorable, destiny-changing expressions: "Mr. Watson, come here, I need you!" from Pa Bell; "A day that will live in infamy" from President Roosevelt; "I think she's got it, I think she's got it" from Rex Harrison in *My Fair Lady*; or even Neil Armstrong's "One small step for man, one giant leap for mankind." Well, add to those "Someone should invent a paper plate that will not blow away" by yours truly.

As soon as I uttered those words, I looked at Jane, she looked at me, and we began to smile, laugh, and embrace. We had it! The one brand-new and exciting reason a supermarket would bring in a second line of paper plates.

If you recall, I mentioned an idea is two percent, the execution ninety-eight percent. But in this instance there was a minor gap between the two: we had to create a new product. No problem. We'll enclose some small nails and a tiny hammer with each package, or better yet a bottle of glue or assorted paperweights. Hmmm. I don't think that will fly . . . as a matter of fact they're not supposed to.

Wait a minute. Who would have more knowledge about making things stick than the Minnesota Mining and Manufacturing Company? I phoned them, saying I was a VP of Cornell Paperboard and had an idea for a commercial application. They were most pleasant and suggested I come up and meet with them. I went off to Minneapolis to present the idea. Their reaction was immediately enthusiastic, and I received the most-favored-customer-to-be treatment. Within a very short time, perhaps a week or two, they phoned to tell me they had developed an application that would, in their opinion, indeed do the job. Whereupon I invited them down to Chicago for a meeting with June Osborn and Paul Wilkins, the vice president in charge of manufacturing.

What they created was as near perfect as I could have hoped for and best described as a band-aid, pure and simple. Peel off the first layer of paper, set the plate on wood, plastic, metal, or glass, and it would adhere firmly. When pulled away, it would leave no mark. A big WOW! They had done it; no question, it was a major accomplishment with a potential for millions of paper plate applications. We proceeded to test it on every conceivable surface, and it passed like a winner.

June Osborn gave the project his complete support. After all, Cornell Paperboard and 3M were a good mix, very compatible. We had to invest quite a few thousand dollars in the machinery and equipment necessary to affix the tape to the bottoms of the plates as they came off the line. June approved the expenditure without hesitation. Then it was up to me to plan the product's introduction.

Come along with me, jump inside my mind, observe everything that was said and done. You will be the beneficiary of an experience that comes close to being the greatest fucked-up marketing program in the annals of product introduction.

Are you in? All set? Okay, let's go. First we realize there are three days of the year when paper plates sell like popcorn before the movies: Memorial Day, the Fourth of July, and Labor Day. Let's shut our eyes and think of the fact there are thousands of markets and supermarkets that sell millions of paper plates for those days. All we have to do is be on the shelf along with the one other brand they sell. It's possible to believe we would get half of the business, and we should. We have a gimmick that sticks out (and on) like no other, figuratively and literally.

Now cool it. We have creative work to do. Creative means we have no national advertising budget and very little promotional money. What's new? We wouldn't know what to do with it if we had it. And we love the challenge, don't we? (Sorry. I forgot to tell you there is a bullshit section in my mind that I try to keep closed, but it opens every once in a while.)

What are we going to name this baby? How about Sta-Put paper plates? Do you agree? Good. Yes, very good, especially since we can't think of a better name, and that really says it.

Okay, what about packaging? If everyone else packages plates in clear-view cellophane, let's make ours attract the eye. How about red and green, with StaPut in red, bright red? Good.

Did you know there is a national convention of food brokers in early January in Chicago? The timing is perfect for launching the program for the spring and summer seasons. But we don't want a typical booth setup to meet our brokers. No, we want a private room off the convention floor that will accommodate a hundred or more people for one hell of a group presentation. If it's successful, the whoops and hollers will magnify the reaction to a point where there's the possibility we will be on allocation before we start. Don't be stupid. You know what that word means. Oh, I'm sorry, you'd just forgotten. Yes, it has been a long time.

Now we had better start communicating. We'll send a letter to invite every food broker to a special one-time meeting at the convention, at which time we're going to knock them on their asses with the most exciting development the paper plate industry has ever seen.

You realize, of course, that out of the hundred-and-some-odd brokers representing us (all who had ever produced an order were the odd) the orders were few and far between.

A few days later we're going to hit them again. We're not going to knock 'em on their ass, we're going to blow their brains out. The next letter will tell them only broker principals will be permitted to attend, and they must show positive ID before being admitted. Furthermore, the RSVP card must be personally signed by them so signatures can be compared at the entrance. Brains will begin to fly all over the place when they get that one.

It would only be kind and decent if we gave them one more shot, a coup de grâce, if you will. We'll send a Western Union telegram, and if the Indians have cut the lines, we'll send García. The message will state, "Confirming Superior Plate presentation. Absolutely no one will be admitted without positive ID as principal of your firm to witness dramatic introduction of greatest invention in paper plates since the industry was formed."

That should do it. It did. They all replied affirmatively.

All right guys, what are we going to do next?

Next we're going to call Pinkerton.

"Pinkerton, we need two uniformed guards with shotguns. No, we're not protecting the Hope diamond, we're guarding a new paper plate. You wouldn't advise shotguns? Okay. We definitely want sidearms and the most lethal looking nightsticks you've got. Fine and dandy; we're sending you our confirming order."

Now I'm driving you hard, but don't fall asleep. Hey wake up! We're going over to look at our meeting room. The big event is tomorrow.

It'll do. We want a hundred chairs. I know it's not enough; let people stand. It'll create a sold-out, standing-room-only atmosphere. We need atmosphere. It's the only no-charge item on the list. The room has a two-step-up stage and a draw curtain. Great. We'll ask for a long picnic table and a large, stand-up electric fan.

Off we go to the market. We're going to buy paper napkins, cups, plastic forks, knives, spoons, and set that mother as if we're holding a state dinner, including our soon-to-be-famous StaPut paper plates."

It's showtime.

"Pinkerton, we want you to be so tough on them about getting in that they become totally pissed off. Come to think about it, give them a GI inspection. Check their business cards and ask for their driver's licenses. We don't care, we want tight security. We must say, you are very imposing— six feet four, blue uniform with badge and sidearms. Don't use them. Apply the nightstick if they give you a hard time."

Okay, we're ready to go.

The room filled to capacity including the front rows. (Sorry, no buck underneath them, we're running a tight ship.) There they were, brokers from all over the country; we hardly knew any of them. They sat down exchanging war stories as salesmen do, waiting for the last of them to pass through our ironclad security gates.

Excuse me, fellas, but I'll have to ask you to get out of my mind for a little while. There comes a time when I have to be entirely on my own. I'll bring you in as soon as I've finished my spiel . . . no, pitch . . . no, presentation . . . no, it's a State of the Union address.

I walked to the podium, waited for the murmuring to subside, and then started by saying, "Good morning. I want to welcome you on behalf of our company and apologize for any slight inconvenience you may have encountered in getting here."

A few had actually been denied admission at the door. The assembled group was well aware that those Pinkerton guys meant business.

"We have taken these precautions because, as you know, we are in a highly competitive business. We need every minute of secrecy to enable you to be the very first to spread the exciting word of what we are about to present."

I had them in the palm of my hand. My fingers were itching to close, but first I had to tell them how terrible things were, and how wonderful they were going to be. I gave them industry statistics, market dollar volume, estimates of growth in the supermarket outlets. Then I mentioned the problem of brand identification: the paper plate was the forerunner of all the generic products on the market today, dealers had needed only one brand. Until then.

"Today the Superior Paper Plate Company is introducing the absolute positive reason for your markets to place a second line on the shelf."

Dramatic moment. Pause. Turn, walk to the stage. Slowly draw back the curtain, bringing into view a long buckboard table with a dozen place settings of paper and plastic.

"Gentlemen. Everything is ready for a traditional family picnic. You can almost smell the aroma of the barbecue. And then, all of a sudden, just when everyone is about to sit down, a wind comes up and this is what happens. Watch closely."

I had to add that. It wasn't necessary. Their eyes were glued on the whole scene, but once a pitchman, always a pitchman.

I pulled the switch on the giant fan hidden behind the partially opened curtain. In an instant, everything on the table flew off the table as if hit by a hurricane. Everything except the StaPut paper plates.

"Gentlemen. Behold the StaPut paper plate." I did not have a chance to say anything else. They got on their feet with yells, shouts, and applause.

This was one of the most exhilarating moments of my entire career. I stood there basking in the fire of their excitement. The combustion of the brazen letters, the demanding exclusivity of the telegram, the Pinkerton guards, the dramatic, windswept presentation was just too much. They really went bananas.

When they all quieted down, I proceeded to tell them the product was developed in combination with the magnificent Minnesota Mining and Manufacturing Company, lest they think it was created in someone's kitchen. I showed them the packaging, emphasizing the eye-catching colors in contrast to present shelf dwellers. And when I told them the pricing would still be competitive, at least for the introductory period, the room again shook with their approval. Man, oh man, was I ever having a good time, and there was more to come!

"Gentlemen, production is scheduled to start within thirty days, at which time we will send you sample packages for your presentation to your accounts. At that time we will send a letter to the president of every supermarket chain in the United States and a similar one to their heads of merchandising and to their paper plate buyers. The letter to the president will read as follows . . ."

I proceeded to read a letter I had partially plagiarized from a perfectly classic one for a president of a company. It can and should be used again whenever you need to have a letter get through to "The Man."

The dynamite of the first sentence makes it insistent that they read on. Pow!

> While I appreciate that you cannot be aware of every facet of your company's operation, I am nevertheless tempted to bring to your attention a development that can have a major impact in one of your departments.
>
> In combination with the Minnesota Mining and Manufacturing Company, the Superior Paper Plate Company has developed the innovative StaPut paper plate. We will shortly be presenting it to your merchandising people.

*Knowing you will be curious, we are pleased to enclose
a small package of the plates for your enjoyment, with our
compliments.*

Now how beautiful is that? The whole thing was beautiful. I can't help it, modesty doesn't become me. I knew down to the marrow of my bones it was terrific.

They must have felt the same way. The meeting was over, but a good number of them stayed, waiting in turn to talk to me.

One of them seemed a cut above average in presence. He expressed his compliments and congratulations on the meeting and then went on to say, "Marc, I represent one of the largest food brokerage houses in New York and, for that matter, the country. We have over eighty men in our organization covering all of New York City and New Jersey. We also represent many of the finest lines on the supermarket shelf. What we would like to do is put on the same show that you have done here for all of our merchandising people in the markets."

Hmmm . . . shades of old Toots Shor's. I replied by telling him of that experience, and then he really became excited. Enthusiasm can be tempered by cost. So I asked if his company would share the cost of the affair. He replied, "Definitely," and we shook hands.

When it was all over I found myself alone in the meeting room. All the echoes faded away, and I reflected on how sad it was that no one from the company had been there. Jane was home, and I had no one with whom to share and exchange thoughts on the experience. I felt a surge of pride on what I had done, decided to decorate myself, walk tall, and go home to a hero's welcome. That's where I've always gotten one, win or lose.

In the ensuing days before production started I must

have personally signed over five hundred letters to the super-market executives. The big New York kick-off at Toots Shor's was set up, and our broker told us that anyone who was a somebody would be attending. It all looked pretty good.

As the early morning plane left Chicago for New York, I amused myself by counting paper plates. Let's see. Two hundred of the top chains with fifty, or in some cases one hundred or more stores, multiplied by one hundred plates per package, multiplied by this and by that, gave me a rough estimate of over one hundred million plates . . . cool; not too shabby for starters.

"The best laid plans of mice and men oft go astray," is an understatement of great magnitude. Nothing compares to the climax. Climax, not as in orgasm, but climax as in the most gigantic bomb ever dropped on one of the most carefully and brilliantly conceived product introductions (if I may say so) in the history of merchandising.

Look, fellas, if you haven't already done so, you'd better get out of my mind now while you have the chance. No need to go down with the ship. I know it's a fine thing I do, for I don't want you permanently scarred.

Me, I'll StaPut to the very end. And you, you can watch from the shoreline and benefit from the experience that will never permit you to be overconfident in any of the battles of your life. Prepare, train, study, think, fight, earn your confidence, but avoid going beyond that because some-times, not always, the fickle finger of fate is out there, and it might go right up your gazoo.

My plane landed in the early afternoon. I was met by my broker, who filled me in on the evening program as we drove into the city. He had done everything I requested, including setting up the picnic table and the big fan; all was ready at Toots's except bringing over the StaPut paper plates.

We sat together in the hotel room discussing our plans when I walked over to the box containing the samples the factory had sent by air freight the previous day. I casually opened a package. Just as casually I pulled the tab on the bottom and set it down on the cocktail table.

Son of a bitch! It didn't StaPut. I mean it slid off the table as if it were on ice. Oh, my God, what's going on!

I tried one after another, opened every package in the box. Not a single one worked.

Oh, that horrible sinking feeling! I jumped at the phone, called the factory.

"No, Paul's out to lunch. He'll be back in about half an hour."

That seemed an eternity. I paced up and down, sweating. What to do? We didn't have time to have the company plane fly in from Marion, Indiana, even if we had a plane, which we didn't. What went wrong? The hell with that. What could we DO?

There was only one thing possible. Put some glue on the tab and press down. Then honestly explain what had happened. But I still didn't know what had happened. Finally the phone rang.

"Paul, we have a problem," and I laid it on him.

"Hold on, Marc, let me check. . . . Marc, it's worse than that. We received a bad run of the product from 3M. I just closed the line down, but it's too late."

"Too late? What do you mean?"

"I mean every one of the sample packages that went out yesterday and the day before to the supermarket executives and the food brokers nationwide came from the same run."

Thud . . . plunk . . . bang . . . and crash. I hit bottom. And part of me is still there today. It groans a bit, and I can hear it especially on Memorial Day, the Fourth of July, Labor Day. What could I say? "I don't believe it, it's unbelievable, ridiculous, it can't be." The words rushed out in a torrent, to no avail. My paper plate died before it had a chance to live.

How ironic that the first production run of thousands of StaPut paper plates packaged in hundred-unit quantities, totalling many thousands, were perfect. But when the factory put the next batch of 3M rolls on the machines for the six-unit sample packages, we ran off thousands of NoStaPut plates, and out they went with our wonderful letter and all our hopes and dreams. The hopes dashed; the dreams turned into nightmares.

I could handle the damn meeting that evening, but my best efforts could not rectify the disaster once the mailing had been received. I can visualize exactly what happened. The pretty green and red package was placed on the president's desk with the letter.

He took one look and said, "Now that's a bright idea." He read the letter and said, "Let's see how it works," and opened the package. He tried to make it StaPut, failed. In an instant the light of interest went from bright to black. It was over right then and there, confirmed by the managers and buyers who had the same experience. It was a crying shame, and I cried shamelessly, as you can easily understand.

Yes, the meeting that evening was relatively successful. Yes, they all came. Yes, they all went so far as to applaud, not as heartily as our brokers group, for after all they were buyers, not sellers.

The magic moment when I switched on the fan and blew everything off but the plates was still the highlight of the presentation, which carried as its theme "We have the reason to place a second line on your shelf."

It was then I gave them the honest account of what happened; explained the need for jury-rigging glue on the tab for the demonstration; and assured them that their orders would have the thoroughly tested and correct application as provided by the world-famous 3M company, which would positively stand by its products; and promised that new samples were going out to them, etc.

Yes, we won them over. Not totally. Not the way it could have been. But how often does that occur even when all is perfect? I left that night down in the dumps, but on the outside I still maintained the appearance and voice of a winner. Best acting I've ever done.

Back to the plant and office to assess the results. Of course, we sent out new samples with a covering letter, but the impact was gone, and so was the need for a computer to add up the sales. Quite a few new chains placed orders, the most prominent being Jewel Tea in Chicago. But overall, it wasn't even close to the projected potential. New York turned out rather well, thanks to the special effort, but even then it was below expectations.

Another way of summing it up was, it wasn't a failure, nor was it close to being as successful as we had planned. I shake my head when I think that, without the disaster, we would have become a giant in the industry almost overnight. I would have been the boy wonder of the paperboard industry. But it simply wasn't meant to be.

There was, however, a substantial increase in volume over the previous year. This became apparent in the spring and summer, the paper plate season. On early spring weekends I would drive with the family down from Barrington, stopping at Jewel Tea stores in Des Plaines, Arlington, all the towns leading into Chicago, and investigate sales. It was apparent that we were getting our share, one hundred percent more than we had gotten before. I tended to believe, since our cost was the same as the competition's, that we were doing very well indeed. After all, it was just a matter of being on the shelf.

One fine day in midsummer, a contingent of 3M executives came into the office to inform me I had won the Commercial Application Award of the Year from their company. I received a laudatory letter from their president, and an entire Westinghouse Dream Kitchen, consisting of every known major and small appliance of the day, as my prize.

# Chapter 9

Amidst our daily trials and tribulations, when a child is born, all else fades away. For all the beauty of manmade works, nothing compares to nature and giving life to a human being in your image. And so it came to be that our fourth child was born in May of 1959. Jane had a habit of going into labor at three o'clock in the morning—bad timing. This time I found the car out of gas and had to empty the lawn mower's gas into a bucket and make the transfer. We had just enough to get to the hospital on time.

It then became a question of a name for our pretty little baby girl. As I would go into the hospital to visit at day's end, the nurse would ask for the child's name. On the third day, the nurses became incensed and insisted that we come up with one immediately. We had given this a great deal of thought, but suddenly I was inspired. I had it. We'd call her Pandora. If you remember Greek mythology, Pandora opened the box that permitted all the evils of the world to escape; only hope was left. I named her Pandora with the hope she would be the last one, and she was. Jane had some mild objections, but they subsided. Pandora has grown to womanhood cherishing her name, and we cherish her.

A few weeks after the 3M award ceremony my old friend Paul Wilson, of my New York days, telephoned me. He was now senior vice president of that extremely prestigious executive search organization, Boyden Associates. He told me about an opportunity that he believed I would find very interesting and that could lead to the making of a small fortune if everything came together.

I was intrigued and told him I would certainly be interested in hearing about it. We arranged a meeting within the week in New York. It's rather nice when people come after you instead of your going after them. No unanswered letters, no waiting for a reply to your phone call after you have left a message, no brief encounter after a long wait in an outside office. On the contrary, you have a warm welcome, introductions to one and all, luncheon at the Union League Club, and then "What we had in mind . . ." Then it's down to business, after you've been softened up. Yes, it's rather nice.

Paul's client was a manufacturer in Mount Clemens, Michigan, who for many years had produced a machine called Ironrite, an elongated mangle with thick, tubular rolls. A woman who was coordinated enough to use her arms, hands, and legs all at the same time could iron her weekly wash in less than half the time it would take with a hand iron.

This contraption had a retail price of close to four hundred dollars, and several thousand were sold a year. It was beyond my comprehension. I told Paul I was a pretty good salesman, but I wasn't a magician, and selling more than that would be a job for Houdini.

"Hold on, Marc. We agree. What interested us was this," and he pulled out a picture of a miniature version of the one-man brass band. (I had to admit it was only slightly more attractive than a toilet seat.)

"Take into account, Marc, that over two million hand irons are sold every year. This new unit, to be in production shortly, will retail for ninety-five dollars, not four hundred."

Hmmm. My interest was piqued. I recognized the new machine was the only alternative to a hand iron. Okay. What was the proposal?

Did you ever know a man who could make you hear beautiful music just by talking? The melody was a fifty percent increase over my present compensation, with an incentive program that would more than double that. Stop the music; the drawback was having to live in Mount Clemens, or near the plant. This required some tossing about.

We, or he, concluded that I was the man for the job, and Paul set up an appointment with their president. The meeting, a week later in Mount Clemens, went extremely well. Apparently I impressed him; within a few days he advised me that I would be their new vice president in charge of marketing.

In the interval, Jane and I had had long, realistic discussions about the decision to be made. On one hand, we lived a pleasant, serene life in a lovely home and community. On the other, we were almost flat broke. We could live as a family in comfort and joy in our beautiful house, but our financial situation did not allow for the same status once we left the driveway. In effect we had everything going for us except money. That had to be fixed!

The warm feelings all over, the praise, medals, titles, recognition, exciting and creative ideas, were all without substance. The measure of a man's success in the business world is how much money he is earning. And goddammit, I was getting tired of my disguise and the cosmetic effort to be one of the Joneses.

Jane and I decided to concentrate on the money. We would return to Barrington Hills, or its equivalent, when we had the money.

I told June Osborn about my opportunity. He accepted my resignation, but first offered to raise my salary if I would stay on. I explained how much I appreciated his offer, but that the opportunity, if successful, would develop into a monetary reward far beyond normal. And I would accept the risks involved. What I did not tell him was that I no longer saw a future with his company—status quo perhaps, but I'd never become rich. Frankly, somehow, the green eye along with my disappointment in the StaPut campaign combined to give me my first twinge of an antiestablishment feeling. Fortunately it never became more than a twinge, for that is as stupid an emotion as jealousy.

The fact of the matter is that we are the establishment—you and I and every person on the planet Earth. To be "anti" is in essence to be against yourself. Our real complaint is with the part we have in the establishment. Oh, I'm sorry I'm not a general, why am I just a Pfc? Can you tell me why I'm not the conductor instead of the second fiddle? Why am I a backup quarterback, a copilot? Why not in a box instead of the second balcony? Why am I covering the godforsaken Buffalo territory?

All right now, all of you who believe the world owes you not only a living but the very best, please stand over there. Good. Now the rest of us will continue to climb the damn mountain to achieve whatever our goals may be. It's easier now that we've gotten all the idiots out of the way. We still (forgive me) have to work hard, make sacrifices of all kinds, get beaten up by others and by conditions.

Generals don't join up on Monday and earn their stars by week's end. Maybe if you practiced more, you would have at least made first violinist. If you really wanted to make number one you could have, unless you really did not have it in you—most likely the case. However, a good backup is vital to any team's or company's success. If I were a captain and I knew I had the best damn copilot of the line, I'd sure let him know it. He's very important. And if I were the copilot, I'd know I was important and be happy in my work. Quite possibly you have never sat in a box. Try it once; you'll never want to go back to the peanut gallery. Lastly, the Buffalo territory, you poor S.O.B. Don't fight it, it's no use. Take solace in knowing there are many happy people in Buffalo. Live out your life as best you can. Someone has to do it, so good luck and God bless. Aside from that one unfortunate exception, the point is, we are the establishment. It's up to each of us to decide which part is best for us. It ain't all red-eye gravy on top of grits. Me, I just plan to keep climbing, even without a ladder. I've made the decision, it's my nature. What's yours? Don't kid yourself. Come clean. Make the decision and go for it. Be the best you can be, whatever it is.

My attitude toward my new position was quite different than it had been when I made regional sales manager, national sales manager, or my first VP title. I viewed myself as a pro. No more "Gee whiz, we can do it, rally 'round the flag, boys." No, this time I was a cold pragmatist, a surgeon to cut off the waste and fat, an antibiotic agent to prepare the ground for launching the product.

The factory and its sales force were picture perfect for this type of management. The factory turned out the same twelve thousand units of a single product, year in and out. The salaried sales force was barely making the calls necessary to sustain this lousy volume of business. There were about twenty salesmen and a manager. I would hate to have seen a motion picture of their individual days' activity lest I throw up on the factory floor, which was dirty enough as it was.

Within a few days it was clear to everyone in the plant that I was not going to win any popularity contests. The first thing cleared and cleaned was the factory floor. The second was going to be the sales force.

I spent a week going over yearly sales records by territory and generally familiarizing myself with the marketing operation, which amounted to little or nothing. I couldn't find promotional or advertising activity, anything at all that would help promote the stupid product. It sold basically on word of mouth, and obviously the owners were a closed-mouth group.

I then began to sketch out my ideas and plans for the interim period until the small version of the monster would be produced, which I understood to be three to four months away. When I had solidified the whole program, I went in to see the president and said, "Charles, this is what I want to do, what we should do, to prepare for the introduction of the new baby.

"First, I'm going to hold a general sales meeting here in Mount Clemens. When the salesmen arrive, I'm going to fire every one of them off their salaried positions. I'll then offer them the opportunity to stay on as commission-only representatives, providing they pass my requirements for the job. We're going to save beaucoup money without loss of sales. I believe most of them will stay on as straight commission men, especially after they see the presentation of the new product.

"Two, in the interim period, we're going to execute a campaign directed at the best laundromats in every major city in the country.

"Three, we're going to place four Ironrites in each of these selected laundromats, so they can offer a full, do-it-yourself laundry operation of washing, drying, and automatic ironing. By way of further explanation, at present a woman carries her washed laundry home for ironing. Soon she'll be able to do it automatically in less than half the time.

"Four, we're going to advertise the laundromats selected

to offer this exclusive service in large advertisements in the daily newspapers.

"Five, we will place a demonstration in the laundromats for three days to teach their customers to use the Ironrite. Once a few start to use it, they will automatically teach others.

"Six, the package will include point-of-sale material, colorful posters, window banners, etc.

"Seven, how are we going to pay for all of this? By selling to the laundromats at full retail and taking the difference between profitable distribution cost and regular retail price for the campaign.

"If all of this falls into place, thousands of people in almost every major city will become aware of Ironrite as a result of the promotion. Then we'll be ready to kick off the baby model to a softened-up market at a retail cost of less than a hundred bucks. If two million hand irons are sold annually, and if the dogs like it, we're going to have a win on our hands—a big one."

Of course, the whole program was approved. It became put-it-together time.

Step one was to hold a general sales meeting and fire the sales force. I should say convert them into salesmen, which I did. I told them that, effective at once, they were off salary and were on straight commission as independent representatives. Before they, or I, made a decision about this new mode of operation, we would relate our immediate plans for the sale of Ironrite to laundromats nationwide. All this, I informed them, was groundwork for the introduction of the new Ironrite, which was where the money for all of us was going to be. The long and the short of it was that they all lined up to sign on as independent representatives.

I want to point out that I'm not a where-do-you-get-off S.O.B. We were running a business, not a preschool-hold-hands, all-fall-down-and-laugh session. If it's not in the Harvard Yard book it should be: start your sales force with independent representatives on straight commission. If they become successful beyond your fondest hopes and dreams, it's sure as hell due to the product or service. That's when you convert them into salaried salesmen with an incentive. Conversely, when saturations are reached, when sales really start going down, convert them back to commissioned salesmen, or what will fall down is your company's bank account. And the only thing that will rise is the problem of meeting payroll.

Step two was the advertising program. I decided to go to one of the best, as I had learned from my StaPut experience. Being involved with 3M or a similarly well-known company lends credibility to your program. I targeted the J. Walter Thompson Agency, a powerhouse name and one hell of a large company.

This was as funny as it was ridiculous. If I had a budget of millions, boy oh boy, would they ever love to have my account. But we had no budget, not a thin dime. It was to be all on the come. As a matter of fact, even that was predicated on the results of the first test markets.

The funny part is that you never can tell until you try. I met with the senior vice president of the Chicago office in the Wrigley Building, as I remember. I outlined what I had in mind. Essentially they were to make up our half-page newspaper advertisement leaving the bottom part blank for a dealer testing. This advertisement would be scheduled to appear immediately after we had signed up the laundromats in each of the numerous cities, and after their orders had been delivered and were ready for operation.

I hastened to explain that the reason for the campaign was to set the stage for the new unit, whereupon I presented pictures of the prototype. Although I wasn't prepared to establish the size of the advertising budget, I led the Thompson VP to understand that we planned to make a significant financial investment, for the product was one of a kind in a vast market of hand irons. The guy wasn't an idiot; he knew what I was trying to do, right down to using the J. Walter Thompson name as a tool in the program. But the whole concept made sense. And I guess he thought that if once in a while you take a flyer, this might be one to fly with. That afternoon, I flew back as a new client of one of the world's largest advertising agencies; Ironrite had joined an august group of who's who in the world. Now *that* was ridiculous!

There were just two matters left to handle before we were ready to start the program. I needed three men who were a casting director's idea of perfection for giving a presidential address. These people had to be inspirational speakers whose presence, in addition to manner and dress, exuded integrity and business acumen. I wanted each to cover a third of the country as major-domos at the sales meetings we were going to hold for the selected laundro-mat owners. No one in my outfit except myself could pull this off. The others were too young, too ordinary, too inex-perienced.

Inspired, I ran ads in the New York Times, Chicago Tribune, Los Angeles Times, and the Wall Street Journal. I was willing to bet all the tea in China the response would be sensational, and it was.

---

### If You're Under 60 You're Too Young
### Three Retired Executives Wanted

If you're tired of retirement, if you yearn to get back in the saddle and have the fun of conducting a business meeting, here is an opportunity. Salary: $10,000

---

We were inundated with replies from retired chairmen of the board, presidents, senior vice presidents, generals, admirals. The reaction was wonderful. They didn't care about compensation. They just wanted to put on the harness for a while and run around the business track, just like the old days. Some of the letters almost made me cry, they were so beautiful as the men voiced their longing for the best and most active years of their lives. A random thought crossed my mind then that it was better to wear out than rust out, and I tucked it away for the distant future.

I had enough good men to choose from to run ten businesses; damn, they were good, and perfect for what I wanted. We also received some major dividends. The business editors of *Business Week* and *Fortune* and the *Journal* picked up on the advertisement. One after the other, they ran a story on my concept, followed by quite a few others in similar publications. Pied Piper Van Buskirk leading the geriatric tycoons down the lovely, knock-on-doors, ring-those-bells old path.

In my opinion this is a timeless concept. If there's any tea left in China, I'll bet that in the same circumstances, the same advertisement run today would produce the same results. Amazing thing about the mind: it can stay everlastingly young in comparison to the physical aging of the body. The only thing to do is keep them both active and hold on as long as it's fun. When it's not, the hell with it.

In very short order, we were ready to kick off a test market. I had the layout of the dealer ad, window banners, other point-of-sale materials, and the tried-and-true "You have been selected" letter to the prospects. All set, and away we went to our first meeting of the "selected" laundromat owners in a small town outside Detroit.

It was, without question, a huge success. They immediately recognized the competitive advantage of offering a complete laundry service. They were impressed with our home economist's demonstration, the advertising, the live demonstration program. Every one of them signed up—every one of them.

Talk about a good deal, meaning a fair exchange for both parties, this was a good three-way deal. The laundromat owner had an exclusive franchise for his neighborhood that would bring in additional customers who would spend more money than normal. The customer had the convenience of doing all her laundry—including ironing in less than half the time. And we obtained exposure of a product most people had never seen, advertising, publicity, demonstrations, and sales at full retail with more than enough profit to pay for the whole program.

Now you might be curious about what had happened to my seemingly forsaken family. I had left them in Barrington and would fly over from Detroit on weekends until I had a reasonable fix on the job and living environment. The latter was a definite departure from lovely Barrington. After three or four weeks, enough was enough. We missed each other, and I missed the monsters. I found a tract house in Birmingham, a northern suburb of Detroit, and leased it for six months. Jane came over one weekend to see it, walked in, sat down on the top of the two steps leading down to the living room (sound familiar?), and cried—a real good cry. It was so sad.

One more test market with the same results. Okay, let's go nationwide and hit them hard and fast. Jim Hopkins, that fine Irish lad from my Presto days, called and said he was available and wanted to join me. He was one hell of a good salesman, had a sharp business brain, and he was a friend. I needed all of those hard-to-come-by supports. We laid out an itinerary for covering the country, assigned our silver foxes a schedule along with our two home economists, synchronized our watches, blew the whistle, and over the top we went.

It was all that I could hope for. In the space of about two months we covered all the major and some minor cities in the country, selling to almost all the people attending the meetings. We could have gone on and on, but you begin to reach a point of diminishing returns when you drop the same major effort down to small-town markets.

Although I would still fly out to attend a meeting in New York or Chicago, after the first few meetings the crew took over. I began to think about launching the new, use-it-at-home version of Ironrite.

For one thing, I couldn't resist holding a press party at the 21 Club in New York with my old PR mentor, Lynn Farnell. Newspaper and magazine articles quickly followed, with headlines like "Ironing Can Be Hard on Heart" or "Laundromat Clients Arrive in Cadillacs" or "Tests Show Value of Automatic Ironing." All of this, spread by UPI or AP throughout the country, increased attendance at our sales meetings and gave me confidence that introducing the new product would be significantly easier because of all that we had done.

Within the laundry industry I had begun to make quite a name for myself. This was acknowledged at meetings of the American Laundry Institute, which comprised the top executives of the industry. I got to know one of them rather well and appreciated his knowledge of the industry and his sincerity in welcoming me into the group. His name was Jack Murray, and he was president of the Speed Queen Company of Ripon, Wisconsin. (Later on I had to call on him to help save my ass from a devastating, business-wrecking and life-wrecking fate. But that's another chapter. I can hardly wait to tell you, for it is a perfectly clear and fantastic description of the End Of The World. Some of you may be aware of hell on earth or, conversely, of a heavenly capsule of time, but, fundamentally, damn few of you know about the End Of The World. It's rather an exclusive experience.)

I began to sense an unraveling of my goals from the fact that the starting date for producing the new unit, the reason I joined the company, the whole purpose of the laundromat campaign, was constantly being delayed. And I had been aboard eight months.

I confronted the president, Charles Mollhagen. "Charles, what the hell is going on? We've completed the laundromat program. It has set the stage, which is what it was supposed to do. Now we need the new unit."

His answer was vague at the time but crystal clear shortly after the new year of 1961 at a board of directors meeting in New York City.

Jim Hopkins and I attended the meeting. By that I mean we stood outside the boardroom for over two hours waiting to be called in. When we were, it was a waste of time. I quickly summarized the results of our program. Over eight hundred of the country's best laundromats were each operating with four of our Ironrites. We were ready to market the new home version as soon as it could be produced.

I was thanked for my comments without being questioned and, in effect, ushered out. Out in more ways than one. Out of the program and out of a job. The board's conclusion was that the corporation was not in a financial position to proceed with the new unit because of losses sustained by the corporation as a whole and, in particular, its two other divisions. Stringent reductions in costs were to be immediately placed in effect across the board.

I knew that by submitting my resignation and getting off the payroll I would save the company from collapsing while my desk was still filled and cluttered. As a matter of fact, I got out without too many moments to spare, for shortly afterward the company ceased to exist. I subsequently learned that they tried to sell the never-produced unit to other companies in the industry, investment bankers, venture capitalists, etc. All to no avail. Hell, all you fellows in the buggy whip graveyard, move over, we have a new has-been coming in who lacked the balls to change with the times and couldn't see until the light was switched on.

It was a cold, snowy night as my plane landed at the Detroit airport to the applause of all the passengers. I needed a white-knuckle-where-the-hell-is-the-runway approach like a hole in the head after our miserable day in New York. Jane, as always, was waiting. I was dismayed to see the strain of our problems reflected in her face. In the swirling snow, I vowed to myself that we were going to get out of our miserable situation once and for all.

It wasn't so much that I was, in effect, fired. If you live by the sword, you die by it. I had fired a lot of guys, including the whole sales force when I came in; and then it had turned out to be bandanna-over-my-eyes time. Okay, for whatever reason, right or wrong, good or bad, the fact was I was canned, and I was truly pissed. (Damn it, I'm going to get it off my chest again.) I worked hard; I flew all over the damn country; I was creative as all hell; the program was totally successful. I had primed the market for the big blast, and all I had to show for it was a soaking wet, soggy match.

Open up the Experience Box and put in a new one for the future. Take the time to investigate offers or opportunities. Keep in mind, I hadn't been after Ironrite for the job; they were after me. One has the right to play somewhat hard to get. But not me. If the company employed Boyden Associates as its headhunting agency, had been in business for a number of years, was well known and a listed member of the stock exchange, I accepted at face value that it was financially sound. Furthermore, I did not take the time to call on dealers or distributors where I could have really obtained answers about the company and its products' acceptability. Nor did I ask flat out the timetable for the new product's production. Lastly—of more than minor importance—I did not ask for a contract. I should have, for as I've said, they were after me to change jobs; I didn't knock on their door. No question, I was a dumbshit.

Now let me give you a glimpse of the End Of The World (a composite picture comes later). First of all, the recession of 1960–1961 was in full swing. I was located out in the boonies of Michigan in the dead of winter without the benefit of a golden parachute or handshake, just a good-bye. I did not have the luxury of putting "I'm considering making a change . . ." bullshit in a letter or advertisement.

The most frightening reality was early morning in our tract house. The very moment the sun touched the horizon as it began its day's climb, four screams for food came out of the mouths of ages one-half, one and a half, two and a half, and three and a half. The same rooster cry occurred again at noon, again in the afternoon, once more when the sun went down, plus a small cry in the night for a midnight buffet. We were practically running a damn cruise ship. There was absolutely no chance of getting ahead. Every time we came close, whammo, more bills. We were in the red again.

Things were gloomy. I placed advertisements in the major newspapers announcing my availability, responded to all the advertisements I felt qualified for, and nothing happened. I flew to Chicago and New York, called on Heidrick and Struggles, and Boyden Associates. "Sorry, we have no clients for your classification at this time."

I had the distinct feeling I was then viewed as a three-time loser: Presto, Superior Paper Plate, and Ironrite. "Please go away. We want to play with winners and have no time for people who have questionable backgrounds compounded by the lack of educational degrees."

Talk about being depressed.

A month went by, a cold, heavy, leaden sky, day after day, the way Michigan is in winter. Just as I was about to read a manual on "How to Pump Gas and Clean Windshields," the sun broke through in the form of a laundry and dry cleaners manufacturers' convention being held somewhere in Ohio. It was an opportunity to meet many of the top guys in the industry, quite a few of whom knew or knew of me.

It was a typical industry convention, with large exhibits by various manufacturers. I walked down one aisle and up another, sizing up the various products being offered and the companies involved. There were two problems. I wasn't looking for a position as salesman or regional sales manager. Hell, I was an ex-vice president of sales and marketing, looking for a job at that level. All the companies had those vice presidents; I'd met them at the convention. Problem number two, they all said they could not afford me. My salary level was as high as or higher than theirs, and one per company was enough.

Just about the time my ass was really dragging and my spirits were as low, it happened. I came upon an exhibit under the banner of the Ajax Pressing Machine Company. I had some knowledge of this business, having demonstrated pants pressers in my early days.

Talk about luck. If I had missed going up that one aisle, I'm absolutely positive I never would have ended up making several million dollars, living in beautiful La Jolla, or perhaps never living at all, in the sense of experiencing the world and all it has to offer.

Ajax was one of the foremost manufacturers of steam pressing equipment, the kind you see in laundry or dry-cleaning establishments. My immediate impression was that if I could not get excited about selling nuts and bolts, there was no possibility of going gung ho with a commercial pressing machine. I was about to turn heel and walk away without meeting one of the principals, when he finished his conversation and walked over to me. "I'm John Strike," he said, "and you're the man who developed the Ironrite program for laundromats. I'm pleased to meet you."

The warmth of his greeting renewed my faltering self-assurance. We adjourned to a cloistered area and began to talk. After a few minutes, he excused himself and returned with his brother, Nick, and we got down to cases.

The cases being that they had developed a coin-operated machine for laundromat distribution (My God, how déjà vu can it get?) and needed someone to activate a marketing program. Naturally I was a prime candidate. But hold on, not so fast.

"Marc, we can't afford you." I'm sure I could set that lead to music, I've heard it so many times. I was just about to tell them I'd work for nothing simply to keep in shape, so to speak, when they continued.

"However, we would like you to join us as a consultant for a period of six months, during which time we'll pick your brains and ask your advice. You will be free to pursue other activities, bring in another client. All we ask is that you live west of the Rocky Mountains, because our plant is in Salt Lake City and this is still a slow, prop-plane era."

They offered to pay me $2,000 per month as a consultant, less than half of what I was earning at Ironrite. In today's world that would be, conservatively, the equivalent of $6,000 a month. Comparatively, the cost of living was incredibly low.

Of far greater importance, I would be a free man. No more answering to a president or arguing my plans with various vice presidents. All of those thoughts raced across my mind, and within a split second I answered by saying, "You have a marketing consultant, and he's going to live in La Jolla, California."

We shook hands and I flew home to tell Jane. "We're free at last! We're escaping corporate persecution and geographical prostitution. What a wonderful feeling. From now on, it's a brand-new life for all of us. California, here we come!"

In mind and spirit, we felt we were leaving a very depressing old world, entering the new and unknown, confident in the knowledge that if all failed, I could always find a job as a salesman. That old tan attaché case would never let me down.

Well, all that rah-rah, charge into the wind, boys, is fine and dandy, but here are the facts. I was touching forty years of age, had a wife, four small kids, a house with a mortgage back in Barrington, one 1957 Cadillac with the long fins, about $5,000 in the bank, and no debt except for the house. That was the sum total for forty years. Terrible! And I had been offered six months in which to do something to keep us going, to say nothing of making a million (of which I was, by my calculations, $965,000 short, before the last milk bill arrived).

We directed all of our activity toward our plans to leave Birmingham immediately. First things first. Since we were in Detroit, we'd trade in the old car for a new Cadillac convertible. After all, we were going to California. Next, bring in the movers.

"We don't know our forwarding address. Place everything in the San Diego warehouse until we locate. Oh yes, in regard to insurance, we've moved several times without a scratch. We'll take the minimum policy of $5,000. Thank you very much."

"Oh, Jane, one small item. We can't all fit into the dumb car: there's the two of us, four kids, two dogs (large). I think it would be best if I drive and you fly out with the kids. It will take me three days. If you leave on the third day, I'll have found accommodations and will meet your flight in San Diego."

There were some strong murmurings of "You're leaving me to finish packing, etc., while you have a happy drive to the West Coast in a new Cadillac convertible. . . ." I was lucky to escape with my life.

As it turned out, I barely made it in time. As their DC-6 set down on the runway at Lindbergh Field, I arrived at the old airport on the east side of the field. The doorway to the plane opened, and down the mobile stairway they came.

First off, Jane, holding Pandora in one arm and hand-holding Ann who held Marc who held Amy, all having thrown up all over the plane due to a rough trip. Our dogs had contributed to the scene by shitting in their boxes in the cargo bin and having it all over them when released. I rushed up to my family to say "Welcome to San Diego." Before I could utter a word, Jane stopped, looked at me and said,

"You son of a bitch!"

No question she called me by the right name. It might have been a good flight if the weather had been pleasant, but it wasn't, and that was bad joss, as they say in China.

Don't ask me how, but we all jammed into the car with the luggage and dogs and drove to the one motel that would take a Coxey's army such as ours. It was located on La Jolla Boulevard, where I had signed in for a one-bedroom with living room and kitchen. Bodies and dogs were all over the place. After bathing down the whole crew and fast-feeding them, we settled in for our first night in beautiful La Jolla. We felt so alone.

We had about four or five days to find a house to rent before our furniture arrived. We certainly could not afford to buy one. The next day we drove around town, down Girard Avenue, up Prospect Street, down to La Jolla Shores, up Mount Soledad, down to the Muirlands, and over to Upper Hermosa, Lower Hermosa, and Windansea beach. That pretty much covered the community of La Jolla then and now, although some builders have constructed housing developments almost as far east as Kansas City, and call them La Jolla.

What an absolutely lovely, charming community. We were convinced we had found an ideal place to live. After a very fast look-see, we stopped at an imposing realtor's office. We introduced ourselves as newcomers interested in renting a house before buying one and asked which was the better section or sections of La Jolla. The reply is as applicable today as it was thirty years ago.

"There is no 'better' section; they're all better. It's just a matter of where you would enjoy living the most—up in the Muirlands with a view of the area and city, down in the Shores, close to the beach, or on the beach." There was no wrong side of the tracks.

Very soon thereafter we found out that the town had a sense of humor. Everywhere we went to look at a house the occupants shook with laughter when we told them we, meaning Jane and I and four kids ages one through four, plus two dogs, would like to rent their home.

A few days later our furniture arrived. We asked for it to be placed in storage as we continued to search for a house, but we found out we had better pick up the pace. One night we were awakened by police whistles and shouts. Our motel was being raided as a swinging whorehouse. The motel had a bar and restaurant with live music. We had no interest in the bar, nor did we patronize it. We poked our heads in one night and saw a half-clad girl on an elevated swing going back and forth. It seemed pretty risqué, but we gave it no further thought until the raid. Years later, when people asked where we lived when we first came to town, we smiled and answered, "Oh, in a whorehouse on La Jolla Boulevard." It has long since been torn down and is now a condominium complex. Well, ya gotta start someplace.

Less than a week later, Jane went to what was then a landmark store called The Little Folks Shop. While there she mentioned her house-seeking activities. By luck and by chance the shop owner's husband was there and, being a realtor, informed Jane he might have just the house. Did he ever!

When I arrived back at the motel I found Jane quite excited.

"Marc, I've found the house. It's wonderful, it's on the ocean, it's expensive, it's only for four months . . ." she babbled away.

"Hold on, how expensive?" I asked.

"Three hundred dollars a month for March through June. Oh Marc, wait until you see it."

We waited five minutes, jumped into the car, and drove over to 325 Dunemere, in what is called the Barber Tract, named after the original builder of the house, who owned a tract of land in the area. We found an absolutely gorgeous house and location covering about an acre of land, a charming adobe house with sprawling lawns on either side, one going down to the beach. We rang the bell and met Patsy Woods, who would become a dear friend to this day. She didn't give a damn how many kids we had, and she owned two dachshunds so our dogs were no problem. We hit it off and she agreed to rent to us. I wrote out a check for the four months' rent. We moved into her furnished house a few days later. It was unbelievable. Within two weeks we had gone from the misery of Michigan to the beauty of La Jolla and moved into a lovely house smack on one of the best beaches in California. That one innocent visit to The Little Folks Shop was eventually to lead us to a future of several million dollars in real estate and business . . . only in America.

In 1961 La Jolla was called the Village; it still is. A bit larger, San Diego was known as a quiet, peaceful, Navy town. San Diego was the end of the line for a one-track railroad from Los Angeles. To go anywhere by train you first had to go to L.A. Light industry was the only manufacturing, except for Rohr Aircraft (which could fly out). All other manufacturing was restricted by geography and freight costs. That the city has gone on to become a giant in educational, medical, scientific, and biotech facilities is understandable, all the more when you realize that the climate, the recreational activities, and just plain living for poor or rich are unsurpassed in the whole wide world.

My own war with the world was held in abeyance during those first three weeks in La Jolla. Why not? My family was fun and precious. We were living in a fabulous house on the ocean. The migration was over. We knew La Jolla was where we would live and die. But as in Barrington Hills, we had to earn the right to live there, because it was a wealthy environment. This time there could be no retreat. I was going to make it here and make it big, for truly we were at the point of no return.

# Part Three

---

# The World Becomes My Territory, With the Exception of Buffalo

# Chapter 10

I began to look ahead. The logic of placing an Ajax pressing machine in a laundromat was obvious, and developing a simple marketing program to do so was no problem. The real problem was where would I be after my six-month contract came to an end? Very frightening.

The whole town seemed to be made up of one-room offices occupied by entrepreneurs who wanted to live and do it (whatever "it" was) in La Jolla. Moving there was like bringing your guitar to Nashville for a tryout and a shot at the big time. You gave it your best, and within a few weeks or months you were gone and a new hopeful would take your place.

I started to strum on my brain cells marked "New Ideas." What could I come up with that really "Filled A Need"? If I could just find the "Need."

The answer came out of the blue—Navy blue, worn by the sailors who in those days wore uniforms on and off duty all over San Diego. Holy cow! Their pants had an inverted crease. Turn them inside out, lay them down on the press, and in ten seconds one leg was beautifully pressed. In less than two minutes the pants were done, and the entire uniform could be pressed in about five minutes. It was an absolute natural for the military. Let's go get 'em.

The Navy exchange officer greeted me cordially after I told his secretary I was a marketing consultant. (As opposed to a salesman: there are times when you have to wear different hats; and I learned to wear a closetful of them before too long.)

"Sir, in my considered opinion," (based on no facts at all) "we have a concept that will offer your enlisted personnel a simple, easy, economical way to press their uniforms after they have been washed and dried in the exchange laundromat—in effect offering a complete service. We would like to run a test for a month to determine if we are right. If we are, we will bring in whatever number of machines are required and sign a contract with the exchange to share profits on the equipment."

Since we were the only manufacturers of the equipment, there was no need to follow the normal procedure of going out for bids. After asking a few questions about the machine's operation, the officer agreed to the test. We decided to bring in two machines as soon as possible. I informed the Strike brothers of what I was about. They responded by fast-shipping the equipment. Within two weeks, the machines arrived and were installed. All that was required was a 220-volt outlet and a water line to the unit.

It was a sight to see. Sailors lined up to use the machines morning, noon, and into the late hours of the night. I would say, conservatively, that the machines ran 15 out of 24 hours. Now that adds up. The charge was 25¢ for 15 minutes or $1.00 for an hour. Each machine returned $15 per day, which meant $30 for two, multiplied by thirty days, or $900 per month.

It all sounds so tacky, so look-what-the-little-people-do-to-make-a-buck, almost degrading, a stupid vending machine made me $15 per day. I was so picayune in the scheme of things. I might as well have opened a shoeshine stand.

Before I began to drown in self-pity I said to myself, "Hold on. Just a minute. You've found a formula. All you have to do is duplicate it over and over again in the vast military complex, where they really have a need for this service."

When you believe in what you've done and what you can do, you exude a contagious enthusiasm that opens doors, minds, and pocketbooks for whatever project you are presenting. My dumb coin-operated pressing machine did all of that. I provided a most welcome, good, and needed service. The military personnel instantly recognized what it could do for them, and had no hesitancy in paying for its use. Lastly, the Navy exchange made a profit without a capital investment. Now how good is that? Everyone benefited, which is the essence of a saleable product or program.

I watched those two machines like a hawk for two weeks. For one thing, I had to keep in mind that first reactions are not always enduring. Would the line of customers continue or fade away? What about problems, if any, with the machine itself? How often was service required? All of these questions would be answered by test marketing, which I was doing; at least I thought I was doing it.

No question, I had a winner. I asked the factory to ship two more units, which they did, and our volume doubled. I realized I could be involved with a truly big moneymaker. As fast as I could I went to the Marine Corps at El Toro and Camp Pendleton. Within a few weeks I secured contracts with each of them to place units in their barracks, since there were no laundromats on the bases. The Marines were a real market. The creases in their fatigue uniforms were sharp enough to shave by. I mean those Marines were sharp when it came to appearance. Perfect customers. Well, almost.

It was one thing to wrestle four of these three-hundred-pound machines into the Naval Station laundromat with the aid of some casual labor, but quite another to install them in individual barracks. Lifting them up stairways, maneuvering them into rooms, and installing them was not my bag. I primarily worked with my brain and my mouth. Anything mechanical, beyond screwing in a light bulb, was beyond my ability.

I recognized the problem and solved it by asking a tall, rugged, retired Marine to join me. Me, not my company; I still didn't have one. His name was Chester Halcomb, and he looked every inch a Marlboro man. He had risen through the ranks of the Marines as an enlisted man, was made an officer and gentleman during World War II and the Korean War, and then was reduced in rank to master sergeant when the need for "Johnny, get your gun" was over. That's the military system. It isn't arcane—everyone knows what to expect—but it's tough on the family, as they say.

Chet was a terrific guy. He talked like Gary Cooper in *High Noon* and worked in some assistant capacity at the exchange warehouse for service equipment such as mine. As time went by, we were looked on as a Mutt and Jeff team. I would tell somebody all we could and would do on this and that. They would then look at Chet with his Rock of Gibraltar appearance, and after he softly said one word or two words, their doubts disappeared. It was that simple.

I keep telling you about "formulas," and that when you find one it becomes a matter of duplicating and multiplying to make your fortune. Let me give you a few examples, all of which started with a single idea, store, or service. How about McDonald's, Kentucky Fried Chicken, Budget Rent-A-Car, Midas; the list is endless. A formula is not exclusively for ideas or service concepts. It's about people as well. Chet was a formula, and people like him, as I will relate, built the foundation for my future company and its success.

I've always believed in the old expression—similar to "Life has its ups and downs"—"You have to take the turkey with the cheese." A philosophical cliché, until it really happens to you. I received a double dose of a downer with plenty of cheese just about this time.

One morning we woke up to the newspaper headline "San Diego Warehouse Burns to the Ground." It was the warehouse holding all our earthly possessions: all our furniture, ninety percent of our clothing, memorabilia, family pictures, letters, books, and the stamp collection started by my grandfather, which was probably more intrinsically valuable than everything else put together. And would you believe that our Westinghouse Dream Kitchen in the original cartons burned to ashes? Devastating. On top of that, the insurance had expired two weeks before the fire. We had absolutely nothing except the clothes on our backs. From that day forward, whenever I read about, or see on TV, people who are in tears for having lost their home due to fire or storms, I cry right along with them.

We might as well bundle all the bad news together and get on with it. I told the Strike brothers I had decided to execute the idea of placing the units on military bases myself and received their enthusiastic consent without outlining the conditions as to costs to me, terms, payment program, etc. In the meantime, they continued to send additional equipment that I quickly placed at the El Toro and the Camp Pendleton Marine Corps bases.

About two weeks after the fire, John Strike came to La Jolla. I took him on an inspection tour. From the beginning I had kept them closely informed about what and how we were doing. I had held nothing back, including the amount of money the machines were producing. But reading is one thing, and seeing is another. I mean, those coin boxes were filled with quarters every time I opened one up during our trips to the various locations.

I'm confident it won't come as a shock when I tell you that the Strikes called me shortly after John's visit and advised me they were going to be my new partners and asked me to fly to Salt Lake so we could discuss and agree on a partnership arrangement. Next to not wanting a hole in the head, a partnership with them came in a close second.

When I arrived in Salt Lake I received a very warm and cordial reception from all three Strike brothers and their father. The elder had immigrated from Greece around the turn of the century, landed in Salt Lake, and got a job working on the railroads. Literally, he was a striker. That meant he would handle the huge sledgehammer and strike the large bolts into the wooden railroad ties. His original name had been one of the long Greek ones, and when the time came to change it, he decided the name Strike was most appropriate because of his successful endeavors.

The outcome of our meeting—after a bit of a fight— was that we would form a partnership with my holding fifty-one percent control. The company would sell me the machinery, which I would pay for out of earnings. They told me their attorney would draw up a partnership agreement that they believed, based on our future growth, would be a profitable and exciting venture for all of us. I had mixed emotions, a forty-nine percent mix. But under the circumstances, my options were extremely limited.

With their approval in hand, I was determined to place as many machines in operation as I possibly could. If I had to share the pie, I wanted it to be one helluva a large one.

Would it not be interesting to read a book made up of business mistakes? Actually you could fill a room with volumes about one goof-up after another. You would think, after intensive research and study, that you could avoid every mistake that had ever been made, leaving only the right decision to action. Well, here comes the first of many mistakes in my new venture.

I contracted with Army and Air Force bases to place the units in all available locations. The Navy and the Marines were, as I've said, perfect customers who used the hell out of the machines. The Air Force turned out to be the worst, closely followed by the Army. The Air Force worked under and on airplanes in fatigues that would grease up and soil in no time. When out of uniform, they all wore wash-and-wear clothing or blue jeans; they had absolutely no reason to use a pressing machine. I had placed about fifteen of them on the line at March, Norton, and Vandenberg Air Force bases before realizing I might as well have placed them in a nudist colony.

We went back to fill the sure-shot locations, the Navy at Long Beach, Moffett Field, and Alameda, and then on to the biggest adventure of them all, Hawaii.

I left Chet to service as best he could all of our locations in California and took off from Los Angeles on one of the first Pan American 707 Clipper flights to Honolulu. In only a few hours, we landed at the old airport and taxied up to the small bamboo terminal, a scene right out of The High and the Mighty. The week before I arrived, getting to Hawaii had meant a nine- to ten-hour flight on a DC-7, or a sea voyage on the lovely SS Lurline.

In 1961, Honolulu was just beginning its tourist boom due to the introduction of jet travel. There were only three hotels of consequence on Waikiki—the Moana, the Royal Hawaiian, and the Halekulani. To say Hawaii is beautiful territory is an understatement, and I'd best leave the descriptions to the poets, composers, and authors such as Michener. Me, I had a job to do and decided to treat it as if I were in Kansas City, lest I go native in a hurry. Within four days, I had secured approval and had contracts in the works with the Navy for Pearl Harbor, the submarine base, Barbers Point, and the Kaneohe Marine Corps base. I avoided the Army and Air Force.

I jumped the first plane home with an estimate requiring forty of the units a cost of approximately $35,000, including ocean freight. I had no doubts about the success of what would be my biggest and most concentrated operation. I was totally confident that those bases would be the top producers of any in the country. My God, the military would press a uniform and walk out in the pineapple juice (meaning rain) and come back and press it again, a fantastic moneymaking machine.

Thus began the saga of our adventures in Hawaii that has, over the years, brought me back to those enchanted isles well over a hundred times. I'm what they call kama-aina, the nearest thing to being native born. And I have privileges. For example, when the flight attendant hands out the forms for declaring any animal or whatever you are bringing in to Hawaii, I have for the last fifteen years put down one rhinoceros (small) and one baby white elephant (fairly large). So far they haven't pulled me aside for a talk. When you're building and winning, everything is fun. I had a labor of love and fun, a really happy time. Why can't it always be that way?

I received no word regarding our partnership agreement, and I certainly wasn't going to bring it up. The Hawaiian units were shipped. Checking the shipping schedule, and allowing two days for off-loading, Chet and I flew to Hawaii for the installation at the various bases.

We found a small but new hotel off Kalakaua Avenue, the main drag through Waikiki. The next day we went to the Matson dock, and there they were, all forty, in wooden crates, very imposing. Now what? How do we . . . who do we . . . what can we do to get this junk moved?

Chet said, "No problem. We'll go out to Kaneohe (the Marine base), where I'll find some old friends."

I'll never forget the scene at the Matson dock the next day. Three large Marine trucks, each carrying four men, came in convoy, drove up to the equipment, and started to load up. Unbelievable; those crates were so big and heavy! They made three trips back and forth to Kaneohe, dropping the units off at the designated barracks. The next day they returned and did the same for the naval station at Pearl Harbor, the submarine base, and Barbers Point. I mean they uncrated and lifted the equipment right smack where it was to be located, all in three days. In concert with the delivery, Chet had picked two Marines to help him install the water and electrical lines. They had it down pat and knocked off one after another. Totally amazing. Once a Marine, always a Marine, and Chet sure as hell was one of them. These men were all off-duty at the time, and we paid them. But the cost was ridiculously low in comparison to a typical freight company, if we could have found one.

Somehow, while all of this was going on, we began to look for a retired Navy chief or Marine master sergeant to be our manager for Hawaii. His job would consist of keeping all the machines running and clean, collecting the money on a weekly or semimonthly basis depending on usage, depositing it in our new Hawaii bank account, and sending us weekly reports with financial information, parts requests, etc.

We quickly found that there are chiefs and there are chiefs. We spent three very interesting days on the project. There were chiefs who, recently retired, would hang around the NCO club drinking beer with old mates and had absolutely no intention of doing anything else. Their future was behind them. They were secure in their pensions and planned to simply enjoy life.

We met the right man on the third day of our hunt. As I remember, we asked him to come to our hotel that evening. George Brown had served for just over twenty years. After the first few minutes, Chet and I knew we had found our man. George was at Pearl Harbor, a destroyer man who had married a local and was raising two children. He was one of those guys that you believed would carry out any job you could throw at him. He was another Chester; how good and lucky could we get? After a day of training and visiting the sites, we left George and flew home knowing we had done an outstanding job, but not knowing it was going to develop into the worldwide operation that it is today.

# Chapter 11

One might have the impression I was raking in money left and right. I was, but before I could put it in my dumpster, it would blow away. Expenses of all kinds kept cropping up. I needed an office and a secretary and a bookkeeper, a truck for Chet and one for George, insurance, and every miscellaneous expense imaginable in starting up a business, plus the cost of home and family. I was of course no longer receiving a consulting fee. We lived off the revenue of the machines, and after all was paid out, we were out of money.

The answer was to increase the number of machines on each location to a point where we more than covered our fixed expenses. For a simple example, if two men could service two hundred machines, and our break-even point was one hundred, with all costs except equipment figured in, we would then be in the happy state of making a lot of money. Oh, there was one small item; I almost forgot. We weren't paying for the equipment. It was all being shipped to us on memo billing. How nice.

You are now invited to take a ride on my roller coaster. All set? Off we go! During the climb up we receive a telephone call from Nick Strike.

"Marc, we have decided we can't go through with our partnership arrangement."

The first down-we-go and up-we-go is sheer exhilaration. Look at us, we're flying, we're free. It's all ours. We're really in business. Boy oh boy! At last!

Nick continued, "Marc, what has happened that is our young brother, John, has just been promoted to our parent company, American Laundry Manufacturing, as a top executive."

"That's wonderful," I injected.

"Yes," he said, "but we all believe it would be considered a matter of collusion if we were to proceed as planned."

"Yes, I can understand that. However, what do we do now? It seems as if I am going to be left with quite a large bag," I replied, knowing they had thought that problem through. (Hold on; we're just about to go down a big dipper!)

"What we're going to do, Marc, is personally loan you $10,000 to be applied as a down payment on all of the units we have shipped. Then we're going to place the balance due on a typical time-payment program that will extend out five years. Based on the dollar volume you are doing, this should present no problem. As a matter of fact, it should be terrific."

Sorry. You can't get off the roller coaster, we're being taken for a ride. Try not to be sick. Keep in mind we'll soon be in the driver's seat, completely in charge. . . . Okay. It's over. You can get off now, before it's too late. Hurry!

So it came to pass that I cut all ties to a system that had employed me, sent me a semimonthly paycheck, contributed to my health insurance, given me an expense account, established a year-end bonus, paid my vacations and sick leave, and would have topped it off with a pension if I had stayed around long enough. I must have been out of my mind, absolutely no question about it.

It became increasingly obvious that we were spread too thin, except for Hawaii. On the mainland, one base had four units, another twelve, and still another, a hundred miles away, offered six installations. The real money was being made by the military laundromat operations and on large bases with barracks installations where the combination of washers, dryers, and pressers would produce maximum returns with a greatly diminished cost of labor. The contracts for military coin-operated washers and dryers came up for bid and renewal every three years. The companies who held those contracts had enjoyed many years of almost uncontested bidding.

As I made the rounds of all of the bases in southern California, I quietly signed up as a prospective bidder on the forthcoming contracts. All of a sudden, the first one popped out, and we were invited to bid on a powerhouse of a contract. The laundromat at the San Diego Naval Station was probably the most lucrative installation on the West Coast. We knew what we were getting into; the business there went at full bore—morning, noon, and night, without letup, seven days a week.

I had been operating and contracting under the heading of Marc Van Buskirk and Associates. It made sense to me to change this into a corporation. I did so immediately, calling on the services of Shall, Nielsen & Boudreau, a prominent law firm in San Diego, where I met Richard Gore, a soon-to-be partner. He drew up the articles of incorporation, and presented me with the corporate seal for International Vending Corporation, dated October 16, 1961—seven months to the day from our first arrival in La Jolla.

This was decidedly a loose corporation. For one thing, I was president and treasurer, Jane was vice president and secretary, and the board of directors was made up of members of the law firm and practically any pedestrian I could find on the street. I thought of naming one of my kids to the board but had the idea we might have to change diapers during a board meeting.

In naming the corporation "International," I had drawn on my childhood vision when collecting stamps. Certainly what we offered was international in scope. Why not think in terms of bringing it to the Far East, Europe? Anything and everything is possible. Besides, the name had a mysterious and prestigious sound to it.

Now we get to the really funny part. The corporation was capitalized by the issuance of 10,000 shares of common stock wholly owned by the principals, each share worth one dollar. This was arrived at by taking the $10,000 loaned to me by the Strike brothers as capital. I sure as hell didn't have it. I then wrote out a check in this amount and sent it along to them as the down payment on all the dumb pressing machines I had placed in the field.

The time to fall on the floor laughing was when I looked at my first complete balance sheet. It had absolutely no balance. The liabilities were horrendous. There were no assets, unless you counted—which you could, I suppose— the $10,000 capital investment, unless you took into account that it was owed by me personally. Oh yes, I was asked to sign for the loan as a corporation as well as to sign as an individual, meaning personally. Not having any earthly possessions of consequence except the clothes on our backs, I had very little to lose if things went to hell. As a matter of fact, they were already in hell. I was bankrupt, but fortunately I didn't know it.

There was no way I could file for Chapter 11. I had nothing to reorganize. No sir, I was a prime Chapter 7 candidate. It was clear as the white of the driven snow: all I had were liabilities. As a matter of fact, the corporation owed about $90,000 to Ajax Pressing Machinery Company. Woe was me. Talk about being short of my million-dollar goal. I was now just about one million, one hundred thousand short, and counting.

All of this sounds a bit grim, and it was. But I concerned myself only with cash flow. By my simple calculations, if I brought in more cash than I paid out, I was in business. Tax requirements, depreciation schedules, all of that could be sorted out later on. Right then, did I have enough cash to meet the payroll and every other expense of a new business and still have some left over to feed my starving kids?

(Actually, they were far from starving. If anything, they were at the start of becoming uniquely spoiled, as only children raised in La Jolla can become. Sooner or later they realize they are not part of the real world, but by then it's too late.)

So I carefully filled out the form for the proposed contract. The most relevant question was the percentage of commission to be paid to the Navy exchange on monthly revenues. All else was incidental. Here was the moment of pure truth; the bid was critical. I estimated, based on the scraps of intelligence I had gathered in talking to the present contractor's serviceman, that they were under contract in the twenty- to twenty-five percent range. Since bringing in new equipment was not one of the requirements of the contract, I assumed that the present contractor would be in a position to easily raise his percentage to the exchange as a result of having fully amortized his equipment costs over the length of his contract.

I decided to go with a bid of thirty-one percent, allowing the present contractor a normal five percent increase; it seemed an intelligent way to go. All bids were to be opened at a certain date and time without bidders being present. But the hour and day passed without an announcement of the winner, which I found rather puzzling. We were subsequently told that the exchange did not think it had received enough bids and would therefore try to attract more participants. In effect the exchange was going out for bid again. Their letter to me included a new form to complete and send in.

Hold on, something was fishy about that. Why didn't they commit on the bids they received? I know there were at least two—the present contractor's and my own. Nothing was said about a minimum number of bids being required. Was there a leak? Was this a signal to the present contractor? I had not the slightest doubt about the integrity of the exchange, but the procedure was most unusual.

On the second bid I raised the commission to thirty-three percent from thirty-one percent, reasoning that even if the other bidder knew about my competition, I might still beat him out by one percent.

The results were announced: we won! I never found out by exactly how much, but I had the feeling that my original bid would have been more than sufficient.

I have to point out that the military business, especially when it came to vending equipment, was in its embryonic form. Not too many concerns in the industry knew such business existed. It was somewhat mysterious. And horror stories circulated about the pitfalls of maintaining equipment around young, kick-it-in troops and sailors.

I was absolutely ecstatic. The volume of business the contract would produce, combined with the income from the pressing equipment, was like bringing in an oil well. No question, this was the formula to duplicate on as many military bases as I could acquire. But before taking over the voild, mein friends, I had to purchase and pay for the equipment necessary to fulfill the contract. No problem. All I needed was about twenty-five thousand American dollars.

Within twenty-four hours I knew I was in deep trouble. No problem, my ass! First I visited the Bank of America in La Jolla, where I kept our so-called corporate account. After the loan officer took one look at our statement, I found out my banker wasn't really my banker. And I had thought this bank was founded by an immigrant Italian who built his magnificent bank by issuing loans to industrious, hard-working young visionaries of start-up enterprises like mine. Wrong! I imagined that the bank changed that policy as soon as they could get that crazy man committed to a loony bin, some fifty years ago. Since then, they have been on the straight and narrow. If I had had twenty-five thousand or more in their bank, plus an equal amount of hard-rock collateral, I would have been granted the loan, and they might have thrown in favored-client status as well.

Hmmm. The situation was becoming a bit serious, and the contractual clock was ticking toward starting day. I decided, with not a little reluctance, to suggest to a social acquaintance, a rather well-known banker around town, that we might do business together. He was a member of the Beach & Tennis Club, as was I. We played tennis, attended the same parties, lunch groups, etc.

I should have realized that the fundamentals of my position and financial statement were not singularly negative. They encompassed the entire range of the banking system, I might add, from the Federal Reserve Bank down to a pawn shop.

"Marc, the only way our bank could consider approving this loan would be if you would sign for it personally," the friendly banker said, adding, "Of course we would need your personal statement, but—subject to verification—I see no problem."

As I said before, I would rather deal with a Shylock in these circumstances than a banker who traveled in my circles and had been after me to do business with his bank on numerous occasions. Now I watched his discomfort, for he was shocked by what he had seen. I quickly decided to get us both off the hook by telling him I had a strict policy of not personally guaranteeing corporate financing and that I would prefer to lend the company the necessary funds from my estate investments. I barely squeaked by, and only on the basis that I was seeking a loan for growth, not to save the company. There's a big difference, I can tell you.

I was getting pissed off. Here I was, sitting on what promised to be a lucrative contract with almost zero possibilities of failure, and no bank would extend the necessary financing.

The next tier in hard-to-obtain financing at somewhat acceptable interest rates was a leasing company. I found one in La Jolla, owned by two fine gentlemen who certainly had established a line of credit with the bank based on hard-rock credentials. They were prepared to take the risk the bank could not or would not take. They saw the same statement I gave the bank, and their glasses were not rose-colored. On the other hand, they appreciated the facts I laid out about the contract and concluded they had sufficient control over the equipment to insure a reasonable degree of protection. I do believe, however, that their affirmative answer was based on their belief in my ability and—more important—their perception of my integrity as a businessman. Come to think about it, way back then and through the many years in business, no bank, financial institution, factory, or creditor has ever lost a dime in doing business with me or my company. I am as proud of that as I am of having made millions of dollars the hard way.

If there was any irony involved, it was their borrowing the money from my bank to loan to me with at least a six- to eight-point spread. Has anyone ever said life is fair?

It all came together: the new equipment arrived on schedule and was installed when the clock struck the hour of the day called for in the contract. The volume of business came in exactly as outlined in the contract. Best of all, my two fine gentlemen at the leasing company were very impressed and assured me of additional financial support for equipment when I was awarded new contracts. That's what I call coming together with a bang and a half!

The pace began to quicken, and we were on a roll. Vandenberg Air Force Base called to say we were being awarded a contract, and this was followed by the giant Fort Ord. In both instances the leasing company granted me the necessary funds, but the interest charges were gnawing away at my gross profit to an unacceptable degree. Still there was no alternative; it was the only wheel in town.

We were in a money business. By that I mean we handled thousands of dollars in coins every time our people collected from the equipment. It dawned on me that certain controls had to be put into effect. For one thing, I noticed our monthly collections were higher than those of the preceding contractor. Not greatly different, but enough to be noticeable. This meant there had been a certain amount of skimming off the top by the previous serviceman or by the company he represented.

This led me to two actions to defend ourselves and the exchange against downright thievery or fraud.

First I informed our retired Navy chiefs and Marine master sergeants that we were entrusting them with the responsibilities of handling large sums of money for the company and the military exchange. To the extent that they used bad judgement and were found guilty of playing partnership with our money, they would certainly be prosecuted. In addition to that, their record, along with all charges, would be brought to the attention of the Pension Review Board. Maybe they weren't concerned about going to the pokey, but when I mentioned the Pension Review Board I made honest men faster than you can make instant coffee. Nothing and nobody was going to jeopardize those hard-won pensions—nobody. . . . To this day, I'm not certain that there is such an entity as the Pension Review Board. Could be.

Next, I proposed a program to the exchanges that protected everyone. I told the exchange officer that henceforth we would keep the keys to all the coin boxes in a locked box to be placed in the exchange safe. Furthermore, on the day set up for collection, our serviceman would make the rounds in the company of a military MP. The keys would be returned to the safe and the money counted in the presence of exchange personnel. Once the total amount was signed for by both parties, our serviceman would deposit the money in the bank on base to be transferred to our bank in La Jolla. A pretty neat system, and I instituted it on all bases in the contract.

All that you have read thus far and all that you read after—however interesting, entertaining, informative, or beneficial—pales in comparison to the following vignette, under the heading of "Creative Financing."

The term *creative financing* was unknown back in the 1960s. I think it came from the real estate business and its attempts to find money for down payments. It wasn't the monthly payments that snuffed out prospective buyers, it was coming up with the down payment. Child's play in comparison to my problem. First, my company was over $250,000 in debt on a $10,000 capitalization. Second, we weren't making acceptable profits, for my salary made big dents in the company profits. Third, debt payments were ten to fifteen percent higher than they should have been. One wouldn't have to be very bright to conclude, after looking at our financial statement, that we were not a quality loan, as the saying goes among bankers.

Quality. For chrissakes, I was as close to Willie Sutton, Bonnie and Clyde, and the James Gang as anyone could have been. However, I would like to believe I was more on the side of the law than on the outside as I lifted approximately $500,000 from my friendly banker with a creative financing concept that is as workable today as it was thirty years ago.

Before you say, "chicken feed," let me tell you that in 1962 a buck was almost a buck. I bought my home on the beach for $75,000. (Read on and I'll tell you what I sold it for in 1988.) You could purchase one of those beautiful Mercedes 450SL's for $9,000, and any other car from a Mercury on down for less than $5,000. Movies were 95¢, an orchestra seat at the Metropolitan or a Broadway show was $9. A Brooks Brothers suit with a vest was less than $100. Need I go on?

What I'm trying to say is $500,000 in 1962 was the equivalent of over $3 million today, without exaggeration. As you can see, I'm having fun. Again, if it isn't fun, the hell with it. That goes for games, business, people, loves, friends, and places. Life is too short.

Okay, let's get on with it. First you find a friendly banker. I discovered that the more loan money they have, the friendlier they are; when they're tapped out, they won't loan money to themselves in any circumstances. My friendly banker was Bill Black, president of the brand-new Bank of La Jolla. For the bank's grand opening, he offered all depositors a free checking account, an almost unheard-of program back then. Within a week's time, his bank acquired millions of dollars in deposits.

My goodness. What were they going to do with all that loanable money? Of course they could buy Treasury bills, nice and safe, a bit conservative, but every bank has them, a necessary part of the image for the bank examiners. The real moneymakers are good-risk, high-quality loans with collateral that permits interest at prime and above, preferably above.

Shall we make this call together so you will hear it first-hand and book it for your present or future financial requirements?

"Good morning, Bill. I've heard you have created a run on all the other banks in town with your new 'Free Checking Account' program. Is this true?"

(One has to follow form with a jovial remark or two to open ceremonies with bankers or at board of directors meetings.) After the appropriate reply, we settle down when he asks, "What brings you in?" or "What can we do for you, Marc?" Now we're getting serious, for we're about to talk about money. Just a sec, he needs to put on his banker's face, a semifrown, a slight look of disbelief, the steely gaze of a guard, shotgun on arm, protecting other people's money with the flashing thought that they may be watching or listening in.

Steady as she goes, keep your cool. Stand tall, relax, smile. Fire when ready. . . . Ready . . . fire!

"Bill, I'm happy to tell you we have won the contract for laundry equipment at Vandenberg Air Force Base. This contract has a history of providing the contractor with a gross income of $70,000 a year over the five years of the contract. We have won, Bill, by offering the U.S. military exchange system a twenty-five percent commission of the gross receipts. Now, the cost of equipment we have to bring aboard amounts to $35,000. This is the loan amount we require, less ten percent up front on our part, for this is a United States government contract.

"Oh, there is one more major item, Bill. Here is a letter addressed to the bank from the contracting officer at Vandenberg Air Force Base, wherein he has agreed to send the monthly gross receipts directly to the bank. The bank would deduct the monthly loan amount due and deposit the balance in our account."

It's almost enough to make an old banker cry at the sheer beauty of it.

I mean this was *powerful* creative financing. I had explained our situation to the base exchange officer and requested his cooperation. He agreed. As a matter of fact, he was enthusiastic, for the government's twenty-five percent came right off the top before he mailed the U.S. government check to the bank. (Notice how many times I say "U.S. government", exchange officer, government contracting officer . . . hmmm.)

Bill said, "Loan approved," and we were under way. Month after month the bank received the check from Vandenberg, and on the basis of this very satisfactory experience, approved all other contracts we were awarded with the same arrangements and stipulations.

We went full bore after every military contract we could obtain: Pearl Harbor, Barbers Point, Kaneohe, Pensacola, March, El Toro, and—as a departure from the military— the University of California campus right here in La Jolla. Over a period of two years, we were sitting on loans to be paid for equipment worth over $500,000, plus an additional $200,000 of previous debt. This had all been done on a financial statement showing a $10,000 capitalization, which was personally borrowed money without any visible or invisible assets.

You have to understand that from the bank's point of view, it was pretty much an airtight loan. Worst scenario, I could go bankrupt, but the government's military checks would still come into the bank, made out to the bank, and the contract would continue long after the loan was amortized. Yes, there was some risk. An earthquake could destroy the base; the Russians could drop the bomb; Congress could close down the base, but that takes a year or more, if ever; or an unknown plague could kill off the human race. Aside from the ultimate, a contract with God, this was the next best thing. Try it. It works wonders when you need a loan from a bank or anyone.

One would begin to believe I was a four-star entrepreneur. In a relatively minor way, that was true. However, in the midst of my self-serving accolades, three unexpected negative developments occurred that just about knocked me on my ass. I can tell you, you're not a fighter or a success until you have had the hell beaten out of you at least once.

First, there was a meningitis outbreak at Fort Ord, California. They literally closed the base down, sending troops to other locations around the country for an indefinite period of time.

Compounding the problem was the fact that I had spent thousands of dollars in plumbing and electrical equipment to prepare the forty barracks, three decks high, with laundry facilities, water lines in and out, electrical outlets, and air vents. And that's not all. I had invested almost $50,000 in washers and dryers. Woe was me!

To almost put me down for the count, those barracks were occupied by Army recruits whom I had counted on to do their laundry in the barracks because they had little free time to roam around or go off base.

Little time? They had no time. They woke up at 5 a.m. Every minute was scheduled until they hit the sack at 9 p.m. The returns on each machine were so low it would have taken five years to pay them off. I was in deep trouble.

To make matters worse, the damn pressing machines began to break down, one after another, as if the factory had built in a one-year obsolescence factor. They may have been fine for a civilian outlet, but on a military base the rough, tough handling turned them nonoperational faster than we could repair them.

I began to bear a strong resemblance to Mr. Ponzi. This pyramid I was building depended on all previous blocks holding up and contributing their proper share of the cash load. It reminds me of my seawall; it was strong enough to withstand a high tide or a storm, but when both came together, good-bye wall. It was almost good-bye Marc, and everything I had in the world—business, house, and all earthly possessions.

I began to fall behind on my payments for the pressing machines, needing every dollar to meet the payroll, taxes, phone, and every other business expense we had to deal with. The next priority was the bank; this was sacred. We had to pay the bank no matter what. Alongside these expenses were the payroll taxes, required by the government and state without interruption. Try skipping the payroll taxes, and the president will call out the National Guard to support the IRS, the DEA, the FBI, and the local SWAT team; not paying those taxes has to rank as the most heinous crime in the annals of the justice system. My best advice is hold up a bank, get that tax money; do everything, anything necessary, but pay Uncle.

Before all of this culminated in a near disaster, a wonderful series of events took place in Hawaii. My chief in charge, George Brown, was doing his work at such a level of excellence that it came to the attention of the exchange officer at Pearl Harbor, who had a problem. He needed a contractor to offer an out-of-warranty repair service for all of the appliances he and the other exchanges were selling. On my next visit (I made one every three months), he proposed we take this project over, and we did. Or, I should say, George did. Within two weeks, he found retired Navy chiefs who formerly had been electronics or plumbing mates. No sweat. They were so good, they could repair an atom bomb. We leased three trucks and were under way, and it was profitable. George would have them line up the trucks on base at 0:800, hand out the calls to be made, and off they would go. Once this operation was an obvious success, the exchange officer came to us again, asking us to take over the delivery of the major appliances and large electronics items he had sold. This required a two-and-a-half-ton truck with lift equipment and a team of two. Again George had the operation set and running within two weeks.

Finally it dawned on me, there we were, servicing equipment on base, repairing appliances, and delivering them. Why not sell them to the exchange in the first place? Wake up, Marc! That's where the relatively big money was to be found. One quick survey revealed that the exchange carried only Whirlpool and G.E. appliances. Oh boy, oh boy! Let me at 'em. I'm going to go after KitchenAid, Speed Queen, and Amana.

How did I go after them? I picked up the phone and called their VPs of marketing.

Good morning, my name and company is . . . and we want to be your military representative overseas. (God forbid I should mention the United States military exchange system; did I want to totally destroy their distribution and dealer network? I'm being sarcastic, and rightfully so. But in 1962 these manufacturers considered their mode of marketing to be sacred: they sold to their distributors, who in turn sold to their dealers. The untouchables were the mass markets, Sears, K-Mart, etc., and most decidedly the military exchange system.)

As it turned out, none of these manufacturers had a distributor of any consequence in Hawaii. I had struck gold on the first call. With KitchenAid's approval in my pocket, I hit Speed Queen and advised them about acquiring KitchenAid. Got them. Amana joined the party as fast as I could tell them about the first two. Sort of reminded me of how I sold all the New York distributors the Presto iron after knocking off the first one or two.

It took more than a phone call to nail it down. In each case, I had to visit the factory and meet with the headquarters executives and the manager in charge of export. Hawaii was a state of the Union, but these factories still considered it overseas. And they weren't alone. Twenty-six hundred miles from the West Coast, with jet travel just beginning and all shipments going out on the Matson Line: man, that was overseas. That was export without any government duty, foreign operations. And what made it more so was the "military exchange system," so very mysterious in the eyes of these companies, so wonderful in mine. There was my future, beyond all doubt. An organization that was recession- and depression-proof, an instrument of the U.S. government that could never go bankrupt, one that sold to young homemakers who after a tour of a year or two overseas would be replaced by new homemakers who would also need refrigerators, dishwashers, washers, dryers. It was one helluva market and growing. "All of this and much, much more," as the commercial says, was presented to them. And the more I presented it, the more I believed it myself.

So I became the duly appointed military representative of three major companies. Armed with my old attaché case, I became a salesman again.

# Chapter 12

Thanks to the reputation George Brown had developed for our company, within three days I had sold three lines of merchandise to all military exchanges in Hawaii. Same formula. I showed the orders from the naval exchange at Pearl Harbor to the exchanges at the submarine base, Barbers Point, and Kaneohe. One after the other, they signed up and placed orders.

Hot diggity damn, this was exciting! All I had to do was obtain orders and send them to the factory. The factory would ship and bill the exchange. The exchange would pay the factory. And the factory would pay us a commission. Beautiful: no inventory, no warehousing, no people, just lil' ol' me. Wow!

This was the start of an adventure into a new world, one that would bring me around the old one, from Japan, Korea, Okinawa, the Philippines, and Guam on to all of Europe, with stops in Alaska, Panama, and Puerto Rico. The new world was the old one with one big difference . . . the money to be made was unbelievable. All I had to do was work like hell—morning, noon, and night—and I can tell you that becomes a labor of love when you see all you have accomplished.

There is one thing sure as hell about retired Navy chiefs or any retired military personnel: they can't sell for shit. They can repair a ship's engine, shoot off cannons, prepare meals for hundreds, lead and control men, but they can't write an order if they are on allocation. The ability simply isn't in them, and furthermore, they don't want to. So I had to do it. And I loved it all!

As a result I found it necessary to fly over to Hawaii just about every two months. ("Tough!" you might say, raising an eyebrow.) The fun was writing up orders, holding impromptu sales meetings with exchange salespeople, putting up point-of-sale material, making certain I did everything possible to help the products sell. I knew that my competition did very little or nothing along these lines. Very quickly all three catalogs of products became best sellers. How could it be otherwise with KitchenAid, Speed Queen, and Amana?

During my very next trip after obtaining the initial orders, the atom bomb went off in La Jolla. I was in our little office in Honolulu when Jane phoned.

"Hi, hon', is everything all right?" I asked.

Her reply is written verbatim, for it was and is etched in my memory forever.

"Marc, are you seated? If you're not, you had better sit down."

"Okay, what's going on?" I asked.

"What's going on, Marc, is the sheriff has been to our house and placed a lien notice on the front door. He's also been to our bank, where he placed a lien notice on the checking and savings accounts for the business, on our personal account, and on the savings accounts of all the kids including Pandora, who has a total of one dollar and seventy-five cents. That's what's going on."

The shock waves went through me in rapid succession. Hold on, heart and guts; if this is the end of the world, we're all going together.

"Try not to worry," I said. "I'm sure I'll be able to

straighten out the mess. In the meantime, doesn't one of the kids have a piggy bank you can bust open?"

"Don't be funny, Marc. I can't pay the milk bill."

"Okay, okay, I'll get it fixed. I need another day here to obtain orders from the military. I should be home the day after tomorrow. Love you, bye."

I hung up with that kicked-in-the-stomach feeling. What obviously had happened was that the Ajax Pressing Machinery Company had turned me over to a collection attorney who nailed me to the cross hard and fast. My monthly payments to Ajax had slowed down to a crawling stop as I had to take money from Peter to pay Paul. And then Peter petered out.

All this started when the pressing machines began to break down all over the place, combined with the closure of Fort Ord due to a meningitis outbreak after I had spent a ton of money on rehabbing barracks for a large quantity of laundry equipment (which was also on my unhappy accounts payable list). Talk about rippling effects; this was a tidal wave. Oh my, oh me.

First things first. I stopped the money flowing into our bank from all the collections we made on various bases in the contract. This I arranged from Honolulu with a few swift telephone calls before returning to La Jolla with, I might add, a bushel of military orders. On my arrival I expected to see undernourished, starving waifs down to their last slice of stale bread. No, they were all fine. Jane used charge cards left and right. Amazing what you can do without cash if you have to, until the bills come in.

Second, I opened another banking account for the business and personal finances. I picked a bank far away from the scene of the crime, hoping the sheriff wouldn't find me.

Third, putting a seizure on the bank accounts was one thing, but a lien on the house was far more drastic. The final act, if this ran its course, would be that the house would be taken away from us and sold to satisfy the creditors' claims. To sleep on the ocean is to go into dream-land minutes after your head hits the pillow. The sound of the waves breaking on the shore, the coolness and smell of the ocean air, and the droning noise, however light, of the surf going back to sea, all combine to create a rhythm that constantly adds to and draws on your senses, lulling you to sleep faster than all medicines and in spite of all troubles of the day and the world, with one exception. Losing the house! That will keep you awake all through the night . . . and it did.

Fourth, I talked to my attorney to find out where I stood. Ed Butler, a member of the fine firm that I had used to form my corporation, and I were La Jolla friends. (He subsequently went on to run for mayor of San Diego, albeit unsuccessfully, losing to Pete Wilson, who moved on to the governorship of California. Ed later became a superior court judge and rose to judge of our appellate court here in town.) Well, Ed looked the situation over and gave me the look of an attorney who knows his client is going to the electric chair.

I would have to handle this myself.

"Give the attorney in Los Angeles a call and tell him I would like to meet with him," I told Ed.

He picked up the phone and made the call with the friendly and objective chatter two opposing attorneys will use when they're not in the courtroom. Ed ended the call by asking him not to go too hard on me. Thanks a lot.

Having two or three days before our appointment, I set about lining up my defenses. Most important was to secure help from my old friend, Jack Murray. Jack, as I previously related, had been president of Speed Queen when I served with him on the American Laundry Association board, a group of industry executives that met quarterly to generously foster programs for the good of the overall industry. This went back to the days when I was vice president of Ironrite. Jack was a helluva nice guy and followed my program at Ironrite with sincere interest and encouragement. He was now a top executive of the McGraw Edison Company, which happened to own, among other major companies including Speed Queen, the outfit that had attached everything I owned in the world—the Ajax Pressing Machinery Company.

I picked up the phone, dialed, and had the good luck of getting through to him. He was pleased to hear my voice and asked how I was and how things were going for me. I told him the family and I were in good health, but I thought my business was going to die sooner than expected.

I then went on to explain my plight and told him that if he could do anything to establish a reasonable attitude on the part of the Ajax attorney and the company, it would be deeply appreciated. Of course, I succinctly explained my side of the problem—equipment failure, etc.—and that my intentions were to work our way out of the situation. He, of course, had not been aware of my being shot down, because he was about ten layers up in the corporate table of organization, far removed from run-of-the-business problems such as mine. The man displayed his quality to me when he said, "Marc, let me look into it. I'll see what I can do."

I hung up knowing I had done the right thing by calling him. For chrissakes, what are friends for if you can't call them when in need? And man, was I in need!

This was to be my first experience in digging my way out of a financial hole. It wasn't a hole, it was a Wilkes-Barre mine, another never-to-be-forgotten experience. Like a first bicycle, first car, first kiss, or first love, the intensity of feeling was overwhelming.

I arrived at the office of the attorney representing the Ajax Pressing Machinery Company in Los Angeles with great apprehension, of course, but also with a determination to make one helluva pitch on my behalf. But it wasn't just a matter of what they might do. Hell, they had already done it. My house and everything we owned was under lien. I owed them a bunch of money, and the lien would not be removed until they were paid or until we went to court and the judge officially gave them all of my property to settle their claim; a pretty sad situation.

It wasn't only sad, it was frightening to be in his office. He was a specialist in law. Just as there are doctors and dentists who specialize in their respective fields, this guy specialized in legally collecting bad debts, a much higher form than the petty, lowlife collection agency.

To make it even more frightening, he was all of five feet tall, with pitch black whiskers covering his face, in a black suit, seated behind a desk in a throne-type chair with a backrest about eight feet high. The overall combination gave an impression of the first toll-booth stop on the way to hell on earth. This guy had been around the track so many times he undoubtedly knew every possible why-we-went-down-the-tubes-and-can't-pay story ever told. There was no way I could bullshit him. But I did have one slingshot at him. It was a matter of presentation and timing.

He was somberly pleasant, if that's possible. He got up, walked around his desk to shake hands, and we were on a first-name basis right off. He waved me into a chair, offered me a cup of coffee, which I declined, and we got under way.

"Marc, it looks as though we have a rather serious problem here. Can you tell me why you haven't paid on your obligations to Ajax?" he asked, though not in an intimidating manner of face or voice.

I replied, "The basic reason is that the equipment is falling apart faster than my men can repair it. As a result the revenue has fallen drastically."

"Well," he replied, "this is puzzling. You have had this equipment in operation and have been paying for it for almost a year. Now you're telling me it is not operating."

"That's correct. Furthermore, it's almost as if the machines have a built-in obsolescence factor that always kicks in about the same time. I believe this is related to the type of people using them. These units were not designed or constructed to hold up with tough military personnel," I answered, somewhat preparing him for my most important argument.

He pretty much took all of that with a grain of salt, not that it helped the taste or the digestion, and quickly responded, "You knew the type of customers you had from the very beginning, and you continued to contract and order additional machines. Under the circumstances, why did you do that?"

It was almost as if I had written the script for how I wanted the meeting to go. "I'd rather not answer that question," I said with whatever reluctance I could put on my face.

"Are you kidding? Are you serious? What do you mean, you would rather not answer the question? Come on, let's have it!" he said. There was the first slight hint of a pit bull.

"Because it could be very embarrassing to certain people at the company," I said, playing my next-to-last card. Whether or not he knew what I was going to lay on him, I couldn't tell.

"I suggest you answer the question now and in full if you know what's good for you." He said that quietly, making it all the more ominous.

Okay, here goes. I looked him straight in the eye for a

few seconds, as long as I could, to make what I was about to say more dramatic.

"I'm really reluctant to answer your question because it personally involves the Strike brothers and it could be extremely embarrassing if the situation were to end up in court. You have attached my house, all my bank accounts including my children's, and if it comes down to going to court and losing, I'll manage to pay off my indebtedness including court charges, but I would hope it doesn't come to that."

(Between you and me, I would have had absolutely no problem in managing to pay off Pandora's bank account lien of $1.75. Beyond that, it became questionable, and then, impossible. If he had come to this conclusion I could just hear one of the kids saying, "Daddy, Daddy, why do we have to move?" I was somewhere between having nerves of steel and taking a deep drag of laughing gas to give me courage.)

I figured if he accepted that fantasy, I would have a bit more leverage when it came down to dollars and cents and common sense. At least I had nothing to lose by telling him I wasn't planning to beg for mercy and that a compromise was a reasonable solution. I didn't know, though. This guy was tough and looked about as compassionate as a hanging judge. I'd better get right to the big bang and light the fuse.

"As you know," I began, "I came to California as a marketing consultant for their company. Shortly after, I conceived of and executed the military test program. I told them I wanted to resign as a consultant and go into this business for myself. During a brief interim period, the younger Strike brother came to San Diego, and I took him around to the various installations. He watched the military personnel using the machines. I opened the coin boxes. It was quite an eye opener, and he could multiply with the best of them.

"Within a week, I received a call from the Strike brothers informing me that they wanted to be my partner and asking that I fly to Salt Lake City to discuss the program. Well, I didn't have very much choice, so off I went.

"After a brief flap about who would have fifty-one percent of the company, which I was insistent on receiving because I was doing all the work, we shook hands, and a partnership was formed.

"I advised them that we would have to expand the number of locations if this were going to be profitable for all of us. They agreed this was the course to follow. As I departed they informed me they would draw up the partnership agreement and send it to me as soon as it was prepared. Within a month I had substantially increased the number of locations. I was beginning to wonder where my partnership papers were when I received another call. They informed me they were unable to proceed on the agreement because their younger brother had been selected to be the CEO of a major company within their corporate complex. To proceed would create a collusive situation, and the family's pride in his achievement precluded any questionable activity," I ended.

Questionable, hell. This was blatantly going outside the rules of appropriate corporate conduct, and it was made obvious by their pulling out before it actually happened.

He remained silent through all of this, so I went on.

"They said they wanted to do the right thing in the circumstances and that they would personally loan me ten thousand dollars to be used as a down payment on all the equipment. They then set up a time payment program with the credit arm of the corporation.

"The rest is easy to understand. We had far too many

machines in operation. For a while they were profitable at the Navy and Marine Corps bases. They died on the Air Force installations, where crawling around airplanes does not lead to pressing machine use. Many of the machines were put into these locations after we agreed on the partnership program. All of this, combined with mechanical and construction failure, brings us to our present situation."

To close the lid, I concluded by saying, "Overall, this was totally unfair to me. I should have been wary of Greeks bearing gifts, as the expression goes. All I have is an empty bag. That's why I think we should avoid going to court, and try to reach a compromise."

Not too shabby a pitch. I gave myself an eight.

He smiled and asked, "What have you got in mind, Marc?"

"Based on what I have already said, I was thinking in terms of ten percent."

"Think again, Marc. That's totally unacceptable," he said.

"Okay, twenty-five."

"Be realistic."

"I am. If I go any higher I'll be back in the soup a few months down the road."

In the end, in matters of this kind, it's never as bad as it could be and never as good as you'd want it to be. We settled at forty percent.

I'm quite certain that my friend Jack Murray paved the way for the reasonably happy ending. Reasonable? Pandora was ecstatic! She went on a blow-it-all shopping spree. The lien notices went off the house and bank accounts. The ordeal and siege were over. The only visible reminder was a slightly worn carpet due to my nightly pacing back and forth.

That beautiful passage from Saint Exupéry's *The Little Prince* is far more applicable: "It is only with the heart that one can see rightly, what is essential is invisible to the eye." In my heart I realized I had nothing more than a tarnished victory on my hands. I could see that I could not continue to borrow from Peter to pay Paul. Once is the limit. And lastly, in distant shades of black and blue, I had committed the most common of all errors in building a company, over-expansion without studying and testing the market.

I had squeaked by and out, but I had learned my lesson the hard way. I would hope that reading about this experience will implant the lesson in your mind. If so, that would be the easy way. Come to think about it, if all the do's and don'ts were published and followed, everyone and everything would be successful. The hard way would be no more. However, let's just phase it out gradually.

If you have begun to believe I was a better salesman than a businessman, I'd have to go along with you. But hold on. Those were just the first, start-up years. Furthermore, I want to say again, I did not anticipate the meningitis outbreak and the closing of Fort Ord, which ruined my cash flow. And I did not anticipate the breakdown of the pressing machines. Remind me next time to set aside reserves for such contingencies.

Please? What are reserves?

In the aftermath, I wasn't at all anxious to go after new contracts. It was time to renew our efforts on the ones we had going, lest we fall behind and be sued again. We had reached a point of having more laundry vending equipment on military bases than any other company in the country. But more machines don't necessarily mean more volume or profit. More can mean more employees, more trouble, more trucks, more repairs, more complaints, more insurance, more vandalism—all adding up to being down and out.

A case in point: Pacific Southwest Airlines, a fine regional airline, had a great idea to buy a radio station to extensively advertise the airline. Then PSA purchased hotels on the West Coast to give passengers the advantage of special rates for staying at a PSA hotel. It all made sense, except that for some reason, nothing happened. PSA sold the radio station, the hotels, and then itself. But for a brief time, it was really big time. C'est la vie.

What the hell was I doing in this business? It was no longer fun. It was about as creative as walking in place or going around in circles—very dull. If it made a ton of money, it could overcome the pain-in-the-ass feeling I had about being in the stupid business, but it didn't. Oh, yes, it was bringing in a good income. Jane and the kids were well taken care of; we had no complaints financially. But I wasn't about to become a millionaire.

For example, I anticipated that my profits would increase substantially when my equipment was amortized and after I received a renewal of my contract.

Man, what a dreamer! By the time this happened, the large civilian operators had found out about the good pickings to be had on military bases and had come after the contracts, meaning I had to make higher bids to win the contracts. I had to push my bids way up. Reminds me of that old cartoon of one bum telling the other he had always been the high bidder. How true. Winning was also losing. The commission to the military was higher, and so was the ever-increasing cost of repairing three-year-old equipment.

If I could have pushed myself out of this trench warfare business long enough, I might have heard the lovely sounds and felt the tingling emotions of my old world of selling: hearing a group of salesmen attending a meeting; the one on one; the give and take of a sales presentation;

receiving a "yes, put me down for the program"; the leaving with a beautiful order in your bag that gives you a warm glow you somehow feel in your face, a sense of anticipation to tell your boss about your success, and a can't-wait-to-get-home desire so you can share the news and be enveloped in admiration and love.

Rather than gloss over what I went through, I'd better come really clean. (It's good for one's conscience, not that I was aware of having one.) The company was going broke. While I mitigated my indebtedness to one company, all the others were bombarding me with requests for payment. I had the never-ending cycle of payroll and payroll taxes; God forbid I should miss paying on that.

The gravity of the situation was overwhelming. My world was falling apart in a maze of financial demands. Try sleeping with all that on your mind. But within thirty days, I refinanced my mortgage, obtained a second, and borrowed $15,000 from three old friends from my Presto days. Back then, that kind of money was a big deal, but they gave it without question. I just phoned them and said, "I am in trouble and I need help." Would you believe two of them were my salesmen who had made good? Jim Hopkins had formed a successful employment agency business throughout Chicago; Richard Warren had become vice president of marketing for Presto; and Mort Phillips had been active in many enterprises since leaving Presto. Mort was a millionaire many times over. One indication of why he was, was that he (not-too-seriously) asked if I thought he was a bank. My friends didn't ask for interest or security. They just mailed me a check the same day. On that day, my company was saved.

I was a pretty beaten-up guy, I can tell you. Where was the confident, cocky, I-can-do-anything person of just a few years ago? I'll say it once more: you're nothing until you have gone through some storms of life. You have to persevere.

You have to think, fight, work your heart out, never stop believing in yourself, and start again. First of all, you will gain priceless experience to use in the future. And second, how beautiful it is to fly or sail out of a storm that has tested you until the sweat runs down your back. Only those who have been tested like that really know, don't we?

Finally, and I mean finally, I heard the bugle blow "Charge!", the one you hear today at football games. This came in loud and clear all the way from Hawaii in the form of ever-increasing orders from the military bases for major appliances.

If you're in sales, come along with me to dreamland. Floating in space are the best-known, most desired major appliances that everyone wants and must have. Images of people with a smile of satisfaction as they make their purchases surround you. Salespeople busily write up orders with people standing in line. Hear the buyer say, "We need to order another container, and another." Go behind the door that says "Business Operations" and shut it tight. Don't let anyone know that we obtain an order and mail it to the factory; the factory ships and bills the government; the government pays the invoice to the factory; and the factory sends us a commission check. No factory workers, no union, no machines, no repairs, no work in process, no inventory, no nothing. Just a piece of paper in the form of an order in an envelope that doesn't need a stamp and comes in month after month.

Wake up! That's for real! That's exactly the way it was. All I had to do was enlarge the territory and duplicate the program. Where, oh where, had this gold mine been all my life? It mattered not, for I was going to stake my claim everywhere I could find an overseas military exchange. Considering the size of our military operations overseas, the potential volume of business was tremendous.

But before we gallop off, we'd best take a break and see what's happening on the home front.

First of all, everyone in the family was healthy. Only rarely did one of them come down with a bug of some sort. I attribute that to living on the beach, in the sun and the ocean air, with just plain good food, exercising in all the sports. La Jolla was an incredible atmosphere for raising kids. It still is.

La Jolla was so peaceful and pleasant. After a while we developed a wide circle of friends and nodding acquaintances. Of course there were cliques and small groups set in their privacy based on the old tried-and-true social standards of wealth, which could break down all sorts of barriers to inner circles. Anyone whose financial position was a bit obscure was scrutinized and evaluated on the basis of house; type of car; and city, town, or area they came from. Locals were few and far between, and almost everybody came from somewhere else: Grosse Pointe, Santa Barbara, Tuxedo Park, Barrington Hills, Greenwich, Dallas, to name a few gate openers. But of course one's place of origin had to be supplemented by clothes and all the trivial folderol that, in the minds of many men and women, establishes you as one of the acceptables. I wonder how my farmer friend who hitched his horse to my car and pulled me back on the road would fare in a plastic society-rating system such as ours?

All of you who are climbing life's ladder to reach a position of fame and fortune or just simple recognition, success, and accomplishment are subject to the same type of scrutiny and get-off-there's-no-more-room-at-the-top resistance. Some people tire of the struggle, stop fighting and clawing, accept whatever position they may have achieved, and live out their lives rather pleasantly. A few who have made it to the top have found out there is no peace—the war goes on, one battle after another for more recognition, status quo, and greater wealth. The majority stay on, for they enjoy it. Some make worthwhile contributions to all classes of society. Lastly, there is one in a hundred who packs it all up after achieving his goals and retires well before his time to golf, fish, travel, or contemplate his navel. Fortunately for those who choose to get on the ladder, the vast majority of people do not get on. They have no interest whatsoever. They don't give a damn about becoming a bossman, a top achiever, a star, or the richest man in town. They are happy as clams being Mr. and Mrs. Average, doing their job, caring for their family, having their friends, making their home comfortable, watching TV and the antics of the people on the ladder.

While all of this may certainly pertain to the entire country or world, it's particularly true of La Jolla. It's ironic that of all its wealthy inhabitants, very few have made their fortune here by their own industry. More likely, according to the natives, it's been made by investments, speculation, or inheritance.

This must add up to quite a number, for La Jolla (population 25,000) seems to have more banks per capita than any other city in the country, roughly fifteen or more. The sales of scissors for clipping coupons is just amazing. One would tend to believe that we were an offshore banking company that launders suspicious money. Come to think of it, there *is* money to be made in the laundry business. . . . Furthermore, La Jolla has more real estate offices, more lawyers, more doctors, more private schools, and over forty travel agencies. Half the population must be out of town at any given time. Although real estate is expected to be more expensive in seaside communities, the language of real estate people goes along the sounds of one-two (1.2), two-two (2.2), three-four (3.4), four-four (4.4). I must agree that sounds better than two million two hundred thousand. My God, can you believe that? Carry the same houses back over hill and dale to nowheresville and the prefix drops off, just like that. Certainly this is the way it is today in La Jolla. Back in the mid-sixties, things were pretty much the same except for the inflationary real estate prices and property taxes that are being paid today.

So it's off to work I went, to Hawaii to take a hard look at why we were doing such great business with the military exchanges on our appliances. The answer was in two words: quality and reputation. Although the military would always go out for bid and accept the lowest bid when seeking contracts, they also had a tendency in those days to buy the least expensive store merchandise. I believe we were among the first to bring in well-known, high-priced appliances. For example, my competition was Whirlpool and G.E., fine companies who make products and price them for the mass market at lower prices than Amana and KitchenAid or Speed Queen. Now, you'd have to be blind not to see the difference between a Chevrolet and a Cadillac. It's a bit more difficult to see the difference between an Amana refrigerator and a Whirlpool. But the difference is there in many important ways, for example in copper tubing rather than plastic. I could go on and on comparing products, but it boils down to value for the dollar. Of course you get what you pay for. The image has always been that a military family can't afford more expensive merchandise. How terribly false. They can't afford to buy cheap is more like the truth.

How do you spread the word, tell the quality story, point out the features? The hard way, of course. First you go in and wipe down the display until it shines, then you detail. You put up point-of-sale material: posters, placards, banners, and brochures inside the units. What's next? You hold sales meetings before the exchange opens: explain the sales features to relate to the customers, explain the warranty, describe over and over the quality and your exclusive improvements over the competition.

The exchange personnel were not dynamic salesmen. They did not work on commission or an incentive basis. They were just nice people trying to do the best they were capable of, if you know what I mean. To the extent I could etch in their memory one or two of the selling points I presented, I was ahead of the game and, I might add, the competition. That's the way it's done. There is no other way; absolutely, positively, guaranteed. Then and only then does a factory receive its money's worth from its national advertising, and then and only then does the dealer receive his money's worth from the local advertising. I'm referring to maximum results. If you accept less as satisfactory you are in the wrong business. As a matter of fact, you don't belong in any business.

Flying back to the mainland with a bunch of orders in my case was as pleasant then as it is today from wherever I've been. Your world—our world—is so very small. A simple matter of writing up orders can fill you with well-being until you overflow. You must surely feel as I do when this happens to you.

Perhaps the 30,000-foot altitude purified my mind, because I could distinctly hear the clank of two brain cells; one said, "Sell out all of your vending operation ASAP" and the other, "Build up your sales representative business." Okay, I thought, if that's the plan, I'll work it. And I did.

# Chapter 13

Within six months I had sold just about all of my contracts and equipment. Actually it was rather easy. The civilian vending companies were anxious to expand into military bases because they could use their civilian servicemen to cover the bases, an advantage I did not have. I sold out at a fair price, all facts considered: the used equipment, the monthly volume, multiplied by the remaining period of the contract, less commissions due the exchange, etc. The only problem was that my indebtedness to the banks and leasing companies was substantially above what would make me happy. As I remember it was about seventy-five thousand dollars, less departure pay and bonuses for my managers, the wonderful chiefs and master sergeants without whom I would never have had the guts to start and accomplish all that we did. Although the monetary figures were not at all impressive back then, and certainly aren't now, we were the largest contractor in the coin laundry field with the military exchange system at the time of the sellout. Of far more importance, we had earned a reputation for honesty, hard work, and for doing what we said we would do. Now that's precious. I believe we are regarded the same way today, some thirty years later. It has to be true, or we would have been kicked out a long time ago.

Is it not reasonable to assume that if your products sell well at military bases in Hawaii, they will on all other military bases? I can tell you that is absolutely correct. There is only one problem. You can't just pick up the phone and call other bases and ask if they would be so kind as to place an order in the mail because of your experience with the Hawaiian exchanges.

No, my friends, you have to physically go there, stand in line to see the buyer, show him your Hawaiian orders, tell him why he should bring in another line—make your pitch. In those days, all the military exchanges were autonomous buying operations. Today, they are pretty much centralized: one call, one pitch, one yes or no, and you have them all or nothing at all. There was no easy road then, nor is there one today.

I'm appalled, and at the same time amused, at the salaries or fees paid in today's world to a few performers who are considered stars. I've never experienced jealousy or even envy, for I realize a star represents one in hundreds of thousands. I will admit that when I read or hear about these financial distortions, I have moments of depression. I ask myself, What the hell I am doing one or two steps up from a barrow peddler? My hard-earned, relatively small amount of money was coming in, and seemingly large amounts went out just to survive. For God's sake, we're all trying to survive. The hell with the big guys, the lucky ones, the God-given exceptionally talented ones. We can't even be given our daily bread unless we get up early, go out into the unfriendly world where competition for each of life's good qualities comes on en masse and tries to beat the hell out of us for everything, including our share of the bread. Now this all sounds rather miserable and hopeless, but it isn't. Just think. Look around. You're part of the competition; you're holding your own. You're making progress to a point where you can look down and say to yourself, I'm better off than a lot of people. It's all relative. You should feel better. Start looking up and go after them. You're as good or better. There is no turning back. You've gone too far. Come on. Let's go for it, whatever it is.

Flush with cash in the bank, a most unusual state of affairs, I thought it would make sense for me to become the civilian distributor of all three lines for the state of Hawaii. I approached each manufacturer. Would you believe they said yes? Of course you would. First, because none of them had a distributor for the state. Second, they knew me and what I had accomplished with the military. Third, I had enough money (I'm tempted to say financial strength, but I really shouldn't) to get under way with a modest inventory from each company. For example, I could say, "I'll take one of those, two of that one, three of that best seller." I certainly didn't want to be overinventoried.

In my opinion there was a definite synergizing factor. My manager, George Brown, was such a workaholic that he could easily handle the civilian end of the business, providing I would undertake a commuter program between the mainland and Hawaii, which I did. It added up to about five trips a year, although that wasn't enough. Being a distributor absolutely requires a hands-on, everyday operation. Here I was trying to run it from the mainland. Totally absurd, incredibly stupid, but I did it. And I paid for it over and over again.

At the time it seemed logical, all the more because the state of Hawaii in 1963 was going into its boom. Jets were coming in from all over the world; high-rise condominiums, new office buildings, and hotels were going up left and right. It wasn't uncommon for me to see a dozen or more topping-out cranes in Honolulu and the suburban areas every time I flew in. It was a madhouse of building, and businesses of all kinds were starting up. The prosperity of the state was never better.

In addition, I was determined to introduce these appliances to the Pacific overseas bases. To reach those bases I had to go by way of Hawaii. The products involved were renowned as the finest of their kind in their respective industries, so how could anyone not leap at the opportunity, especially in a market that was growing dramatically?

I would have to say, without question, that Hawaii is a unique market. Yes, I know every market is unique, but this one took the cake and still does today. Rounding Diamond Head as you fly in, you see a maze of high-rise hotels, condominiums, and single-family dwellings stretching back and up into the hills, so Honolulu looks like any big city on the mainland.

One top executive after another, seeing this, is convinced that it holds terrific business potential for his company. It makes no difference what kind of product or service he offers. Look at the size of Hawaii. Wow! How cruelly deceptive, horribly so, and as a result far more new enterprises fail in Hawaii than in any other market in the United States. When you subtract the military, city, state, and government employees, you've reduced the state's population by two-thirds. Then within the remaining group nearly everyone has a son or a nephew in the National Guard or Reserves, with proper access to the various exchanges throughout the island. Lastly, if you discount thousands of tourists who come in and buy matching muumuus and walking shorts to wear with black socks, you are left with a very charming, albeit small native population who, since Captain Cook's visit, are dyed-in-the-wool G.E. customers. G.E. salesmen must have been on the second ship to arrive.

That's not all by a long shot, for the natives are not friendly to start-up businesses that are owned by haole newcomers from the mainland. They have a good reason. They have been taken over and over again by numerous fast-talking mainland salesmen selling a bill of goods without service or parts to support whatever product or project was involved.

It gets worse. A staggering number of new retail stores and service businesses close shortly after opening. They aren't even given a chance. It's almost as if a sign is on their door that says "Newcomer. Buy at your own risk." Invariably, those who did buy soon learned to never depart from the old firms of Hawaii. I like to think that the expression "fly-by-night" originated in Hawaii with the fast-buck group who came in, did their thing, and took the red-eye back to the mainland. Aloha.

If New York was known as a melting pot of the world, Hawaii definitely established itself as one for the entire Far East, if not the world. The term "local" refers to a minority white colony and to the vast majority of Asian Americans. This group, as you know, includes descendants of the original Hawaiians who migrated centuries ago from volcanic islands in the South Pacific. Very few native Hawaiians can be counted today, and they are treated with great respect by all the rest of the population. From the Hawaiians, we go to the thousands of Japanese, Chinese, Filipinos, Samoans, Guamanians, and the infinite number of mixtures that have developed since they all came together. That's Hawaii.

"You lucky, you live Hawaii" was a headline for an advertisement coined by an excellent advertising agency in Hawaii. The headline has never been improved on, for it says it all. Because most inhabitants are Asian, a business-person certainly needs one or more of them, all if possible, to be the contact with customers. The comfort and trust level is much higher when doing business with a member of own's own race, especially in Hawaii. People there have what is known as an open-heart policy, meaning they open their hearts and all that may imply to all Asians, but probably not to palefaced humans.

With just the bare essentials—two servicemen and a local secretary—we were under way, only to wonder when the phone would ring, or when, if ever, we would see a live potential customer.

At least from a location standpoint, I had a bit of luck. I rented an old tin warehouse with a storefront right smack on Kalakaua Avenue, the main drag going to and from the airport and to points south of Waikiki. There was very heavy vehicle traffic, but little foot traffic. With all the signs and window displays we could muster, I figured if people drove by often enough they would surely remember where we were located if and when they needed a major appliance. Figure again, Marc!

Another major decision: we were not going to sell to appliance dealers. There were only three or four of them, and they looked like flea markets. If any of them had a credit rating, it was very negative. The mom-and-pop dealers in shorts and bare feet had little hole-in-the-wall locations, selling to members of their family, or hui. They would order one unit at a time and never pay for it until they needed another. One hell of a dealer network. The great advantage we had was that we could buy as a distributor and sell at competitive retail prices, thus obtaining the profit of a distributor plus that of a dealer.

The only requirement to achieving a successful and very profitable operation was to sell a good number of our major appliances. This wasn't an easy task, for as I've related, Hawaii was a subsidiary of G.E. when it came to appliances.

Another interesting aspect of being in the appliance business in Hawaii in the mid-1960s was the advertising cooperation that all of the appliance distributors received from the Hawaiian Electric Company (HEC), the utility for the islands. At that time, HEC was trying to build up the "load," because its generators were not working at anything close to capacity. In other words, the more electrical appliances that were in use, the greater the load. The greater the load, the more and larger bills the company could send out to residents each and every month. Toward that end, HEC offered to pay fifty percent of the cost for distributors' or dealers' newspaper advertisements. Because nearly every manufacturer had a cooperative advertising program based on fifty percent of the cost based on accrued purchases, it was a beautiful invitation to advertise without cost, as long as factory purchases generated sufficient advertising dollars.

It was so ludicrous. Every day of the week, including Sunday, the *Honolulu Advertiser* was filled with page after page of advertisements for refrigerators, freezers, washing machines, dryers, etc.; it made me wonder whether I was reading a newspaper or a catalog. I have no doubt that the big guys, like the G.E. distributor, made more money through advertising discounts based on quantity insertions than they did on the sales of their appliances. We, of course, were limited by the small fund generated by our meager sales. I keep telling you, it's a cruel world out there.

I also have to tell you that once HEC reached total capacity of its generators, the advertising ceased. No more co-op, thank you very much; please advertise on your own. The other switch was to create its own TV and newspaper campaigns suggesting and recommending ways of cutting down on electric bills. HEC was the good guy, trying to save homemakers some hard-earned dollars . . . trying to stay current.

Being aware of these adverse conditions, I nevertheless decided to make an all-out effort as the distributor for Hawaii. My ace in the hole was the military business. So all I needed to do at the civilian level was to break even. I would have the benefit of the manpower covering both aspects of the business without additional costs, and sales with the military should strengthen as a result of our advertising and visible location. All very ethereal. I should have cut the deck again.

You may wonder when the hell am I ever going to have an easy win and, with a suddenness you only read about, become a millionaire. You'll have to bear with me again. It will happen. There is a speck of dawn, not enough to light up the dark jungle path I was plowing through, but at least I was moving by instinct (which sheds a light of its own).

Shortly after we were under way in Hawaii I received an invitation to attend my first Amana distribution conference, to be held at the Doral Country Club in Florida. Now, this was going to be exciting as well as inspirational. My patron, meaning my regional manager at Amana, who was in charge of distribution on the West Coast and Hawaii, was a topflight person by the name of Gene Whittle.

Everything about Amana, from its people to its products, service, and style of operation was first-class. For the most part, the Amana people were country boys from Iowa. The leader and founder of the company was George Foerstner, a self-made man who, in his garage, invented the cooler or freezer as we know it today. From this came the company known as Amana Refrigeration, located in the Amana colonies of Amana, Iowa.

The colonies had been settled by the earliest Amanites, a religious group of people who came over from Europe and finally found their sanctuary in Iowa. There they pursued their religious beliefs and a unique way of life. It was an adaptation of a communal society, a first in America, but totally on the benign side. One colony made clothing; another made furniture; others handled almost all the farming, food, and various other needs of life and homemaking, all of which were exchanged among each of the six colonies.

Everyone knew they were making a fair exchange, for the quality of everything was superb. The reason, which remains true today, is the religious belief that you prove your belief and love of God by the work you do with your mind and hands. Anything they did with their hands had to be the best they could do. There was no Detroit slap-it-together attitude and sloppy assembly-line work. Amana Refrigeration, as a company, became famous for quality craftsmanship, and it maintains that reputation today. I know I would buy anything I needed out of the Amana colonies. All you have to do is go there, meet the people, and you know.

This little ol' Hawaiian boy arrived at the Doral Country Club for the Amana distributors conference and entered a room filled with prosperous-looking men. It seemed to me they were all smoking long, heavy cigars. I was immediately impressed and intimidated, all the more so because I represented a .001 BPI, the business potential of my market in relation to all others in the United States; they don't come much smaller than that, and go up to 10.00 for New York City. These guys were the big guys in distribution. They did a volume in the millions of dollars, and in addition to Amana, also distributed RCA or Zenith and other big-ticket products.

Furthermore they were not the dead-in-the-ass, catalog-page-turning distributors of my early days. They were alive, hard-kicking promotional outfits that took the factory programs and executed them the way they were told to do, by the numbers. If they didn't, the factory would give them hell and threaten to take the line away. The factories rarely lose. A distributor would be crazy to disagree, not buy his quota, or not have his organization go all out. Not to do so would be to goof around with a few million dollars. There wasn't a looney in the crowd.

Just an instant before I began to feel dizzy and faint as a result of quietly reviewing my inadequacies in relation to the group, Gene Whittle drew me aside and gave me the all-that-glitters-is-not-gold story. In effect, he told me that although some of them did a tremendous volume of business, they had difficulty in paying their bills. Really? Well now. I began to feel quite comfortable and decided that henceforth I would not accept things or people at face value, including myself. But I did accept a cigar, light up, and join the boys in the back room.

The Amana meeting was really exciting. The company was beginning a boom period that would last for over twenty years, with millions upon millions added to their sales volume year after year. I mean many millions, for on top of their growing reputation for quality, they found the formula for hitting a jackpot with a promotion called the Amana VIP. Sooo beautiful, so natural, so fun, and sooo many orders written.

It all started perhaps a year or two before I arrived, when George Foerstner, Amana's president, got together with Jules Boros, the golf pro at the Doral, one of the leading money-makers on the professional golf circuit. Foerstner and Boros signed up almost all the well-known pros to endorse Amana, most visibly by wearing the Amana VIP insignia on their golf hats. Every time a TV camera would pan in on one of the pros at an important golf event, "Amana VIP" would show up clearly. Actually only the top, well-known pros were invited into this august group. Those were the days before endorsements by sports pros were routine and commonplace. I imagine the contracts signed were minimal in their compensation to the pros, but keep in mind that in those days there were no $500,000 tournaments.

Behind the playing field, in the offices, the calculators were primarily used for multiplying—multiplying the number of Amana dealers who would have to purchase X number of Amana products to qualify for the Amana regional golf tournaments held in every section of the country to decide who would attend the fantastic Amana VIP Pro-Am in Iowa and have the opportunity to play a round with one of the world's leading pro golfers.

Now, even if you let your imagination run amok, you still won't reach the level of excitement and volume of business the promotion generated. The Amana dealers were golf nuts. They went bonkers. To go to the regional tournament to qualify was an event in itself. They placed enough orders to fill their warehouses and garages, thoroughly preempting any possibility that their competition could obtain a sample order. The qualifying tournament was held at a prestigious country club or resort over the weekend, and the dealers were treated to accommodations, meals, and an awards banquet featuring good food, drink, fellowship, and the naming of the winner who had earned the right to go to the big tent in Iowa. It was to die for! Of course, not being privy to how handicaps were determined, I can't say for sure, but I'm almost certain that many of Amana's largest dealers made the cut.

Come August every year, all good Amana dealer golfers go to Mecca, in this case the Finkbine Country Club in Iowa City, Iowa, where the Amana VIP Pro-Am is traditionally held. Here again, they are wined, dined, partied, housed, and allowed to play with the gods of the game. I guess you have to be in a Pro-Am to experience the thrill, but it's a lifetime memory. The climax finally comes on the last night, when Hollywood and country music stars offer their best performances at the awards ceremony. This is followed by a Las Vegas–style gambling setup where if you lose your given stake, you just go back for more; it's the only gambling joint in the world where all shooters are winners.

The following day all the dealers go home, giving every consideration to doubling next year's quota to qualify. . . . And then they do it.

What an absolutely fantastic promotion. It rendered all that I have ever done totally minuscule. For one thing, I estimate Amana wrote up over ten million dollars worth of business from dealers who attended the qualifying rounds and the Amana VIP in Iowa. Taking all expenses into account (I'd say $250,000), the promotion would have to be nominated to the Promotional Hall of Fame. Now remember, I'm using 1966 money. Back then, ten million was only mentioned when you spoke of government budgets; $250,000 expended on one promotion called for a Price Waterhouse audit.

Amana never had an advertising budget that inundated the country with TV commercials or newspaper and magazine advertisements. They considered it enough to make a subconscious impression about quality and craftsmanship. This impression was combined with a strong network of dealers who bought Amana up to their yin-yangs as a result of the VIP program. They had to recommend and sell an Amana appliance so they could reorder and participate in the next tournament.

# Chapter 14

Armed with the excitement of the new year's Amana program, brochures, price lists, promotions, etc., I returned to Hawaii. After obtaining orders from the military exchanges, I planned to take my first trip to the Far East: Japan, Okinawa, the Philippines, and Guam. To do this, I first had to obtain the consent of Amana's export department, then headed by a fine gentleman named Ben Douglas. I decided to make a special trip to Amana for this purpose. I phoned Ben, set the appointment, and within a few days flew to Amana. (There were no advance-purchase airfare requirements in those days. One fare fit all flights.) I was warmly welcomed by Ben. We hit it off together from the start, and by the afternoon I left the factory as Amana's worldwide military representative.

Now all of you who have been with me these oh, so many years, vicariously being banged from pillar to post, enduring the pain of one disappointment after another until you are mercifully Novocained by rejection, may realize we're at the beginning of a new era. However, I can understand and fully appreciate that there may not be many survivors who have the energy and desire to see this story through to the end. I salute all of you for being with me, for your patience and unswerving determination to follow me with unflagging hope and belief in spite of my manic-depressive tales of success and misfortune.

All aboard! We're leaving on our first flight to the mysterious Far East. As we take off from Honolulu on a Pan Am Clipper and turn west, we can sit back, relax, and enjoy the next ten hours of flying time to Tokyo. The world is one big territory.

Actually, Japan wasn't in my plans for business, due to the fact that its electrical current was and is 220 volts. All of our appliances operated on 110 volts. For this reason, few Amana appliances were sold to our military in Japan. Military consumers had the option of purchasing Amana export models in the 220-volt configuration, but they usually decided not to, because the products would be useless when they received orders to return to the States. To compound the problem, military quarters on or off base were so small that an Amana refrigerator would take up almost all of an average-sized room. For all of these reasons, it was not a viable market.

My first impression of Japan and its people remains unchanged these many years. In my opinion, shared by many, they consider themselves a superior race and almost totally reject equal or reciprocal interracial relationships of any kind. It's a one-sided proposition: they will sell to the world most aggressively but will resist buying anything that isn't Japanese with unbelievable determination. The only exceptions are what they do not possess, manufacture, or grow—for example, oil or some kinds of food. Nationalism, thy name is Japan. The lowliest potwalloper in the lowliest restaurant in Japan is shining that pot as if the entire nation depends on him. They are a hardworking people, and I remember riding a taxi in from the Narita airport late of an evening, seeing that many of the office buildings lined up on either side of the highway were still occupied by very busy-looking people. The Japanese either used three shifts of office help or they had sleeping quarters next door.

Most likely the latter, for when I say late, I mean nine or ten at night.

Another source of amazement was to go to Tokyo station in the early morning and see the thousands of commuters coming to work. Those people didn't walk; they hopped, skipped, and quick-paced to just about a run. They were all so young, in their twenties. Middle-aged or elderly were nowhere to be seen. Obviously, this first mature generation after the war was dedicated to building a new Japan. And so they did. As a matter of fact, they succeeded far beyond whatever they might have accomplished if their fathers had won the war.

It is inconceivable today that the two most powerful nations on the planet Earth, aside from the United States, are Japan and Germany, both of whom exemplified to the ultimate degree the brutality of war. Both were taken from the ash heap and brought back to reignite the greatest explosion of economic growth in the history of mankind.

The timing could not have been more perfect, and the Marshall Plan worked wonders. For one thing, it gave the Japanese state-of-the-art steel manufacturing while our own mills were cranking out product the same way they had done it for over fifty years. The Japanese could out-produce us, steel mill for steel mill, as the net result of new automation while our plants used old equipment. That was bad enough, but when the Japanese labor rate was seventy-five percent below ours, well, the party was over for us again.

I'm not through with them. They were still copiers. It all started with the automobile. In the early fifties they brought the first Japanese cars to the West Coast priced $1,500 to $2,000 below cars of the Big Three. Of course we laughed. Their quality was everything we imagined it to be before the war . . . or was it?

The West Coast population, always known for its avant-garde buying habits, started to purchase a car by the name of Toyota. Lo and behold, it ran pretty well—as a matter of fact, damn well. The next year the price went up three or four hundred dollars, but so did the prices of our cars. The Japanese cars began to catch on. Their distribution expanded to the East Coast as their prices rose. The midsection of our country remained true to Chevrolet, motherhood, and apple pie—a bit more difficult. But even the last holdouts joined the stampede to buy Japanese. In the meantime, the Big Three of our automobile business were sitting on their fat asses still burping and farting from overindulgence in easy sales and the stress of operating on allocation, which they had enjoyed since the end of the war.

This malaise drifted over the entire industry from the top down to the assembly people, who made lousy automobiles. The disease spread in the minds of American consumers to the budding electronics business, where everything made in Japan was believed to be far superior to our product when, for the most part, we had invented the damn industry. Whatever we made, they copied and improved on, at least temporarily, until we woke up and found we were and are being hosed by the nation we re-created.

There's more. They outadvertised, outpromoted, and out-everythinged us with the oodles of money they saved by not having to pay taxes on a level anywhere in the vicinity of our country's. As a matter of fact, the Japanese government subsidized them to the extent of picking up the shipping charges on exports. Can you believe that? Then also believe that production came in just about duty free. For God's sake, they operated with huge profits that provided advertising and promotional budgets we couldn't even come close to matching. It gave them the money to provide company housing and all the amenities their workers could ask for plus the unspoken, unwritten understanding that their jobs would last for life; there was no fear of being laid off. In return, the manufacturers received unswerving loyalty and devotion to quality production.

On top of it all, by way of further explanation to this musical—this incredible, unbeatable rise in the fortunes of a country and its people—is the fact that to this day we have held the defense umbrella over Japan. We maintained a defense force of men and women throughout the world, a major share of our overall budget then and now and the reason our businesses are taxed beyond their ability to compete.

The Japanese have rejected the concept of conquest by military force and means, using our dropping the bomb and its horrendous loss of life as the reason to never again become a militant nation in the eyes of the world. Very commendable, economically advantageous, and very self-serving, thank you very much. And best wishes to the friendly folk who gave us Pearl Harbor.

I realize this may all seem quite prejudiced, and it is, but not to the point that I want to play bang bang with lives. I just think that we need a major tune-up in our trade relationship. The trade deficit is millions, billions of dollars going out of the United States to Japan. There are only two ways to make profound adjustments, and only one is practical. The first one is to slap a tariff on their exports as they have done to us. The nearest we have come to that is to put a limit on how many cars they can ship into the United States. The Japanese reacted by raising prices drastically to make up for loss of sales. What did we do? Detroit raised prices at a time when it had the chance of a lifetime to beat the pants off the Japanese. The Japanese became frightened enough to prepare for future moves in this direction by building their own plants in the United

States. As an added inducement and attraction they started up physical fitness programs for factory workers. It's all one wonderful, happy factory. I sure do like what you do for me, Toyota.

Today, after years of our presidents and Congress demanding and threatening Japan to open its markets, reduce and eliminate tariffs, nothing has been done. I'll give you a hundred dollars every time you see an American car going down the Ginza; you give me a penny for every Japanese. You won't have taxi fare home; I'll make a ton of money. Even if all the government negotiations were to work in our favor, they would still amount to nothing. Japanese will not buy American. They will buy only Japanese—cars, electronics, everything they make. We don't stand a chance of success unless, by their taking a pro-American pill from childhood on we eventually feel a slight dent, just a touch of improvement perhaps three generations from now, but I doubt it.

On my first, exploratory trip I visited the military exchanges at Yokota, Yokosuka, and Tachikawa without obtaining orders, for reasons mentioned. But I did make favorable introductions for the future. It was so good to come aboard a base overseas. The sights and sounds made me think I was calling on the San Diego naval base, Fort Lewis, or any of our mainland bases; hamburgers, French fries, and hot dogs made me feel right at home in a traveling salesman's world.

Next stop, Okinawa. This was our island, for we paid dearly for it in lives during the war and had not yet officially turned it back to Japan. Everything outside of our huge military complexes was decidedly Japanese in structure—a hodgepodge of flimsy houses, businesses, stores, and bars (frequented by the single troops), all facing the one dusty paved street that led from the airport straight through Okinawa.

Inside our bases, it was a relative garden of Eden. There was military housing surrounded by well-kept lawns and flower beds, troop barracks as far as the eye could see, well-paved roads leading to theaters, golf courses, tennis courts, swimming pools, schools, playing fields, and clubs of every type to suit one's purpose in life.

Of overall importance to me was the fact that on these large and magnificent bases, all of which had the electrical current compatible with my appliances, I could write up some business. I scored a heavy order for Amana without any problem.

Fortunately the buyer told me that he had owned an Amana and thought highly of the company.

"How very nice," I murmured as I wrote up a container-load order.

Interestingly, they sold few dishwashers because every military family had full-time Japanese servants. That's right, servants. There was no need for the housewife to wash a dish, make a bed, clean the house. They had it made, paying all of fifty dollars a month for wages. The military families lived in attractive GI housing, had free medical services, could use all facilities at next to no cost, and of course enjoyed the wonderful advantage of going to the exchange and commissary to fill their needs at extremely attractive prices. How good could life be? Beautiful. And those people knew it and appreciated it as only regular, long-term military people could, following the philosophy that the last assignment and the next one are the best. You can't beat those people; they're terrific.

This was to be the first of many trips to Okinawa. On leaving, I knew I would duplicate this business in the Philippines and on Guam. It would be just like the Presto days; by showing the orders obtained from one major base to another, I would hardly ever fail.

A wave of nostalgia must surely envelop anyone who talks or writes about experiences in the Philippines, and I am no exception. Let me float a few memories that stand out as I think back over the years.

My first touchdown at Manila, to an airport surrounded by hundreds of children behind the airport fences—children everywhere, no matter which way I turned. The Philippine immigration officer asking if I wanted to exchange dollars for pesos. The ride down Roxas Boulevard, named after the Philippine patriot that General MacArthur restored to the presidency after we recaptured the country. Seeing my first fantastic sunset on Manila Bay. Visiting and having lunch at the old Army Navy Club on the bay, noting MacArthur's name listed on the back wall as a president of the club in the 1920s. Going out to see members playing tennis, with a ball boy at each end of the court to retrieve balls. Finding out I needed a chauffeured car to drive out of Manila to Subic Bay and over to Clark Field. Taking leave of the hotel in the early morning, threading through heavy traffic made up mostly of Jeeps left over from the war and decorated lavishly with rainbow colors, all carrying passengers up and down the crowded streets. And on the return trip to Manila, stopping the car to watch a small boy try to mount a water buffalo by shimmying up, hand over hand holding the tail, with his feet on the hind leg, falling three times, and kicking the buffalo's leg in frustration; so funny.

Arriving in Manila for the flight to Guam, I was the last one to board a plane that had just come in from Saigon, and I got the only seat left, next to a pretty American girl. Subsequently I asked her how she enjoyed the Philippines and how long she had been there.

"Several months," she replied.

Taken by surprise, I asked what she was doing there.

"I'm with the Peace Corps."

Oh, wow. I'd never met a member before.

"Which facet of the Peace Corps are you in?" I asked.

"My job is to teach birth control to the Filipinos."

"Oh, my God, are you ever going to need help," I said. "The country is inundated with hundreds of thousands of babies and children."

"Yes, I know," she said simply.

"What can you do? Have you taught them the usual and known methods of birth control?" I asked.

"That's not the problem," she said. "The problem is not education. The problem is inherent in the life of every person in the country. There are no homes for the elderly. They do not have a poorhouse, to say nothing of government entitlements such as welfare, social security, food stamps. No kind of care whatsoever for old people. They therefore have their own system.

"Families have a minimum of ten kids, knowing that some will die before their time and that others will be unable to care for themselves. But out of the ten, there will be a few or even one who will give the parents loving care until their lives come to an end.

"There is nothing we have been able to do, or perhaps under the circumstances we prefer not to change the system. It's all they have," she concluded with a moist eye, along with a small smile.

"Are you planning to return?" I asked.

"Oh, yes," she replied. "A close relative passed away and I'm going home for a short while. When I come back I plan on marrying my fiancé."

"That's exciting," I said. "Is he a member of the Peace Corps?"

"No, he's a young Filipino attorney," she replied.

Of course I couldn't resist. "And how many children do you plan on having?"

"Why ten, of course!" she laughingly said. And we laughed our way to Guam before saying good-bye.

Our conversation refocused my thoughts about how lovely, gentle, wanting to please, and smiling the Filipinos are with their "Yes, sirs" invariably voiced with sincere respect whenever you speak with them. The Filipinos really do have a charm all their very own in the world. One can easily understand the reasons why General MacArthur said, "I shall return." I myself have returned many times, and can only hope to go back again.

Guam is somewhat of a hybrid. We own it. It's American—not a colony or a commonwealth, but perhaps a responsibility we inherited. It's difficult to determine its character. There are two major military bases, Anderson AFB and the Guam naval base. Both were rather active, to say the least, back in early seventies, when we were bombing the hell out of Vietnam. The taxiways leading to the runways were filled with monstrous B-52 bombers waiting to take off on their way west. Those guys were on a nonstop round trip scheduled for twelve hours or more and at the halfway point had to bomb targets through all the antiaircraft fire and missiles the Viet Cong could launch at them.

And there I was, driving along the road paralleling the runway, on my way to open my salesman's attaché case, bring out my brochures, and ask for an order. Doesn't seem quite as important, does it? But it is. Because everyone has to do the job he or she was destined to do, for that job becomes part of the master plan for life going on. And it does.

Once the day's work was done, you might say all was done. Guam, as Guamanians will remember, was an island with one hotel, the Cliff. If you didn't have a reservation, you were almost held up at the airport in Honolulu or wherever because your choice was either the Cliff or the beach.

The two military bases were at opposite ends of the island. The small, family town of Agana was totally void of activity after dark. Your only sources of comfort were your fellow peddlers of the road, the bar, and the hotel restaurant. Not very much different than a rainy night in anywheresville on the mainland, except you were surrounded by thousands of miles of water.

These were the days just before the invasion of the Japanese honeymooners who found Guam to be the closest warm-weather island to Japan. All of a sudden, hotel after hotel went up. The island was jammed with them and is to this day. It has turned into a Miami Beach. And so the world turns and changes.

Everyone's first trip to the Far East has to be memorable, and mine was no exception. The people, their customs, religions, dress, language, food, and smells are all brand-new and very exciting, doubly so for me because I had opened new territory, obtained orders, and made expenses. All in all I found it an extremely satisfying experience.

The satisfaction has to be measured against being away from home for about three weeks, flying seemingly endless hours, being alone, tired. I knew this was the way I'd been running my life from the beginning, that I should stop complaining. "I will," I thought, "when I finally add up our bank account and find I'm a millionaire."

Undoubtedly physical exhaustion from such long trips, combined with the seemingly endless stress and frustration of running a business, takes its toll on your spirits, your dreams, your hopes, your love of the game. You can end up feeling like someone whose grand illusions never will be realized. I hasten to make it perfectly clear that this depression is normal. When you are young, it can come and go in a minute or an hour or a day, until you write up your next order. When you are older it can come on just as fast, but it will hang on a bit longer, giving you an opportunity to reassess position, ability, and determination. Obviously if the latter two are positive, you naturally resume working with renewed confidence that you have made the right decision and will eventually succeed.

I must confess all of this is a bit of rah-rah. During my periods of depression, I didn't have the confidence that I would succeed to keep me going. I had the same old fear that I would starve to death along with my wife and kids, for those were the days before food stamps. I had no options. None. I had to hit the road, knock on doors, ring those bells. There was no turning back . . . back to what?

To home, of course. Home on the ocean in La Jolla. To my wife and kids and all the joy of living they represented. It was growing up time for them. All of them were in school for the first time. A time for midnight hand fishing for the grunion that made a fleeting swim to shore to lay their eggs in the sand and then swim away with the tide. You can imagine the squeals of delight as the kids, searchlights in hand, found the fish and scrambled to pick them up. We would take the kids to the Beach & Tennis Club for swim meets, started them off on tennis lessons and every kind of lesson for the proper bringing up of children without robbing them of childhood.

A year or two slipped by; the last of the vending contracts were disposed of. All creditors who loaned me money to pay for the equipment were repaid in full. We had no debts except a mortgage. Commissions from our sales to the military exchanges in Hawaii and the western Pacific bases came in on a steady basis, sufficient to carry on a good life in La Jolla. I'd fly back and forth to Hawaii about every two months and add a visit to the Far East at least twice a year.

The memories tumble over one another when I recall those seemingly placid times, of taking the family on one of the last voyages of the old *Lurline*, watching with delight as the kids participated in all the shipboard activities, the coke parties (that means Coca-Cola), costume parades, hula lessons, games, and of course the shipboard shows every night with Hawaiian music, hula dancing, and songs. Everyone on the ship was up at dawn on the morning we were to arrive, fully expecting to see natives wearing grass skirts and leis on head and shoulders, swarming out from the beach in outrigger canoes, so intense was the buildup and anticipation. Although that no longer happened, the entire Royal Hawaiian band waited at dockside to greet our arrival. That welcome was so memorable, so lovely, that a first-time visitor was immediately inoculated with the charm of the island. It is said that one shot will last a lifetime.

We had acquired a beautiful apartment at the Colony Surf, a truly special condominium hotel complex on the beach at the foot of Diamond Head. It was all fun and games when we were there together. The Outrigger Canoe Club, next door to the Colony, had a reciprocal membership with our La Jolla Beach & Tennis Club. It was fantastic and still is. Every morning, off the children went to eat slushes, hoho's, hamburgers, to endless splashes, sundown kid parties, and dinners surrounded by Hawaiians singing about old Hawaii. We'd thank God for them, those peaceful, happy evenings; they were precious.

# Chapter 15

You may have long since wondered when and how in the hell I would move out of perpetual mediocrity into the shoes of a millionaire. I know I wondered for just about twenty-five long years, most of which were dedicated to survival and reduced to infrequent dreams of the unknown million-dollar world. You will be happy to know my time had finally arrived. One last chance, if you will, for me to capitalize on my years of experience in selling and marketing with a product designed especially for me, as you will soon agree.

It all began at an annual distributors conference of Amana Refrigeration at Miami Beach, Florida, in January 1968. I had attended these events since becoming a distributor for Amana in Hawaii and enjoyed meeting and knowing many of the principal Amana distributors. I could not quite feel I was one of them because my market, Hawaii, was, is, and always will be one of the smallest of all.

However, to boost me up a bit, I was also Amana's international military representative, and this gave me a presence along with the fact that my tennis game was good enough at the time to make me part of a doubles group including Tom Phillips, the CEO of the Raytheon Corporation, parent company of Amana. I would sit with the export department vice presidents, Ben Douglas and Eldon Pugh, who were among the finest men I've ever known in the business world.

Why do I say that? I say that because shortly afterward, when they were sending me checks for hundreds of thousands of dollars a year, they could have, at the stroke of a pen or with just a telephone call, eliminated me as a commissioned representative and turned the operation over to an in-house activity employing three or four men and paying them less than fifty percent of what they were paying me. That's why I think they were great, as well as the whole Amana outfit. I also like to believe that the three or four guys who might have replaced me could not have done the job anywhere near as successfully as I. What the hell, I know it, and as this story unfolds, so will you.

Beyond the camaraderie of a sales conference, Amana always highlighted its business presentation with a new concept or product. One year they introduced the side-by-side refrigerator. Another year they brought forth the automatic ice-and-water dispenser. In 1968 they outdid themselves and no doubt were invited to sit at the left hand of God.

Ladies and gentlemen, Amana is proud to introduce the greatest invention since fire: the Amana microwave oven—the Radarange.

Wow! Now I have an idea of what it's like to become a born-again Christian. The love of everything reenters your life, including the love of Mike. In this case, Mike was a product as revolutionary as the electric light bulb or any other magnificent product that has changed, forever and for better, life in the civilized world.

As I listened to Lou King, Amana's vice president of marketing, give his presentation (not a pitch or spiel—much too important), I realized I was looking at a pressure cooker that could also bake a cake. In addition it could roast turkey or beef. In effect, it could do everything a pressure cooker could do and, as they say, much much more. Déjà vu was hitting me right smack in the face! All I had to do was duplicate the old pressure cooker program from over twenty-five years ago, and sure as hell the same thing would happen. Talk about excitement! I went right out of my mind. We had struck gold, oil, and diamonds; totally fantastic!

As some of you may know, the microwave oven was accidentally invented by a Raytheon scientist who noticed a chocolate bar begin to melt in his shirt pocket as he tested a magnatron tube in a radar system. This led to an experiment with popcorn that popped all over the place, and the rest is history. Amana, under Raytheon, superbly engineered and produced the first tabletop microwave oven the world had ever seen, a dream for a creative marketing man. That's me!

Before the meeting ended I was climbing the walls without a ladder until I was given the okay to take one of the samples with me to Puerto Rico when the conference ended. There was a military location over there called Ramey Air Force Base, as well as a naval exchange in downtown San Juan. Within a few days I'd have the answers about the Radarange's acceptance.

Me and my hundred-pound Radarange box took off from the Miami airport the morning after the gala farewell dinner at George Foerstner's magnificent Indian Creek Country Club, an affair remembered by all from one year to the next—truly magnificent parties.

Upon arriving at San Juan, I switched over to a flivver plane for the flight to Ramey, where I spent the night. The next day I went to the exchange and met with the exchange manager and his merchandise manager. Olé, olé! The moment of truth.

I made what is called a cold call. No one knew me or had ever heard of my product. I mean cold. Fortunately I was on the other side of the moon, a base on the extreme western end of Puerto Rico far removed from the main-stream of a heavy flow of visitors or salesmen. I've always found people to be warmer and more receptive in relatively isolated locations.

I introduced myself. "I've just flown over from an Amana sales meeting in Miami where they presented The Greatest Invention Since Fire, and you are the first military exchange to see and hear what this is all about. What I want to show you is a fantastic new way to prepare food that one day the whole country will use as easily as the gas or electric stove."

They say one picture is worth a thousand words. I can tell you a live demonstration beats a picture, black-and-white or in color, every time. Of course, I was prepared, having stopped at the base commissary to explain and receive a go-ahead to purchase the few articles I needed for my demonstration.

Within a few minutes I had prepared three simple items in the Radarange. I met with no resistance; on the contrary, they said yes to everything I suggested. I told them all I wanted was to demonstrate the Radarange on Saturday, take what they call special orders from all who wanted one, and then write up an order from their office for the total, plus some for word-of-mouth sales created by satisfied customers. They agreed with enthusiasm to the whole concept. It was so exciting!

The next day I returned for the first military exchange demonstration of the Amana Radarange. A very young man by the name of Ed Cart was assigned to help me set up my demonstration table. (He subsequently rose through the civilian ranks of the system and today is director of retail operations for the Navy exchange system around the world.)

When the doors opened that morning, I fleetingly recalled the same thing happening many years before in

Wilkes-Barre, Pennsylvania, where I eagerly awaited the first customers for my stupid pants presser. Once again, I had no posters or display materials. There was no advance publicity or advertising of the event. Just me and, on a table, my Radarange with a display of uncooked food and a sign showing the military retail price of $395. To say the least, that was a lot of money for the military in those days (and even in these days).

In they came, and as they started to pass by they saw me holding a bowl of cake mix in one hand and stirring it with a long spoon in the other. Of course they stopped for a second, long enough for me to look up, smile, and ask, "Have you ever seen a cupcake bake in thirty seconds?"

Well, those people weren't going anywhere; they were my prisoners without bars. But I wanted more. So I kept stirring my mix as more people stopped to see what was going on. The group kept growing. I remembered using the same ploy at the World's Fair with a pressure cooker many years before. Hmmm.

"Well, now we're ready," I said.

And I poured the mix into a cupcake holder, opened the oven, placed the cupcake inside, set the time for thirty seconds, and pressed START. Did I ever start something! Within twenty seconds the cupcake began to rise right before their eyes. The exclamations, the astonished expressions, were almost as if they had seen a miracle in the making. They had—the making of my long-sought-after fortune.

Now they were totally enraptured with all I would say and do. "If you think that was exciting, watch this!"

I can't help laughing. Certain expressions are as powerful and enduring today as they were way back then. Can you improve on the tried and true even in this high-tech, everything-has-been-said-and-done-before world, when you simply say "I love you"?

They watched me as I picked up a paper plate and told them I was going to cook bacon in two minutes and that it was going to come out brown, dry, and crisp.

"First, I place a paper towel on the plate and the bacon on top of the paper towel. Next I cover the bacon with a paper towel to prevent splattering. I don't like to clean ovens. But even if I had to, the inside of this oven is stainless steel. I'd clean it with a damp cloth.

"Okay, I place it in, shut the door, set the time for two minutes, and press START. Put your eggs on to boil and breakfast is ready. Yes, if you want six strips of bacon it will take another minute or two depending on the thickness.

"Okay, time's up, the power switches off as the bell sounds.

"I'm going to open up the Radarange and show you what bacon looks like in just two minutes."

Again, gasps as I removed the top paper towel and displayed the really attractive bacon that wasn't dripping in fat.

"Want to taste the bacon, the way it should be?"

And I proceeded to offer pieces that I cut up. Yum, yum, it was good.

"Now let me ask you, how long does it take you to bake a potato at home?"

The reply was about an hour.

"Not really; you have to heat up the oven for fifteen minutes and then it takes an hour. We're going to bake a potato in just five minutes. Watch this."

I then cut a cross in the potato, put it on a paper plate, and again showed them how to set the timer and press START. "It's so easy to use and so safe, even for children."

While the potato was cooking I had the opportunity to give them all of the reasons they should be among the first to own the new Amana Radarange, the greatest invention since fire. I let them have it, one after another.

It cooks vegetables and just about everything in a quarter of the time required for regular cooking. You cook in a cool kitchen—no gas or electric heat. If you live off base, your electric bill for cooking goes way down. The food tastes better because it retains the natural salts and sugars. On and on I went, duplicating my old pressure cooker spiel until the time was up and the potato was done. I opened the door, brought it out, took a towel, because it was too hot to handle, squeezed it together, and the potato puffed up. And again they went bananas.

It was still too early to close. They were not going to pay $395 for a bacon maker or cake baker. They were going to need the all-powerful demonstration of a roast that comes out tender, juicy, and brown. So in went a two-pound roast that I told them would take all of fifteen minutes. In it went, and I then started to answer a thousand questions. Everyone had one, and in addition to answering them in detail, I would pick up the cookbook and go through it with them for all kinds of food. Before we knew it, the roast was done. It came out brown, juicy, and tender.

I let the roast settle while they admired the sight. I listened to them exchange comments, all positive. I then began to slice the roast to the oohs and aahs of the group, cut it into pieces and passed it around. Every single person had a taste. Now it was time to ask for the order. It absolutely had to be casual, no push or shove, almost independent, as if it was a fait accompli. All I had to do was tell them what they had to do to buy one.

I had on the table a standard, yellow, lined writing pad. I had written across the top "PRIORITY SPECIAL ORDER. PHONE WHEN SHIPMENT ARRIVES." It was numbered down the side of the page for a list with headings for names and telephone numbers.

All I said to have them sign up was, "At present, the

only way to obtain the Radarange is to place your name and telephone number on this priority waiting list. The exchange will phone you when the shipment arrives. You are under no obligation. If you change your mind, your unit will go to the next person on the list."

How cool is that! But it's vital you keep a straight face. It's not that you are pulling a fast one. On the contrary, you are actually offering them an opportunity to purchase a truly fine product worth every cent they would pay for it and one that would provide unlimited advantages to the entire family.

As I recall, just about every member of the group signed up. Before I knew it I had six names on the list, and it was barely 10:30 in the morning. That was just the beginning. The next demonstration added a few more, and from then on it was a romp. People would look at the list, recognize their friends' names, and quickly sign up themselves. They say nothing spreads faster than good or bad news, and on a military base I can tell you this is true. Before the afternoon got under way, couples who had had no intention of coming into the exchange began to do so. Their friends and neighbors had told them about the demonstration, so they hastened in and signed up as soon as they saw that cupcake rising with their own eyes. That demo was pure dynamite.

"Blessed are those who believe and have not seen." You'll be blessed if you believe I had thirty-nine sales for the day. Now keep in mind, Ramey was a small, isolated base whose people were normally not the first to see anything, most likely not even the last. But when they did, on a rare occasion, they offered an amazing response. Now you may say, wait a minute, no money changed hands, how and why do you think those thirty-nine were really sold? Because, I would answer, those people were totally sold and couldn't wait to have their units arrive.

To be frank, the normal procedure for a military customer to place a special order would be to write a check for one-third of the purchase price, with the balance due on delivery. But because of the extraordinary circumstances, remote location for one, we waived this requirement. In spite of all the rules and regulations of the military exchange system, no retail organization even comes close to its liberal policies, all in favor of the customer. For example, a customer who made a down payment on a special order could change her mind and receive a refund. The lightest scratch required a hefty markdown. Buy it, take it home, use it for thirty days or more, decide you don't like it and want your money back; no problem. I've even heard of shoes that have been worn for six months being returned for a full refund. For a military customer to shop anywhere else but at the exchange is extremely rare. Moreover, the meager profit the exchange system enjoys is turned over in great part to the Morale and Welfare organization of the military to provide, among many things, funds for family emergencies, child care, and all kinds of recreational activity. It's a testimony to the excellence of the military exchange system, whose mission is to serve the military personnel and their families. They do this with a dedication that is nothing less than awesome.

My demonstration was the talk of the base. All the managers of the exchange saw it and were besieged by customers asking how soon they could expect to receive their units. Needless to say, I received an order for thirty-nine Radaranges at the end of the day. My, oh my, what a day, what a revelation. The only thing left to do was to multiply the total number of military bases by the number to be sold by demonstration and multiply by my commission. When I flash back on all the memorable days of my life, this one is certainly one of the top ten.

I had arranged to put on the same demonstration at the naval base in San Juan the next day, Sunday. I had learned years ago that there is only one day of the week to run a demonstration, and that's a Saturday. Sunday is for church, family activity, etc. Thus the traffic was not as heavy as it could have been, nor was the subconscious mood as strong for buying as it was on Saturday, the day almost implanted in people's genes to buy, buy, buy.

I used the same technique across the board, except for cooking the roast beef before the exchange opened, thus permitting more time to put on one demonstration after another. In total, I believe twelve to fifteen people signed up for the unit. This was truly fantastic, and I obtained an order in this amount from the merchandise manager, Joe Casanazo, and his very young assistant, Freddie Vasquez. (I mention their names because over the course of the next twenty years our paths would cross time and again. Freddie, as an example, subsequently became merchandise manager at the Navy exchange in Taipei. I would visit him there on my trips to the Far East.)

You can only imagine the hero's homecoming I received when I returned to La Jolla. And my success was also a cause for celebration in the Amana factory's export department.

To me this was a major event—a new product with zero saturation and unlimited potential. I knew from my long Presto pressure cooker experience that if I would follow the old demonstration program, it would only be a matter of time before satisfied customers would pass the word and sell those Radaranges until Katie barred the door.

My market was international but not national. In other words, the factory at the time would have nothing to do with the military exchange system within the United States, believing that selling to military would ruin their dealer

sales. They couldn't have been more wrong. But there was
no changing this decision. So I had the world outside the
United States. The major market for the military was the
U.K. and Europe, where we had stationed 200,000 troops
as a bulwark against the Soviet Union and the forces of the
Warsaw Pact nations. That was one hell of a viable market,
and the volume of business from approximately forty
exchanges exceeded a billion dollars a year.

Any super exchange in Europe could do more dollar
volume in one day than a major department store in the
United States could do in a week. Boy, oh boy, I couldn't
wait; but I had to. The factory had to be persuaded to
build a unit that was compatible with both European and
stateside electricity. They agreed to the project, but it would
take about two months to have it engineered and produced.
While this was in the works, I would concentrate on Hawaii
and the Far East exchanges, where the electrical current presented no problem.

I'm sure you realize that all I intended to do was demonstrate the hell out of the Radarange. The product demanded
a demonstration. We could advertise it in magazines, newspapers, radio, and TV, but nothing would sell it faster than
a live demonstration. As I've said before, when it comes to
new cooking devices, a person has to taste the food. Is it
tender, juicy, sweet, colorful, crisp? Only after this judgement has been made, and is affirmative, can you expect to
sell to the mass market. Until then, TV or other media will
get your "gofers," and that's slim pickings.

Here I was in the early spring of 1968, a one-man band
with an engagement to play around the world. First stop,
Hawaii. Absolutely no problem. Our reputation was so
good. Our history of attention to detail in every facet of
marketing our products was totally intense. We held sales
meetings, put up point-of-sale materials, did everything

possible to help the sell-through. We could have sold horse manure wrapped in plastic as a cancer cure. Within a few days I received orders from all military bases in Hawaii and at the same time placed an order for twenty-four Radaranges for our distributorship.

Hold the phone. This was the civilian market, where the price was much higher, and we did not offer the military's liberal return policy. This would be a much harder sell, so twenty-four seemed adequate. I remembered the early days of the pressure cooker, the consumer fears and doubts about something new: people have difficulty understanding a concept that is radically different from the old tried and true that has been handed down for generations. Keep in mind, the first automobiles were met with cries of "Get a horse!" It takes time to create change, no matter how obvious the new advantages are over the old. It takes a great deal of time.

I returned to the mainland and shortly after received the prototype of the Radarange with a 50/60-cycle configuration that could be used in Europe with a voltage transformer. This meant that a military customer who returned to the United States could switch the Radarange back to 60-cycle operation. Perfect. Off we went, Jane and I, with confidence and the anticipation of not only opening up the European military market, but having fun at the same time. As it turned out, it was the time of our lives. But not before we received a lesson in retribution for overconfidence exceeded only by the people who built the *Titanic*.

# Chapter 16

We arrived in Munich, the headquarters city of the Army Air Force Exchange Service (AAFES), one early spring day— meaning cold, raining, and depressing.

The next day, I took a taxi with my Radarange and all the food I had purchased for the demonstration to the building headquarters called McGraw Kaserne, after a deceased Medal of Honor recipient.

Now this was somewhat tough. No matter how close I was to where I wanted to go, I still had to lift a hundred-pound box, and carry the food and other paraphernalia, including my trusty attaché case. Back and forth I went, with no help; that's the job.

Finally I managed to carry everything inside, met the receptionist, and asked for Herman Eisencraft, the buyer for major appliances in AAFES Europe. I had met Herman when AAFES HQ was located in New York City, on Four- teenth Street, no less, and unsuccessfully tried to sell Speed Queen washers and dryers. He was an awfully good buyer but tough as nails, and even tougher as time went on.

The receptionist called his office and pointed to the tele- phone on the adjacent desk. I picked up and said, "Herman, Marc Van Buskirk."

"Yes, Marc, what can I do for you?"

"Herman, I want to show you the greatest invention since fire. It's a microwave oven, called the Radarange."

Before I could say another word, he said, "Marc, special order."

"But Herman, I . . ."

Again he broke in, "Marc, I said special order," and he hung up.

I was flabbergasted. I had flown over six thousand miles from California with my equipment, had set up for a cooking demonstration in the vendors room with all the food I had purchased, and he said "special order" without coming down to meet me or taking a few minutes to look at the product.

I take it all back. In my opinion, he wasn't a good buyer, he was a lousy one. And I think he went beyond tough, I think he was stupid. He might have done a good job buying the same appliances year after year. It was hardly necessary to be a merchandising genius to do that. But once in a rare while, when a concept or invention produces a product with overwhelming improvements or advantages, it should be instantly recognized as something to be seen and considered. I fault him all the more because there had been tremendous publicity regarding its coming on the market. He would have had to be in total isolation not to have seen or heard about this product. Unbelievable. But then everyone makes a major mistake or two in a lifetime. Unfortunately for all concerned, this one held back—for almost a year and a half—a volume of business that subsequently produced millions of dollars for AAFES every year.

Okay, maybe I'm a bit tough on Herman. His was the modus operandi of the exchange system at the time; they routinely waited for a year or two until a product had proved itself in the marketplace before adding it to their stock. I understand that when Gillette first came out with instant shaving cream they advertised it on TV spectaculars, the World Series, Monday Night Football, and even the Super

Bowl, to no avail. Everyone at the Dallas headquarters continued to shave in the same old way.

However, back then I sat down in the dismal vendors room mumbling to myself the usual expletives, starting and ending with "Son of a bitch. I can't believe it." After a few minutes, I put my senses back together and asked the receptionist to call the head of Special Order. Again she pointed to the phone. I picked it up and spoke to a Mike McClain, quickly telling him I had been instructed by Herman Eisencraft to contact him and explained why.

He came down to see what it was all about within a few minutes. (Mike was a youngster at the time, working his way up in the AAFES organization, as all have the opportunity to do if they fall into the pattern—hard, and I mean hard, work, and accepting a nomad's life of being stationed anywhere in the world at two- or three-year intervals. Most of all they had to be determined and dedicated to improving the performance of their predecessors in any way possible—buying better, increasing volume, cutting costs, improving distribution, upgrading the appearance of the exchange, motivating subordinates. No matter what the job is, it's a system that sometimes recognizes good work, and a career in the military system begins to take shape.)

Mike and I had a pleasant start together. I gave him the background on the development of the Radarange and then told him that what he was about to see would be amazing. I proceeded to demonstrate the rising cupcake and went on to microwave every item of food I had prepared, at the same time explaining the features and advantages of the product. It seemed to me that there was no question; he was sold. So I simply told him I wanted him to draw up a schedule of demonstrations on one base after another, offering the Radarange on special order. He said he wanted to think it over and asked that I come back the next day.

Think over what? This was special order: he wasn't placing an order, spending money on an open-to-buy budget. All he had to do was order one at a time after his customer placed her order and made a down payment. For chrissake, give me a break. Sometimes I believe the world rotates on an axis of injustice. When things fall into place as they should, we have a spectacular event worthy of a blasting fireworks display that lights up the whole world.

I returned the next day, went through the procedure of signing in, phoning, and waiting. Mike told me he would be right down, but twenty minutes passed before he came through the door of the vendors room. He apologized by saying that he had started down to tell me they were going to pass on the product, but on the way down had decided to run it past the colonel. Fortunately, the colonel hadn't made colonel for being a dumbshit. After hearing about the product and the program, the colonel simply asked, "What have we got to lose? Let's try it out." That's how close I came to a total rejection. Wow.

Within a day I had a schedule for going from base to base, one day after another, for four weeks. The first exchange to see the demonstration was right there in Munich in an old Gothic building of large, dimpled stone, three stories high. Jane and I arrived on a rainy and most dreary spring morning to start the first demonstration of the Amana Radarange in all of the Old World. It wasn't an auspicious first, to say the least. Fortunately, the building had an elevator to the third floor, where they sold major appliances and where the store manager decided, because we had an appliance, we belonged. Jesus, please forgive the idiots of the world, for they know not what they do.

Aside from the few people who came up to look at refrigerators, we might as well have been on the other side of the moon. After an hour or two of doing our best, I went down to the main floor seeking the store manager, to no avail. Of course, no one was authorized to permit me to make a change of venue, shall we say. It was horrible, but clearly the first floor wasn't very populated either. Overall it was a bad midweek rainy day. Quite discouraged, we returned to our hotel and had a gloomy dinner.

The next day we were up and ready for an early morning train to Augsburg, about thirty minutes out of Munich. We found the one good hotel, checked in, and went out to find food for the day's demonstration. Then on to the exchange. We were well received and the demonstration was up front near the entrance of the exchange. The traffic was light, for it was still midweek, but we put on quite a number of demonstrations to the oohs and aahs of all who stopped and gathered around, but no sale. We didn't even come close. There was obviously a big difference in AAFES Europe compared to a backwater, isolated base in the Caribbean. When they said special order, they meant special order. There was none of this put-your-name-down-we'll-call-you-when-the-unit-arrives nonsense. This was the real Army exchange system, and it was run by the numbers, meaning money as well as regulations. The air was coming out of my balloon pretty fast, and, considering I'd been floating rather high, the thud could be felt on a Richter scale from one end of the globe to another.

Again we went back to the hotel, down in the mouth and feeling the first doubts and questions about what we were trying to do. What's wrong? What can we do? We may be in trouble. It's amazing how cold and tired and depressed you can become when you don't write up a damn order.

We were out of Augsburg at the crack of dawn en route to Stuttgart, with Frühstück (breakfast) on one of the super intercity trains. We arrived in time to throw our luggage into the lockers at the Bahnhof and jump a taxi to the exchange. I was hoping I could somehow buy my food at the commissary. This taken care of, they placed us on a stairway landing between floors, with a single light bulb hanging down from the ceiling to illuminate the demonstration table. Well, at least I'd catch people coming and going. But that was the problem. When they came up the stairs they had something in mind to buy and, of course, first things first. When they had completed their mission upstairs they were on their way out or going home. Whatever the reason, haste was required. No time to be stopped by a demonstrator husking some dumb thing of no importance, and so went the day—many many demonstrations, no sales.

The next day was a payday Saturday. I kinda figured it would be then or never. Jane was a real trooper. She could have stayed in the hotel or gone sightseeing; instead she stuck with me all day long. And when I took a break, I'd come back to find her demonstrating away like a pro. It was when I went for tea with an English salesman who worked the exchange on a daily basis that it happened.

What happened?

Why, when I returned, Jane told me that we, meaning she, had sold our first Radarange to a black lady school teacher who thought it was wonderful, wrote out a check, and happily walked away. We were thrilled, renewed with enthusiasm, excitement. Then it was my turn and whammo, I sold one to a lovely couple. (They're always lovely when you sell to them.)

I can tell you the doubts were removed, the questions answered. The one answer that covered everything was that the only time to demonstrate was on Saturday, preferably a payday Saturday.

Going back many years, you may remember I had come

to this same conclusion on the Greyhound bus from Wilkes-Barre. Pencils have erasers to take care of a mistake. But they're not large enough to keep erasing the same mistake over and over again.

Now we knew we would win. Nothing could stop us. I phoned Mike McClain at Munich on Monday morning and related our experience. After hearing me out, he agreed to set up a new schedule of Saturday-only demonstrations and canceled the balance of the daily itinerary. Next, I called the factory and spoke to Eldon Pugh. He arranged to ship five additional units for the best exchanges in Germany. As I remember, they were Frankfurt, Fuerth, Stuttgart, Heidelberg, and Ramstein. The one I carried was earmarked for Kaiserslautern once things settled down.

Establishing the foundation of any enterprise is always tough. The time it takes is painfully long and expensive. For example, here I was trying to put on a demonstration in one exchange after another; traveling to and from; paying for hotel, food, car, train; encountering all kinds of costs as well as spending days of my life. All worthwhile if the results had been obvious. But as far as I could see, I was peeing in the Pacific Ocean and trying to measure the results before and after. At that particular moment, I was a joke. What I should have done was open twenty demonstrations simultaneously in the top exchanges and run thousands of dollars worth of advertising in all the publications read by the military, in addition to drenching the military consumer with a publicity campaign in print and on Armed Forces radio and TV. That would have done it, just as it had for all previous products I introduced.

"Why didn't you do that, Marc?"

Because I had no money. I was a commissioned representative, not an employee. I was entirely on my own, but that was the way I wanted it to be.

I'm relating the miserable details of my grinding away with my bare hands at what seemed like cement barriers in order to indelibly imprint on your mind, for the present and for your future endeavors, that victories of consequence during your life are few and achieved only with total determination to succeed. Anything less and you end up in the immense crowd of also-rans in a lifestyle of mediocrity. This is not to say you're a failure and will have an unhappy life. On the contrary, you will be relieved of working twelve hours a day, seven days a week, relieved of anxiety and stress, of being endlessly away from home and having a one-track mind and existence, to name only a few of the benefits. As I've said before, it's your choice. Obviously, I didn't have one way back then, or now.

Returning to the trench warfare of the western front, we were ready to bring in more troops. I needed four or five demonstrators on whom I could rely to duplicate my enthusiasm and excitement for the product. Within a few days of advertising in the base papers, placing cards on bulletin boards, I was ready for a hair restoration program. Nobody, but nobody, wanted to work, especially on Saturdays. While the Cold War was in full swing so were the troops and their dependents, who were having a ball. It was a good life to be quartered without cost in the housing projects of the base, shop at the commissary and exchange, use all the facilities you wanted to, participate in any function you cared to join, travel on weekends to one country or another throughout Europe, take leave and visit England. It was a great exclusive for the military and their families. Work on Saturday? Forget it.

There had to be a way. I couldn't give up. Wow! I had an idea. I went to the high school on the base, met the principal, and asked for the name and phone number of the substitute teacher of home economics. It was nothing less than a brainstorm. The substitutes were called in only rarely. When I told them they would be in the forefront of a new concept in home economics, they quickly recognized the truth and joined up with my much-needed enthusiasm. As a matter of fact, I hired two at each base, to have a backup in case the first one was unable to be there on a particular Saturday. Problem solved.

All in all, it was a start. I had four excellent women demonstrating every Saturday at the best and largest exchanges in Europe. The only problem was that the Radarange was on special order. That was the biggest deterrent of all. Some customers would be transferred back to the States before their units arrived. But we did the best we could. The best started to produce some sales. Once the first customers received their units, the pace began to pick up. It was so interesting and reminded me of when TV first came out; friends and family would be invited over to gather around the set for the evening. It was the same thing with the Radarange. The new owners would hold a party, and everyone would end up in the kitchen. The whole evening would be spent demonstrating and discussing this wonderful product.

More interesting by far was that the next day, the partygoers would go into the exchange and place an order. That, my friends, was the beginning of a gusher of money pouring in, up, and around our fragile company. It took time for all this to happen—as a matter of fact, a bit over a year.

During that time I'd go back and forth to Europe to open new demonstrations, on to the U.K., down to Spain and Italy. In between, I'd take off for the Far East: Guam, the Philippines, Okinawa, Korea, Japan. The world was my territory, and I loved every minute and mile of it. We now had about twenty demonstrations under way.

Please don't relax. Hold on tight. This is only the end of the beginning. For just when I was convinced the world was my oyster, we were hit by an overwhelming event.

# Chapter 17

As I remember, I was enjoying a sunset at the Colony Surf in Hawaii, sipping a drink, when Walter Cronkite came on the evening news. He declared in his first story of the broadcast that the United States government had instituted a law requiring that all microwave ovens pass a rigid set of standards to prevent emissions that would be harmful to health, including the category of cancer. I was blown out of my chair. What an incredible announcement. Son of a bitch.

That was just the beginning. Within twenty-four hours every TV newscast repeated the story over and over again. The newspapers carried headlines followed by various madcap scientists all seeming to confirm that using a microwave oven was the kiss of death, whether or not the standards were met.

I can tell you that ever since then, I've rejected anything and everything that appeared to be a certainty. One maniac tampering with a Tylenol bottle and whammo, every supermarket, drugstore, etc., in the country has to take the product off the shelf. It's happened again and again with different products, and it's the end of some of them. That was almost the case with the microwave oven.

The next day I went out to Pearl Harbor, where we had an ongoing demonstration, only to find people watching from ten feet away. No sales, but plenty of concerned, disbelieving people, regardless of what we said or tried to prove.

The factory sent us emission-testing equipment. Even when we applied it to the Radarange while in operation, showing no visible movement along the scale, nobody believed it. Even if they did, they still stayed ten feet back. Woe was me.

Of course the scientists of Raytheon and all manufacturers of microwave ovens came out with all kinds of scientific proof regarding the safety of cooking with a microwave oven, but met only moderate success. Once bad news is planted it's harder than hell to overcome it with good news. Finally, perhaps six months later, the issue died down after the manufacturers all claimed to have met and exceeded the government standards. In the meantime, sales were on hold at an extremely low level.

To establish a reminder of the so-called potential danger of a microwave oven, the government issued orders to post signs wherever a unit was in use, in military dining rooms, fast-food stalls, etc.

**WARNING. MICROWAVE OVEN IN USE.
PEOPLE WITH PACEMAKERS ARE
RESTRICTED FROM ENTERING.**

Ninety-nine percent of the population didn't know what the hell it was all about and of course used their imagination, which created fear of the unknown. Naturally they would damn well not be stupid enough to buy one of those newfangled machines.

No problem. I was so accustomed to being knocked on my ass, it was just routine. I was fine. After a while, though, it does create a dragging sensation.

Actually all a microwave oven did was emit electromagnetic waves like a vacuum cleaner, for example. When you run the vacuum cleaner close to your TV set it distorts the picture. To various degrees so will all other electrically driven equipment. It's totally harmless to humans, as is riding in an elevator, working on a car engine, watching TV, or listening to a radio. All those machines emit electromagnetic waves, more or less. The only thing they affect is another piece of electrical equipment, such as a pacemaker implanted in a person's chest to regulate a heartbeat. And a pacemaker might go out of whack only if a person is within *three or four* inches of the oven. Beyond that, the waves evaporate, disappear, dissolve, vanish.

The sign went up on all military bases throughout the world and stayed up for two or three years, a total overkill situation. The medical equipment profession soon produced a pacemaker shielded against all electromagnetic interference. That made no difference; the signs stayed up until they yellowed and crumbled into tiny pieces.

One has to accept one adversity after another in life with lightness, a shrug, and a smile, perhaps a touch of laughter, a ha-ha or two. Taking such things seriously can drive people out of their minds.

In the final analysis, the product was too good to be denied. When the Japanese manufacturers who had duplicated it came in shooting millions of dollars in advertising budgets, the scare was washed out. Unfortunately, so were the wonderful reasons for owning a microwave oven. The Japanese concentrated their attack on the size of the unit and the fact that their ovens had a turntable to cook the food more evenly. Naturally they sold for less than Amana units. The Japanese paid no duty to speak of, if at all; were subsidized by the Japanese government for shipping across the Pacific and around the world; and paid little or no taxes. These advantages permitted a large advertising budget and lower prices. Over a period of a few years, they tore our manufacturing program completely apart. Today, the microwave market is ninety-five percent Japanese and Korean. A sad finale to a magnificent Amana invention.

Going back to the beginning for a moment, I remember when my regional manager for Amana, Gene Whittle, asked me how many Radaranges I wanted for initial shipment to our distributorship in Hawaii. I decided on twenty-four instead of the forty-eight I had been allocated. My only restraint was that I had to pay for them within thirty days, and shoestrings do not pay the factory invoices. When they arrived I ran my first advertisement in the *Honolulu Advertiser*.

What a fantastic reaction. We sold the entire inventory of twenty-four on the same day. They were all sold to Japanese, not locals. The Japanese representatives immediately took them to the Honolulu airport and sent them off to Japanese manufacturers on the first plane out. Before the next corn crop came up in Iowa, the Japanese were manufacturing and selling Panasonic, Toshiba, etc., all over the world.

The final irony was that when I flew to Japan with my Radarange to introduce it at American military bases, I paid customs duty at Tokyo airport of about four hundred dollars. I don't know what the duty is today, but I would not be surprised if it were the same, although perhaps they have taken pity on us and reduced it a bit. But then you would have to believe in the tooth fairy.

What a magnificent country we have, that allows economic imbalances to continue long after their purpose has been achieved. The original trade agreements were instituted to build up the economies of depleted and ravaged countries so that, first and foremost, they would not turn to communism. We wanted them to embrace capitalism, prosper, and become financially able to import American-made goods, thus building up our own economy. By not demanding that they reduce their tariffs on our exports years ago, we let them become the bankers, and we became the borrowers. It's amazing that we can win in spite of our-selves in the overall scheme of things.

This would seem to be a digression into economics and history, but it has a decided effect on our military exchange business. A prime example would be the value of the dollar in relation to foreign currencies. I recall the German mark gaining strength to a point where you would receive one mark ten to the dollar, down from a high of three marks sixty. When that happened, military personnel were flat broke, with no money to pay the rent if they lived off base, no vacation, nothing to do but stay on base. Of course this directly affected their buying anything but downright necessities. For salesmen such as myself, traveling was horrendously expensive. The cost of goods and services remained the same, except that the dollars we had to change for marks would make us despair. Of course when the dollar was strong, the reverse occurred. Everyone felt rich, spent money on all of their hearts' and minds' desires. Obviously Murphy's Law is international in scope and plays a part in any and every business.

Please come back with me again to a more placid time, before the overwhelming competition and takeover by the Japanese, to when we were still struggling to make the product a household word. I must say, much to my constant amazement, that what is obvious to my eyes, mind, and taste is not shared by everyone. You might ask, "What is?" and never receive an answer.

Aside from the radiation scare, there was a hard-core negative group made up of people who were happy with their present method of cooking. A massive number believed in the art of slow cooking instead of meals in minutes. And then there were the vast number of those who could not and would not put up almost four hundred dollars, the purchase price at that time. It all goes back to shades of the pressure cooker days, of trying to change old tried-and-true recipes, methods, and taste buds. It takes time, lots of time.

One thing was certain: before people could be pro or con, they had to see a demonstration and taste the food. With this as my major plan of operation, we expanded our demonstration force around the world: all over Europe, as far south as Naples and Spain; from Puerto Rico, where it all started, to Panama; and everywhere an American flag flew over our bases in the Far East. Gradually, as had happened in Europe when we first started, the weekly Saturday demonstrations and the satisfied, excited, new owners passed the word, held parties to show off and demonstrate the wonders of their new Radaranges, letting everyone know they were among the first to own one. Funny thing about the military, they do that, probably down to a new washer and dryer. I would suppose civilian families might do the same, but they don't have the camaraderie, and they take too many things for granted. The civilians never have to wonder if they are going to receive a weekend pass.

Finally, about a year after I held my first demonstration on that rainy day in Munich, I received a call from Dallas headquarters informing me that AAFES Europe was placing its first order of the Amana Radarange to be shipped to its Giessen warehouse just outside of Frankfurt. From there the units could be drawn as needed by all the exchanges in Europe. The special-order period was finally over. Jim Howard, the buyer in AAFES Europe, placed the first order for all of forty units, even though we were receiving special orders on the average of sixty a month, and even though the customers had to wait at least two months before their units arrived. There was simply no easy, fast ride. For me it was all in frustratingly slow motion.

I think we would still be on special order today if someone in Dallas hadn't recognized the cost of ordering, shipping, and handling one unit at a time, informed Europe,
and further recommended that they order and place the
product in inventory. This guy was, no question, an outstanding executive. I have to admit, sometimes the system
drives me crazy with its lack of perception about how short
life really is.

The big boys, the ones who have already made their
name throughout the world, have no problem except to
send in a weekly carload of Coca-Cola, Kodak film, Bud-
weiser, Sony, or G.E. this and that. Why is it so difficult
for the new kid in the market? Because it is. It's the law of
the jungle. You have to announce you are there and proceed
to fight and beat the hell out of one and all. Maybe one
day you will become one of them and enjoy your place in
the sun, at least for a while, until a new, improved, lower-
priced, son of a bitch comes along to take you on. You can
count on it; he will.

Now for the good news. After the word went out about
the availability of the Radarange from the AAFES warehouse,
exchange after exchange throughout Europe began to poll
them (meaning order) in ever-increasing quantities. Lo and
behold, AAFES began to send in larger and more frequent
orders until they were ordering carload quantities, hundreds
at a time.

My ship had finally arrived, after twenty-five years of
finding its way through one storm after another. What a
feeling; it's indescribable. We made it. We made it the hard
way. A hundred-to-one shot came in for a person without a
formal education, without inherited wealth or noble lin-
eage, but just an average amount of luck combined with
hard work and an inexhaustible determination to succeed.

I would hope all who have read the saga of my life thus

far can vicariously absorb the exhilaration of my victory. You should really be rewarded with one of your own. I'd then be very happy to know I have been a partial source of your inspiration and achievements.

# Chapter 18

No one has ever accused me of being a "Golly gee!", "Land's sake!", or "Oh my gosh!" type. But once in a while we could look in the mirror and see ourselves as the spittin' image of the Grant Woods farm couple, pitchfork and all. It actually happened to us here in La Jolla. The vice president of these United States of America, Spiro T. Agnew, and his family were going to come a callin' and stay at our barn on the ocean.

How it all came about is a bit vague in my mind, for I was out of town when the play began. A light scenario was none other than that Bob Hope was looking for a summer rental in La Jolla to escape the heat of Los Angeles or Palm Springs. The gospel according to Jane was that a friend of hers—the realtor in on the search—was the mother of Peter Malatesta, who was high up on the staff of Vice President Agnew. The easiest way to describe what happened is that one thing led to another, and we ended up by inviting Spiro Agnew and family to take over our house for a week's vacation as our guests. They accepted the invitation most appreciatively and graciously, and the memorable event was upon us.

Jane went into action immediately. She decided that the house, which I believed to be perfectly fine, most attractive, etc., etc., had to be turned inside out, renovated, renewed, changed, added to, and of course, to say the least, *cleaned*, before the visit that was scheduled within two weeks. All hell broke loose in that department. I may not be very bright, but I'm not stupid. I just tried to stay out of sight and pay the bills.

The house was still being worked on until the very last moment, when the limousine convoy turned down our street. The mop and dust cloth just made it to the closet as the Man drove up the driveway.

We had begun to obtain a sense of what it would be like a few days before their arrival, when the first of the Secret Service agents knocked on our door. I happened to be near the door as Jane opened it. A handsome, movie-cast young man said, "Good morning. I'm with the Secret Service."

Jane, somewhat half on the square, asked for his calling card. He replied by saying he didn't have one because he was a secret person. That split us up. He then showed his ID, and we invited him in to inspect the house and grounds. In the next day or two a swarm of electricians and communications people turned our garage into a high-tech center that within seconds could make phones ring anywhere in the world. An alarm system was set to go off if an invisible line that surrounded the property was breached. By golly, this was big-time stuff!

"Air Force Two is touching down at Miramar Naval Air Station," the Secret Service operative advised from the control room (my garage). From that moment on, the Man was tracked and monitored by mobile radar every minute until the cavalcade turned down our street and entered the driveway, preceded by motorcycle police, of course, and followed by the Secret Service limousine, and—if you please—a large military truck containing all the required foods, wine and other spirits, as well as mess stewards . . . rather a nice way to travel.

Jane and I and the four kids stood in an oblique line to the walkway as the vice president, his wife, and two young daughters came up to us. I stepped forward with hand outstretched and said, "Good morning, Mr. Vice President. Welcome to La Jolla and our home. We're all delighted you are here. May I introduce my wife, Jane, and family, Ann, Marc, Amy, and Pandora."

That was my best shot at protocol. He, in turn, introduced Mrs. Agnew and their daughters by their first names. And all of a sudden, we, meaning my group, and I relaxed. These were real family people; it was going to be fun.

"If you please, Mr. Vice President, we would be happy to give you the escorted tour."

"A pleasure, Marc, and please call me Ted," he replied, which was short for his middle name.

Off we went. We took them through the house, Jane commenting on where things were: closets, linens, and various things houseguests want to know about. I recall his wife acting in a motherly way in controlling their two girls, no different from Jane or any other mother in similar circumstances. When we reached the outside deck, the beach and the ocean spread out before us. It all came together: they knew they were going to have a good time. I must say the ocean was in one of its most beautiful states; the moderately spaced, turquoise, see-through waves splashed gently on the almost-deserted beach. Ours was not a tourist beach, but primarily used by the know-where-it-is locals.

We bade them be at home, feel at home, and took our leave. As we stepped out the front door, a Secret Service agent was standing right next to it, and others were here and there around the house.

We were indeed fortunate to have very good friends and neighbors in Stan and Nancy Moore. The Moores had gone to Hawaii, so they had invited us to occupy their house during the vice president's visit. It was just next door to ours, on the ocean, beautiful, with a lovely swimming pool in a semienclosed courtyard. Perfect for all kinds of entertaining and relaxed living, typical of La Jolla. We weren't the least inconvenienced. On the contrary, we felt as though we were on holiday in more ways than just being in a new abode.

The first day Ted called (sorry about the informality), asking if my son, Marc, and I would care to join him for tennis the next day. We cared to. I told Ted I would make arrangements to play at the La Jolla Beach & Tennis Club. We set a time, and he said he would meet us there. Making arrangements was no problem, as you can well imagine. Half the membership of the club showed up to watch the match. I can't say it was a match. The vice president showed up with a spray of Secret Service agents and none other than Rod Laver, one of the world's best pros. Marc was on the La Jolla High School tennis team, one of the best high school teams in the country (and well it should be, for children here are brought up with racquets in their hands from the day they leave the crib). In those days I was an average club player, pretty good form, able to hit the ball back if I could reach it. (Same as I am today, but somehow my reach has shrunk.)

Marc and I played against the vice president and Rod Laver. We had one hell of a lot of fun. The veep was about my level, and Rod naturally played to our game, returning the ball with a pace adjusted to each of us. Inevitably we would make the unforced errors not of Rod's doing. It was very similar to hitting against a backboard, he was so consistent.

It was a scene. Secret Service agents were all over the place, including on the court, which turned them into semi-official ballboys. Onlookers were everywhere; the largest number possible watched from an adjacent court. It was exciting.

"Is that Marc Van Buskirk? . . . How and why is he playing with Agnew? . . . What's going on?" was the rapid-fire buzz.

"Just routine," I would explain when asked. "I have a wide circle of friends."

I created a vast number of tired tongue waggers about the big event. Naturally reporters and photographers from the San Diego papers plus our local gazette, the La Jolla Light, were on hand, and we became locally famous within a day.

We received a repeat invitation the next day and almost every day thereafter. Not a tightly scheduled arrangement. I'd be in my office when a Secret Service agent would call and say, "The vice president would like to play tennis with you and Marc at 2 p.m. We'll send a car for you. The game will be at the Bishop's School courts to avoid as many onlookers as possible."

And so it went. The vice president would play a round of golf at the country club and then go for a least four or five sets of tennis. I mean, this guy was a bull—tall, well-built, bursting with energy—and a warm person once you knew him. A man's man. One who, I perceived, thoroughly enjoyed his position and lifestyle. My God, who wouldn't?

The week passed quickly. They climaxed a week of leisure activity and visiting with friends by holding a rather grand party at the house—grand not exactly in numbers but in the guest list. Jane and I arrived by walking a few yards to be greeted by the Secret Service holding a clipboard listing the invited guests. After being checked through the looking glass, we entered a kingdom of celebrities—Frank Sinatra, Dinah Shore, Rod Laver, show folk, sports personalities, and politicians. I was figuratively and literally seeing stars. Best of all was being introduced by the vice president to several of them before the mix of a cocktail party made everyone seem average. I adjust quickly, but I was enough of an outsider to be excited and at the same time realize this was just another ordinary gathering in the eyes of those who come from Hollywood or Washington. We had a blast. Life was definitely worth living, and this was one of its highlights.

On the day of their departure they extended most sincere thank-yous for our hospitality. Then off they went into the wild blue yonder toward Washington on Air Force Two—back to another world.

After the visit I found we were established as semi-members of the who's who of La Jolla. Well, that's fine for whatever it means, especially if you don't take yourself too seriously.

The absolutely hilarious residual was when I shortly thereafter left for a trip through the Far East military bases. No sooner had I arrived at the military exchange head-quarters on Guam when I was invited in to visit the exchange officer—not a normal event. (Primarily my business was with the buyer or the merchandise manager.) This time I had the pleasure of meeting all three men in the exchange officer's office. I accepted a cup of coffee and began to answer questions about my houseguest. It could not have been a more affable conversation, understandably, with everyone totally aware I had a friend in the government.

Naturally, I downplayed my position in the scheme of things but at the same time laid on positive descriptions of the vice president. When our chat was all over, I was invited into the merchandise manager's office for an order-writing session. This scenario pretty much repeated at one base after another throughout the Far East and during my next trip to Europe. Ah, life on the road, how sweet it is!

In the fall of 1972 the president's election campaign was in full swing amid the Vietnam War. Protestors were waging their own war against the war. Vice President Agnew was thrashing and bashing radicals, the lot of them, as the strong arm of the Nixon team. The team won reelection but, as we all know, it turned out to be a Pyrrhic victory.

Before the beginning of the end, we received an invitation from the vice president to attend the inauguration, complete with box seats opposite the reviewing stands, and a VIP invitation to the inaugural ball. All of which we were delighted to accept. It was truly memorable—the hustle bustle, the glittering pomp and ceremony, the gathering of prominent people, the influx of youth, the Academy cadets, marching bands seemingly numbering in the hundreds, cocktail and dinner parties going on night after night, a maze of swirling people spectating and participating in the thrilling events that take place every four years in the capital.

In early 1973 Vice President Agnew's wrongdoing began to surface. This was almost at the same time that the first reverberations of the Watergate break-in began to shake their way to the fence around the White House. The vice president allegedly had accepted payments from contractors when he was governor of Maryland, and subsequently received some residual money after he went to Washington as vice president.

Because he had undoubtedly not reported this income to the IRS, he realized he was in an untenable position, so he pleaded "no contest." In effect, he was sentenced to resign his office without further punishment. On one hand, he was lucky not to be prosecuted and imprisoned. On the other hand, unfortunately, he was a first-time victim of a system that had been allowed and understood by almost everyone for over a hundred years in the state of Maryland.

Agnew was my friend. I do not intend to minimize or dismiss the course he followed. Nevertheless, these two factors have to be included in any judgement, not as they pertain to the letter of the law, but as they apply in conditions that were not considered or even argued at the time.

I have found by extensive travel throughout the United States and the world that there are more systems than one can count that civilized humans—individually, as groups, or as nations—consider acceptable. Here are a few examples that range from the extreme to the laughable. Saudis cut off your hand if you steal, your head if you do it again. South Americans and Europeans take siestas that last three or four hours while we run, grub, run back. Bribery in the Far East and elsewhere is an acceptable part of doing business; it's added to the price. In Taiwan to retrieve a box from customs, you go to ten different windows for appropriate stamps and sometimes tip accordingly at every one of them.

It's all rather a crazy-quilt pattern, and the craziest was being the governor of Maryland. There it was S.O.P. to accept gratuities from appreciative contractors who had won their contracts on a fair bidding basis. Because the salary of the governor was only ten thousand dollars a year (less than he could bring home if he received welfare and food stamps), this was the means employed to compensate him without having to raise taxes. Everyone knew this was the system. As I've said, it applied to all governors of Maryland going back to the days of their wearing powdered wigs.

I suppose this would not be enough to excuse the defendant, but if the same system had been in effect in other states, we certainly would have said, "That's the system." (I must say, however, although I'm not even close to being the first one to throw a stone, I'm certainly not the last; I'm somewhere in the middle, where you will find most stone throwers.) On balance, I have to be more than just puzzled that he was accused of accepting payments after being elected vice president, the number two man in the United States. I suppose he thought this was money he had earned and that was due him as a delinquent account receivable.

Shortly thereafter President Nixon's problems with Watergate forced his resignation. Just think; if Agnew had not gotten into the pickle of the Maryland system, he would have become president of the United States, and I would have been the Rebozo of the West Coast. If I thought I was receiving the royal treatment from my military exchanges as a friend of the vice president, what would have happened if my house had become known as the West Coast White House? I'd have kicked civilian manufacturing ass all over the place, probably obtained every major line that caught my eye, and become one of the largest and most successful operations in my particular business.

What actually happened was that when I returned to Guam and all other stations of the line, I was effectively told, "Van Buskirk, no special treatment for you, you bum! Go to the vendors room and stand on line. Wait your turn with the rest of the peddlers."

Oh my, how the mighty can fall, hard and fast.

That leads me to the question I often ask myself: Which would you rather be? A king, a president, or one of the richest men in the world? I've finally decided I'd rather be rich. Yes, I'll have to do without my private 747, the mortgage-free, tax-free White House, the TV coverage of my meetings and parties for the elite of the world, my Secret Service bodyguards, and all the other trappings and hideous responsibilities of the exalted office. I'd rather be rich. Free to come and go as I please. Almost like a salesman with an unlimited expense account.

Speaking of being rich, I woke up one morning in 1973 and found we had just over half a million dollars in our company account. Since we were a wholly owned corporation, that money was mine—all mine. That was progress. I was still a long way from a million, but if I had just for fun calculated what I'd have without my monsters' financial requirements (food, housing, medicine, private schools, summer camp, tutors, orthodontia, clothes, cars, dance classes, vacations, etc.), I might have come close to ringing the big bell. Well, not really.

Even though the kids have contributed various degrees of mental pain, costly amenities, time restraints, confinements, loss of sleep, and general lack of freedom, when I add it all up, make deductions, and divide by four, I find that the joy of them far outweighs all the trials and tribulations by millions of dollars. I can simply say they are more precious than anything else in the world.

The time was right, all things considered, for the grand tour of Europe. For several years I had brought home souvenirs and presents from various countries to give the kids a touch and a flavor of the world beyond La Jolla. I would tell them that their generation was truly fortunate to come into a world that was shrinking like a prune due to jet transportation and international TV reporting. But even now, millions of kids grow up and never leave their home towns. They never even see New York City, San Francisco, the Rocky Mountains, the western deserts, the Midwest farmlands, or watch a wave break on an ocean beach. I think such sights are terribly important for all of them. In the foreseeable future, Jules Verne's concepts of what will be are horse-and-buggy in comparison to reality.

Every family has its best-years-of-our-life memories. This tour certainly takes its place among our top ten. How could we not remember having fourteen pieces of luggage to contend with? (Even though I had given strict instructions about one bag per person.) We flew off to Washington, D.C., as a first stop, seeing America first. I hoped that some of all they were to see would stay in their minds. After Washington sightseeing, we took the train to New York. There they got the tour as only a New Yorker can give it. Finally we made our way to the Hudson River to board the magnificent Queen Elizabeth 2, a brand-new world within itself. The kids went totally nuts. They scurried back and forth from their cabins to ours; there was so much to do, so much to see. Although we were all in first class, they decided the action was down in second. The only time we saw them was at "hot hum" (meal) times. That wonderful ship, then and now, has something to please everyone. We all had a ball.

In London, everything they had seen in movies and on TV came to actuality. They were enthralled with Westminster Abbey, the Tower of London, Buckingham Palace, the changing of the Guard, the bobbies, and Harrod's (of course; even at that tender age . . . actually, the urge to shop is ageless).

In Paris, of course, we visited the Louvre and took the three-minute tour: Winged Victory, Venus de Milo, and the Mona Lisa, where Amy's profile was strikingly similar as captured in one of our hundreds of photographs.

On to Germany, where I left them to their own devices while I made a call or two on the exchanges. Their greatest excitement came in finding the BX cafeteria and devouring American hamburgers, French fries, and Coke. Sometimes it takes so little.

After Heidelberg and Munich, we went on to Lucerne and Vienna, then Italy, all by train. When the young Italians saw three blond American girls they followed us in passionate pursuit. In Florence, of all places, the girls were too tired to sightsee and instead gave themselves a beauty treatment, for after having charmed the Italians, they decided they were ravishingly beautiful. At least Marc saw Florence. And finally, Rome with all it has to offer. Although London and Paris had seemed old in terms of King Henry the Eighth and Marie Antoinette, those cities were just suburbs of the world in comparison to Rome with its over two thousand years of habitation. If we had taken the family on to Greece and Egypt, they might have lost all comprehension of time.

In the years ahead there would be two or three more grand tours, without the fast pace of this first one. However hectic, it was fun and rewarding for them, and vicariously so for Jane and me. Today it is easier to travel than ever. Instilling self-confidence, a sense of achievement, and an enlargement of one's capacity to dream the impossible dream are gifts that remain in your children's minds and hearts for as long as they live.

# Chapter 19

In the midst of the whirlwind of Amana activity, Lou King at Amana called and informed me he had told Gerry Ankeny, sales manager of the Maytag Company, about my company. In those days, Amana and Maytag were among the few major manufacturing operations in the agricultural state of Iowa. Lou found Gerry receptive to engaging us as Maytag's military representative. Besides telling Gerry we were absolutely tops insofar as sales and creative marketing programs, Lou gave him the clincher when he noted that our service and parts record was superb. Maytag, the home of the lonely repairman, was more concerned about service than sales, especially as its Maytags began going overseas.

I phoned Gerry and made an appointment to visit him at headquarters in Newton, Iowa. If ever there was, or is, a company town, it's Newton. Everything revolves around Maytag. Except for workers in the supermarket and assorted shops, the population is all employed by Maytag or associated with companies that serve the factory. Maytag's management system and factory operation is an absolute model of a world-class company. When you combine all of this with a truly super product and an ingenious advertising concept, you have, very simply, a Maytag.

My meeting with Gerry and some of the other executives went very well, all the more because I had the tailwind of Lou King's glowing recommendation. I made the cut and left as Maytag's duly appointed international military representative. Not a little appointment, but a huge one in name recognition for our portfolio and a potentially substantial source of income.

First things first. Arrangements were made for my son, Marc; Brick Tortora, my manager in Hawaii, whose territory also included the Far East; and me to learn all about the product by going through the Maytag factory, including its service, sales, and advertising departments. Maytag's setup for newcomers is intensive; we were totally immersed and came up ready to go.

As fast as I could get to a phone, I called AAFES headquarters in Hawaii. At that time they were in charge of procurement for all American-made products for the Far East exchanges. A young man by the name of Sonny James was the buyer for all major appliances as well as my Amana microwave ovens. He knew we were a pretty reliable outfit; reliable meaning we hadn't done anything bad and would actually follow up and do all that we promised to do. You see, it's so simple to be well-thought-of. Do what you say you will do, and you become reliable. Contrasted to the sixty percent who take an order and run, and then forget, you emerge as exceptional and acceptable.

"Sonny, I've really got good news," I said.

"Yes, Marc, what is it now?" Sonny had heard every opening enticement thought of by man.

"It's Maytag, Sonny. Maytag for the entire Far East, excluding Hawaii. It's a pure, clear winner," I said.

"Okay, Marc. Send me the brochures and price lists. I'll present it to the committee and let you know."

The committee, made up of Sonny's bosses, had the final say; the young buyers just forwarded information about worthwhile products or programs for consideration and discussion.

"Sonny, I'll jump the first plane and come over to make a presentation," I offered. Who ever heard of a product that required hundreds of thousands of dollars in purchases being accepted as a result of a brochure? No one . . . until the name of Maytag was involved. When you've got it, you've got it. Sheer name-brand power.

Sonny said, "No need, Marc. Send me the particulars, and I should have the answers within a few days and will let you know."

Well, you can't beat that. I quickly mailed the Maytag brochures and price lists along with my recommendations.

The following week I received a call from Sonny. "Marc, Maytag's in. We're sending you our first carload orders."

Wow! Not one carload, but carloads! "Great, Sonny. Which models are you ordering?" I asked.

"The top of the line, the 808 series."

"What other models are included?" I asked, with an apprehensive note in my voice.

"That's it, Marc," said Sonny.

"But Sonny, they're the most expensive models of their line; they cost one hundred dollars or more over Whirlpool and G.E. The best sellers are the lower-priced units that for another forty or fifty dollars can really compete with those two. I'd really recommend the lower-priced models. It means less dollar volume on each order, but we know those units will be best sellers!"

"Marc," he replied, "the committee made its decision taking all prices into account. If you want us to cancel the orders, we will."

There comes a time to shut up. I did. I thanked him and told him we would do everything possible to make this program a success. I wiped my brow, not quite certain if I should celebrate or be depressed.

Off went the orders. The first carload was shipped by the factory and in quick succession, about ten days apart, the second, third, and fourth. Just as I was preparing to visit the Far East exchanges, put on my sales meetings, set up the displays, let the people know Maytag's availability, I heard a crash from as far away as eight thousand miles. It came from Okinawa. It was the sound of the second carload crashing into the first, and then was rapidly followed by the third and fourth banging into the first and second.

What caused the crash? Do I have to explain? They crashed because they didn't sell. They didn't sell because, in comparison to the low-end models of G.E. and Whirlpool, they were hideously overpriced for the military customer. At retail, they were separated by almost two hundred dollars.

We had one helluva disaster on our hands. This was the committee's fault. Well, they're human. They may make a mistake once in a while. But why, oh why, with a beautiful product like Maytag? Every woman, given a choice, would choose Maytag, but not for half a month's pay or more.

Unfortunately, the mistake was not corrected. The exchanges never ordered the low-priced models; they just held on, and sold the expensive ones eventually. At least they didn't ask us to take them back, which they are not afraid of doing. They accepted the situation and went on. We also went on until several years later when Maytag bought out the Norge and Admiral lines and consolidated all under an in-house sales operation.

As representatives we live under a Damoclean sword that can at any moment drop on our heads. Maytag's a great company, and the military exchange system is a marvelous organization, and we are a damn good representative firm. But somehow, sometimes, things can go out of sync. This was one of those times.

My business with Amana microwave ovens was improving

every month. Actually it was surging. But so was the competition. The Japanese came on hot and heavy; hot meaning with sizzling prices, and heavy meaning with six sales managers at a time, all bowing together in front of a buyer—a very impressive act. And I'm not kidding.

As you know, somewhat before this invasion I had set up my demonstration force throughout Europe and drew on my experience with the Presto pressure cooker. I knew the microwave oven was probably even more mysterious than the pressure cooker, so demonstrating it would accomplish three very important requirements. First, it would eliminate the fear of using the new and unknown by explaining how it worked. Second, customers who had been shown step by step how to use the product would feel confident of their ability to use it. Third, they would be a bit unsure of another brand for, after all, they knew how to use ours. They had seen and tasted the food. They weren't goin' nowhere but to Amana, that's for sure.

There are times when opportunities knock on the door with a bang and announce themselves. Unless you're deaf, dumb, and blind, you act on them immediately. Though they're too few and far between, they're worth their weight in gold. In 1980, I decided to hold the first microwave oven cooking school. Instead of demonstrating to a few people at a time, we would demonstrate to a hundred or more.

Out went the messages from the base radio station, the write-ups in the base paper, the notices on the bulletin boards, the in-store announcements, the posters at the officers and NCO clubs. Soon almost everyone knew we were holding a cooking school and that some lucky person would win an Amana microwave oven at draw-your-name-from-the-box time.

Before we went all out, I chose to test the promotion at Ramstein, one of the best and largest Air Force bases in

Germany. The master chef extraordinaire for the event was none other than my daughter Ann, who had dazzled us with her microwave cooking, to say nothing of superb culinary art, for several years. She was extremely enthusiastic and excited. Not only about the cooking school, which was naturally fun, but also about the chance to romp around Europe. Besides her three tours with the family, she had gone to the Université of Tours, France. She graduated speaking impeccable French, the Tourraine accent being the purest in all France.

Over three hundred men, women, and children attended our premiere Amana microwave oven cooking school. There was standing room only. Just amazing. Ann had three microwave ovens going at once. She cooked everything: breakfast, lunch, hors d'oeuvres, simple fast recipes, roasts, seafood, and a fantastic-looking three-layer cake, her closing number.

It was a smashing success, and our sales zoomed at Ramstein and everywhere else we held a cooking school. Naturally we scheduled the events one night after another, once the pre-event publicity was in place. We were show folk, doing the Van Buskirk circuit: Frankfurt, Heidelberg, Karlsruhe, Stuttgart, Kaiserslautern, Augsburg, Munich, Fuerth, and Wurzburg. On a map their locations form a square, so we finally ended up where we had started. Indisputably this is the most productive, cost-effective promotion one can plan, particularly if you are introducing a new cooking appliance with all its mandatory requirements for education and its final approval being based on the taste, texture, and appearance of the food.

We absolutely beat the hell out of the competition. The combination of Amana's national advertising, the demonstrations, and the cooking schools established Amana as number one by a wide margin over everyone else. The others were coming on like packs of mad dogs: Toshiba, Panasonic, and Sanyo for starters, followed by the Korean manufacturers. We were a year or two ahead of them in consumer acceptance, but I could see that we had one damn big battle coming up, and I was not at all confident of winning, especially in the military.

The military market reminds me of a faucet and a drain. The troops pour in from the faucet (the United States) down and through the drain back to stateside. At that particular time, just about every military family in Europe owned or wanted an Amana, because we were as closely identified with microwave ovens as soft drinks are to Coca-Cola. The military kept moving. One-third of the troops stationed in Europe would rotate each year. Think about it for a moment: it's a manufacturer's dream market. Every two or three years, there is a brand-new population with zero saturation of your product. Contrast that to Cedar Rapids, Iowa, where once everyone in town owns a refrigerator or a TV set, the only time it's replaced is when it goes totally on the fritz. Give me a military market every time. Rotation is only one of the many reasons why this market is one of the most magnificent sources of distribution and volume our industry can achieve. Unfortunately, not all manufacturers are aware of or completely understand the potential. In addition, many have an unfounded fear of seriously harming their civilian distribution, examples of which I will soon relate in terms from the comic to the tragic.

The cooking school program accomplished its purpose. Just about everyone learned how to use a microwave oven. After all, it wasn't a course in nuclear fission or how to speak Japanese. However, the Japanese manufacturers began to speak to the military consumer. They spoke the language of money and applied overwhelming advertising, inundating every publication read by the military with four-color, full-page advertisements. That was bad enough. But when their layout and copy stressed a larger oven capacity (larger than Amana's) and a turntable for even cooking, they neglected all the good reasons to cook with a microwave oven. They ruined the market not only for Amana but also for themselves.

I'll be a bit incisive. The Amana was big enough to hold a twenty-five-pound turkey. Does anyone cook something larger than that? Ridiculous. But the aperture of the oven was far smaller than that of a conventional oven, which needs great size to circulate hot air around the food. The microwave oven only required a size large enough to fit, as I've said, a twenty-five-pound turkey "on account of it cooks with microwaves." This created an illusion of smallness. And when this point was pounded out, the largest oven scored the points.

Next, the Japanese pointed out that their rotating turntables provided even cooking. They so drenched the consumer with this feature that you'd have thought they were selling turntables, not microwave ovens. Although the turntable may have evened the distribution of the microwaves, its pin, gear, and socket created a grease trap. The turntables also only allowed a dish smaller than the turntable to actually turn. So lasagna still had to be turned by hand, as did a turkey or anything else oversized. Now the good guys at Amana had a better system. It was known as Rotowave. It dispersed the microwaves in a circular shower pattern to give even cooking without the loss of space. And you didn't have to worry about the messy, gooey, oily clean-up required by the turntable.

Do you think I've knocked them a bit too hard? Hmmm. Well, I wish I had at the time, because that's what they did to us with their massive advertising campaign.

Amana could not come close to matching it. So I'm going to bash them one more time. They did it with our American invention and with income and profit received from selling all their products to the U.S.A. They had no tax system like ours, which had to cover the cost of our military budget as we conducted guard duty for Japan. Besides, their government sponsored its manufacturers with every type and kind of assistance imaginable—minimal taxes, overseas shipping, expenses, etc.—while we chipped in duty-free status on their exports. Japan considered its home country's manufacturer an Olympic team that had to win every event, absolutely worthy of all the assistance and backing the government could and did offer. Okay, now I feel better.

When the debris settled and I could see clearly enough to write about the outcome of this confrontation, one conclusion was obvious. The microwave oven was established as being ideal for reheating and defrosting. The original concept of being the greatest discovery since fire was lost forever. For whatever the reason, sales continued to climb for a number of years. We were making a fortune in our own segment of the market.

I'm a firm believer in the good times–bad times theory as applied to life, business, and gambling. We all agree that if you gamble long enough after winning, you'll lose. In business, you have a different set of rules. One of which is, to do nothing beyond what you have accomplished leaves you vulnerable to saturations, an incurable malady, and to competition, who will come after you with multiple duplication, improved product, and lower prices. It's an absolute requirement: you must move ahead. For surely if you stand still, you will fall behind, and then you're gone. All that's left is a memory. I would hope you have stashed enough wood in the shed, so to speak, to weather the rest of your life, which can be pleasant in those circumstances.

In view of the aforementioned guidelines, it's fair to say that good ideas can come in bunches, almost as if one begets another. My next one came about while watching TV in Hawaii. This time it wasn't Walter Cronkite, just the opening segments of the local news hour. The first had to do with the usual: police are investigating a murder. (Sometimes when there are two or more, I'm tempted to call the station and congratulate them . . . two, my that's exciting!) Following this was a fireman climbing a tree to retrieve a cat, with Hawaiian children looking on with concern, then laughter when the rescue was completed.

For some subconscious reason I remembered the same expressions of delight on the faces of the few children who had come to the cooking schools with their parents. The idea flashed across my mind, and the Kids First Microwave Cooking School was born. Oh my, oh my, oh my! With both parents working, the Radarange was perfect for kids to prepare their food. It was safe—no gas or hot electric coils. The only thing they could do wrong would be to overcook the food, no big deal. Just imagine the feeling of accomplishment, the self-confidence generated. It would take the fear out of many future unknowns they would encounter. The pride of the kid, and his parents, in his ability to take care of himself and for that matter his younger brother or sister would be encouraged.

No question, this would be a you-get-a-warm-feeling-all-over type of promotion. Because just about everyone who would attend would already have a microwave oven at home. But I hoped to reap rewards from the good will and word of mouth that would surely occur. I wasn't certain, however, that I could translate that monetarily. Nor was it important that I do so. It wasn't an expensive promotion. And we had actually reached a point where we felt ourselves on a roll. No matter what we did, it would only add to the avalanche of new orders and bang the competition. Remember, all the other guys could do was say "Ours is larger and we have a turntable," a dead-ass bunch in spite of pouring millions into advertising.

One fine midweek day in Honolulu, an advertisement, approximately a quarter-page, appeared in the morning and evening newspapers. The headline simply announced "THE KIDS FIRST MICROWAVE COOKING SCHOOL" and then followed the form of an invitation declaring where, when, why. The "why" outlined our reasons for teaching kids to use a microwave oven as I've just described. The kids had to call in and make their reservations.

Oh, there was a blast-and-a-half line at the bottom of the advertisement that grabbed everyone: "All adults must be accompanied by a kid."

Hundreds of people and kids rang the phones off the hook. By midday we informed callers that the first class was totally reserved, but due to the response we could include them in a second class the following day. That one also quickly filled. Amazing the response when you advertise something people want, particularly when it's free.

Ann, my number one daughter, chef extraordinaire for the little dauphins, was absolutely wonderful in handling the attention span of the five- to twelve-year-olds (somewhere between one and ten minutes, respectively). She wove a program of microwave cooking that mesmerized them with a display of simple kids food, through preparing breakfast, lunch, and dinner items, concluding with her nearly famous baked cake (a bigger wow than a cupcake). The reaction of the kids and their parents was heartwarming. We knew we had made a small contribution to the good of kidkind. We enjoyed every minute of the affair, including the TV cameras and reporters covering the event, and mention by columnists in the newspapers. All in all it was one of our best ideas, beautifully executed and most rewarding in terms of hearing the children expressing their pleasure and appreciation.

I encouraged Ann to begin immediately to write a book, subsequently named *The Kids First Microwave Cookbook*, what else? It was a knockout, and still is. I was carried away with the firm thought we would sell many thousands—twenty thousand to be exact. (That was just about ten thousand too many, based on the last report of inventory in the warehouse. Okay, go ahead and laugh. But *you* try writing a book and publishing it yourself as I did, and let's see how many you sell. Selling ten thousand of anything is not a little thing. It's huge.)

As soon as we had the book in hand, we scheduled kids cooking schools all over Europe, the Pacific, and as far north as Alaska. The turnouts were just as we had experienced them in Hawaii. This time, however, Ann offered to autograph copies of her book. Just about every kid and his mother patiently waited in line for their turn to buy one and chat with Ann. We sold a thousand or two and then made a presentation to *Stars and Stripes*, the newspaper, and bookstore facilities of the armed services worldwide. We ended up selling several thousand, all as a result of the cooking schools. Not too shabby an idea for sales after all.

I'd be remiss, however, if I did not add a postscript to this story by reminding you that we still have a supply of this charming book on hand. Don't hesitate to order one. It's as fresh today as it was then. Now there are new kids on the block who will appreciate it as much as their predecessors. (A salesman to the end, I am.)

La Jolla was becoming a stopover, a place to return to for a short while. Off I'd go or off we'd go, the entire family whenever possible. I have a positively clear recollection of the early struggling introduction of the pressure cooker; its slow and hard battle to win acceptance until it reached its levels of allocation, only to eventually fade away from the needs and wants of the public after they had absorbed all that they could handle, considering that they needed only one and it would last for years and years. I knew the microwave oven would duplicate this pattern. The market was beginning to bust wide open, and it was time for me to spend every day and night on the job. When you find yourself in similar circumstances, give yourself entirely to the cause, work hard, endure the loneliness of travel and being away from family and friends. Forget Sundays and Saturdays. Forget tennis and golf, parties and balls. That's not enough; I'm going to take the gloves off. Plan on working your ass off. Think until your brain, totally exhausted, puts you finally to sleep. If the kids are sick, your wife will have to handle it and every other damn home problem. You're flying, driving from the crack of dawn, making calls, you're the only one in the village, town, or city that is still awake quite late, planning the next day.

The true test of your addiction in pursuit of your goals is when your exhausted sleep turns into a short nap and you wake up in the middle of the night with your eyes still shut thinking about what you are going to do in the morning. You can actually see yourself making a sales presentation with the customer right smack in front of you. Your thoughts can go on to a point where you're writing up the order. Finally, just possibly with the order in your attaché case, will you permit sleep to take you away again, not realizing that in those midnight circumstances you never fail to write the order. Hell, you might as well throw in the dream that you have met and exceeded quota. It only takes another moment or two.

If you think that's tough, years before us, the guys who were determined to be successful make us lily-white-assed in comparison to what they had to do. A train from La Jolla to Dallas took three days, and it wasn't air conditioned. Neither were the hotels. Today I can take an early flight, arrive in Dallas, meet my people at AAFES headquarters by 1:30 p.m., take a five o'clock plane back to San Diego, and be home in time for dinner. I can go on and on, how the old-timers covered Europe or the Far East, to say nothing of Panama, Alaska, and the rest of the United States. We're spoiled rotten. They were really tough men of the road.

# Chapter 20

Let's take a break and lighten up—always difficult for me, as there seemed to be endless mountains to climb with a heavy pack and a hurry-up schedule to reach the summit.

Now I want to step back in time a few years to tell you the story of Paris in the summer. Doesn't everyone go to Paris at that time of year? Of course not. How gauche. Only dumb Americans, including the entire Van Buskirk clan, all eight of us if you include our dog, Taj, and cat, Toncha.

We made the second of our three family trips to Europe on the *QE2* again. The animals enjoyed their private quarters on the highest deck of the ship, which was also ideal for pet promenading. Quite a scene as half a dozen dogs on leashes walked back and forth, all enjoying the sea air while sniffing and making new friends. We dropped them off at a kennel at Cherbourg, reboarded the ship for the ride over to Southampton and London. Once there, Jane and the kids, now teenagers, ran around London while I visited our U.K. military bases in Lakenheath, Alconbury, and Upper Heyford, all very convenient. A few days later we boarded the channel ferry for Cherbourg. We rented a car, retrieved our animals, and headed for Paris.

Actually it wasn't Paris, it was Marnes-la-Coquette, a very charming village, about ten kilometers outside of Paris. The village was known as the home of Maurice Chevalier.

It was also once the headquarters of the famous Lafayette Escadrille, the French air squadron of American volunteers who went to fight the Germans in air duels over France in World War I. I would imagine it hasn't changed very much in the eighty years since that war. You still drive through lovely Saint Cloud park after leaving the main road circling Paris, passing strollers, picnickers, the beautiful foliage of gracious old trees. Past an old tennis club and through the short tunnel at the end of the park is Marnes-la-Coquette. Drive quite slowly. The tiny village consists of a small church, an even smaller post office, a village hall, three or four shops including (naturally) a bakery, an antiques boutique, and a ten-room inn. Last but not least was a noteworthy restaurant, one star in the Michelin guide. All small villages should be so constituted and so blessed.

All of this had come about when Jane and I left the monsters in the early spring of 1974 for a trip through my old battlefields. We started in Munich, where my business had all begun, and worked around the territory. This time we took country roads, stopping to let the sheep cross with their dogs and shepherds in lederhosen. We spent the nights in country inns where German food is really German and comforters are two feet thick. The German countryside in spring, if it's not raining, is so very beautiful. And as in almost all sparsely populated areas of the world, the people are as friendly as people can be.

In sharp contrast to our early pioneering days when we came back to our hotel cold and discouraged, we now basked in the acceptance and success of our work with the Radarange. What a feeling. It wasn't just the fact that money was being made and we were financially secure. (Did I say that right? Have I misspelled? It was all rather new, you know.) No, it wasn't that alone. It was that inner glow, that sense of satisfaction, my mind being so much at peace that

I could actually listen to what others had to say, in addition to being able not only to hear the birds, but sing along with them.

We had some twenty wonderful women demonstrating for us throughout Germany, Holland, and Belgium. We had become strong enough to invite them to a general sales meeting. I held it at the Europaischer Hof in Heidelberg, a most central location and one of the finest hotels in Germany. It was an enchanted world for them. The hotel offered an ambiance, decor, and service that is designed to cater to those who have lived in the most luxurious circumstances. For all others, it's an eye-opening, talked-about experience long after they have returned home. I mean those women had a good time. I held the meeting in the early morning in a formal, oak-panelled room with a board of directors table stretching endlessly to comfortably accommodate everyone. Once I called the meeting to order, I outlined where we were and where we were going.

The agenda was quite simple. The whole idea behind the program was to improve the demonstration. To do this I went over all of the basics and then asked for input from the women about what was new in the cooking demonstration—new foods, recipes, selling ideas, new ways to answer customer questions. I tried to pull everything I could think of out of them. Everyone made a contribution, confirming the old or encouraging the new.

At about 1:00 p.m. we ate our lunch in the hotel's beautiful dining room. The wine and the delicious food made it a ladies' luncheon party at its best. By 4:00 p.m. they were on the way to the Bahnhof for the train ride home, all saying what a wonderful meeting, what a great company. Shades of my old Fuller Brush days.

When all was done, Jane and I headed for the Shangrila of Germany, Baden-Baden and the famous Brenner's Park

Hotel for a weekend. This is a place unique in Germany and, possibly, Europe. A clear brook runs alongside the hotel. On the other side, a peaceful walkers' trail under a canopy of trees leads to the town center. In the center of all is a magnificent building, the casino of Baden-Baden. The charm of the whole area is not easily found elsewhere in Germany. Some very chic shops offer expensive merchandise. Once past them, you are in the concert area, where every day local musicians offer minisymphonies or the boom-boom band performs amidst exquisite banks of flowers. One can relax and listen to the music while munching on ice cream and rich, luscious, cookies and cakes.

It's really all so pleasant. I've made it a point to stop off in Baden every time I return to Europe. I might add it is also a terrific place for people watching, especially at the Brenner's Park Hotel and the casino. Extravagantly dressed people with the stamp of aristocracy all over them conduct themselves in a most rigid, class-distinguished manner. It goes beyond their dress. They converse quietly, if at all, and take in the whole scene without the slightest hint on their faces that anyone else is in the room.

On that particular trip, we visited Paris. I like Paris in the springtime, as the song goes; I'm not too crazy about summer, fall, and winter. We went on a shopping spree to buy furniture and things for the house in La Jolla. Of course we fell in love with far more than we could bargain for. We were having fun buying this, signing for that, looking for more. Then it occurred to us, why not rent out our house in La Jolla for July or August and rent one here in Paris. Super idea. Why not!

We contacted a real estate office and told the agent what we had in mind. She pressed a button and voila! Up popped our future summer house in Marnes-la-Coquette. We drove out the next day, enjoying the ride through Saint Cloud park and the quaint appearance of the village. The house, a perfect example of the French country style, was quite secluded. The owner of the property, a handsomely dressed, middle-aged, Parisian banker, warmly invited us in and began to show us about. It was hard not to like what we saw; the spacious living room was furnished in the soft pastel colors of the French, so very elegant, warm, and attractive, as was the whole house. There was no need to think it over. We made out a check and told him we would enjoy being in his home for the month of August. The house came with a houseman, who was keeper, cook, and handyman. So far so good. We looked forward to our summer vacation as we returned to the States to tell the kids to brush up on their French.

Kids can be so frustrating at times. I had, from the time I started my overseas travel, and even before that, tried to have them understand the importance of speaking languages other than English. We brought in a French tutor, and although they went through the motions, they weren't smart enough to concentrate and improve on what was being taught. As soon as class was over, they forgot all until the next one. OK. They'll end up one day saying, I coulda, shoulda, woulda. Damn it, it wasn't castor oil, but the young are so smart-ass.

But I didn't have to wait several years to hear my kids say something like, "Dad, we should have listened to you and followed your advice." They quickly came to realize that Dad had been right. I had told them one of the reasons for spending a month in France was to improve their French. After all, I hadn't had them tutored for months for nothing.

I told them to go forth to the market and purchase the bread for the breakfast ritual. So they did, only to return half in tears and mad as hell. I asked what happened.

"Well," they replied, "we started to speak in French, but before we said a few words, the man at the market said 'Speak English! I haven't time to listen to your rough French.'"

That mean Frenchman at the market did me a favor. Not that it had everlasting effects.

Within a few days, everyone settled in. Jane and the girls would go off to Paris on the commuter train for shopping, museum browsing, or luncheon here and there. Marc was accepted by and played at the local tennis club as a guest of our landlord. For some reason, I was not included, an oversight on the part of the tennis pro at the club, no doubt. In addition, Marc took off on the summer tournament trail around France, playing in several events, primarily having fun. Summer passed pleasantly.

The only unusual incident occurred when our dog, Taj, disappeared. We began to worry all the more when we found out that the French equivalent of the SPCA (animal protection agency) puts animals to sleep if they are not claimed within three days. But on day three, we received a call from the U.S. Embassy in Paris. Someone from the embassy had found Taj, and because he was so adorable (he really was) took him to the embassy. The person involved must have been in the upper echelon to do that. Fortunately Taj had his dog tags on, with our name, address, and telephone number. The embassy staff called La Jolla, spoke to our tenants, who gave them our number in Marnes-la-Coquette, and phoned us. As I remember, they said Taj was just fine. He'd made a hit with all at whom he wagged his tail. Our caller said that Taj had just left the embassy to be taken home for the weekend by a member of the staff. If we would come to Paris on Monday, we could pick him up at the embassy. My, oh my, our Taj was getting the royal treatment. (Makes me feel proud to be an American to have them do all that for my dog when *I* can't qualify for free room and board in the embassy. Seriously, God bless America, that is so typical of our people.)

The end of the incident was also a laughing matter. That weekend we all bundled into the car for another expedition to Paris. On our way back to the village, who should we see jauntily crossing the Avenue Foche? None other than his royal highness, Taj, on a leash beside the person who had graciously invited him home for the weekend. Amid cries of "Taj! Taj!", we pulled over. Although he was sufficiently surprised to see us, he didn't exactly go bananas in delight at being found. The bum was enjoying his experience away from us. After thanking the person from the embassy, and proving that Taj really was ours, we had all we could do to get him into the car. Rotten dog. Who said he was a best friend?

Naturally while in France I would take off for Germany for a few days to cover my bases. I would have had to be blind not to see the Japanese competition's serious inroads on my market share. One of their advantages, other than heavy advertising, was the fact that they also sold electronics to the exchanges. They had manpower all over Europe, in addition to duplicating our demonstration program. Last, but not least by any count, they had lower prices.

The same situation was taking place in the United States. The Japanese invasion was on in earnest.

It finally dawned on our country's manufacturers that we were entering a new industrial age in which the Japanese were going to reign supreme, not only owning the automobile business, but also having almost complete control over electronics. Those were the days when Honda and Toyota were looked upon as the only automobiles that would pass a quality assurance program; Chrysler verged on bankruptcy; and Packards and Nashes had long since disappeared. G.M. and Ford were reeling from claims that their finished products were junk. This view spread to electronics. Down and out went our TV manufacturers; perhaps we now have three or four left at most. When it comes to electronics, I'd be hard put to name one U.S. manufacturer. Okay, G.E. Who else? Zenith, Emerson: just minor competition. The business is almost all Japanese or Korean. I don't think it's necessary to review again the reasons for the decline and fall of our industrial might in these three fields . . . but I'd be happy to do so.

Finally, after many visits to the Amana factory, memos, and phone calls wherein I asked them, urged them, begged them, beseeched them to allow me to sell Amana to the stateside military bases, they agreed—with certain conditions. The holdup had always been based on their belief that selling to the military exchanges would seriously affect their civilian dealer distribution. The military retail prices would be lower than those in the civilian market.

I would answer by telling them the world was changing, that just about every major manufacturer in our country was selling to the military. That military people will purchase what's offered at their exchange and will not go off base to buy unless it's vital to their well-being. I told them the market would be five times as large as the overseas volume, and that the time to act was now or our Japanese competition would move on the military before we could.

Well, they ran my arguments by all of their executives again and again, without agreeing to it. Naturally, the sales executives in charge of civilian distribution were against the action. The export department, headed by Eldon Pugh, was for the program because military sales were under their supervision and they had monthly and yearly quotas and profit margins to meet. Sometimes it seems that a company has more than one cash register. I believe the yea vote passed by the slimmest of margins, and only after it was stipulated that I must surrender some of my commission to a distributors fund. The fund, in turn, would be allocated to Amana dealers as a compensation salve against any loss of business they might incur as a result of our selling to the exchanges. It's hard to believe, but that's the way it was. Of course I agreed to the condition after protesting, but only enough to give them a sense of satisfaction that their ruling prevailed. As I've said before, you can't beat factories who make good, desirable products; they is the bossman!

Carload orders were being delivered to their warehouses in Virginia, California, and Texas. We went hellbent to open demonstrations at every major military base in the country. At our peak I believe we were demonstrating at over a hundred and thirty-five, including the Navy and Marine Corps exchanges. The volume and profits rolled in. Those were the glory years of our company, not only for the magnificence of our concept and performance but for the Brinks-size commissions that arrived month after month. How far was that removed from my early days of pioneering the microwave oven or going back to the Fuller brushes, pants pressers, pressure cookers, ironers, washers, dryers, refrigerators? I'll tell you, it was almost a lifetime, a thousand light years ago. The only reason I remember is that the memories are sometimes painful; even when I rejoice, they never diminish or fade away.

Truly it was a fantastic turn of events. As a matter of fact, in the 1970s, incomes of over one hundred thousand dollars were as rare as incomes of twenty thousand in the 1960s. But in the 1980s, one hundred thousand was ho hum income, until the 1990s when all of a sudden there was no income of any size to be found. The moral of all this, as I've related over and over again: you have to be prepared to weather the storms of life, for as surely as the sun comes up every day there will be days when you wonder who and what the hell has turned on the hard times.

It's amazing what time and experience can do for you. Here we had well over a hundred people demonstrating away every Saturday following payday, and in many cases every Saturday. We managed the demonstrations from our La Jolla office, in concert with our field managers, who had formerly been our demonstrators in Europe. One of the problems in hiring military personnel is that they are subject to transfer orders. There is a rather constant turnover. But sometimes it worked out favorably when our European representatives were ordered back to the States. They, in many cases, would resume work on their new bases. Some were good enough to be managers, traveling from one base to another, hiring, training, and supervising. It all worked out rather well.

The only slight irritation was sending a check to Amana, based on our commission check, to be dispersed in various amounts to the Amana distributors, who in turn would disperse it on to their dealers. This had to be considered a joke. At most I would believe the distributors used the fund for a dealer party of some kind. Amana must have eventually recognized there was no need for this patronage, for after six months or so they canceled this program, but not before I had funded the party by many thousands of dollars. You might say, "Don't begrudge this, for you were making a ton of money." But I can't help it; I did begrudge it. It may have been well intended, but it was a misguided waste of money that could have been far more productive if it had at least been used for additional advertising or promotion.

Another year or two slipped by, during which, almost belatedly, I recognized that a continuous demonstration program can quickly reach overkill proportions. Eventually everyone had seen the demonstration, either on a large or small base. Saturation levels were rising to a point that obviously diminished sales. As fast as possible, we closed most of the demonstrations, leaving only those in highly populated and visible locations to maintain the program.

Once I had reduced costs, a major item being the demos, my company continued to make very healthy profits. I was drawing salary and bonuses of well over a hundred thousand dollars annually, not too shabby in those years. Whatever I was earning, it wasn't so blockbusting that my lifestyle changed; I didn't go in for yachts, buy second and third houses, become the social party thrower of the town, involve myself in charities and fund-raisers for the arts, opera, and symphony. Nope. We had a long way to go to reach that level. That takes really big money. As a matter of fact, we solemnly believed that even as much as we had was only a hedge against the onslaught of financial require-ments for the kids' education. Whatever they elected to do, it would be four at a time, because they were only a year at most apart. This meant that a freshman would be follow-ing a sophomore, who'd be following the junior, who'd be following the senior. Combine that with all other costs— four of everything, including cars—and we would be lucky to break even.

Next, one live-a-little experience occurred. I was return-ing from Puerto Rico, where I had gone to call on the bases where it all started with the microwave ovens. In Miami, I stopped to attend an Amana sales convention, always an event to look forward to. On the last evening, after it was all over, I returned to my room with the morning paper. Just out of curiosity I went through the classified ads look-ing for any Rolls Royce automobiles that might be for sale. My eyes were stopped by an ad that sounded particularly attractive. For the fun of it, I made the phone call to Palm

Beach, where the car was located. The fellow who answered seemed pretty solid, for all I could tell, and my interest in the car increased to the point of my telling him I had planned to come to Palm Beach to attend a wedding and would phone him again when I arrived. The next day I did so, went to his house, and fell right smack in love with the most elegant, the most beautiful car I had ever seen.

Rolls Royce guys are almost, no, totally obsessive about the car. Let me tell you about this one. It was a 1963 Silver Cloud III, long wheel base with divider. It was all black with a leather interior; with the slightest sniff you could enjoy the richness of the leather. The wood was simply magnificent, burled Carpathian walnut, perfectly matched up front and in the back. Viewing the car from a few feet away gave me a tingling sensation in my face, for surely it was beautiful, exquisitely sculptured, gleaming, and set off with thick whitewall tires. Under the hood it looked like a brand-new, never-left-the-showroom car; the immaculate, semibright, black-painted engine had silver nuts and bolts, white-corded wires here and there. Surely it represented one more reason to believe in God, who placed men on planet Earth with the mind and sense of beauty to create the nearest thing to a living being. It really was beautiful, but seemingly expensive. The man was asking twenty-three thousand dollars. Back in 1972 that was a lot of money, especially when a brand-new Mercury cost only five thousand. I decided to phone the director of financing and get her approval.

"What I thought, hon, is if you think we should buy it, you could fly down here and we could drive it back across the country and have fun. I'll tell you what, I'll call back in a couple of hours . . . give you time to think it over. Okay?"

Two hours later, I called, and one of the kids answered.

"This is Daddy. Please put Mommy on the phone."

"Mommy's not here. She's on the way to the airport."

Jane arrived on the early morning flight and shortly there-after saw the car. She was as excited about it as I was. The purchase was made. We drove over to attend the wedding of dear friends from La Jolla. We spent the night and began our cross-country trek the next day. It was amazing. Every-where we stopped, people would gather round the car as if it were a never-before-seen invention that resembled an automobile. When the owners (meaning us) came out to drive away, the murmuring of the crowd was "They must be a somebody"—all in all, one of the dividends of owning a Rolls. We had a wonderful trip and arrived back in La Jolla without mishap.

The true value and worth of the car came along there-after—not the intrinsic value, but the fun value. We entered it in local Rolls Royce Club meets, where it won first in class without the competition even coming close. From there, we went on to the regional concours d'élégance; year after year it would be acclaimed best in class. Finally on to the national Rolls Royce meet, where it came in second among all the cars in its class throughout the United States. As a matter of fact, it was beaten only by a car that had been completely restored from the bottom up, whereas ours was totally original.

# Chapter 21

Everything was coming up roses and lollipops and green-backs. It was one of those rare periods in life. I was no longer a salesman, I was an order taker. How happy can one be? Happy enough to turn down offers on the car and the house, for my head was barely above money.

It gets even better. The year was 1980 and Amana was introducing a new, advanced version of the microwave oven, a Radarange Plus called the Ultimate. It was a combination microwave and convection oven. It could be used as a conventional oven with the "convection" hot air circulating around the food for the sake of crisp browning and excellent taste and tenderness, combined with microwaving for speed. It could also be used as a straight microwave oven. Wow! What a combination.

Of the many introductions and marketing programs I had thought up and executed over the years, this one above all gave me the rewards of outstanding creative marketing. For one thing, it provided the one and only time my distributorship in Hawaii made any money. That by itself should earn it an exalted ranking. If the man-does-not-live-by-bread-alone theory is important to you, then I can say I basked in accolades not only from Amana, but from anyone who has ever tried to successfully introduce a new product.

Amana generated all the excitement it could for a product at its early summer sales meeting that year. The one glitch on a perfect portrait of things to come was that production was not scheduled to start until the late fall.

My plans began to take shape before I left the plant and the cornfields of Iowa. By the time I reached thirty thousand feet, the concept was firmly etched in my mind. I began to work out the details of what would be the most audacious presentation of a new product that Hawaii, or for that matter the entire United States, had ever seen.

I'll admit to a bit of exaggeration but not a hell of a lot.

The headline of my three-quarter-page advertisement to run on the eighth of August in the *Honolulu Advertiser* screamed in bold lettering:

**We are taking phone orders today starting at 8 a.m.**
**for delivery in September–October 1980**
**of the "Ultimate"**
**The Amana Radarange Plus!**

The absolute audacity of announcing the 8:00 a.m. start, combined with the delivery date a month or more down the road was riveting to readers. They had to read on. Their minds were blown away, no question.

I set up pictures of four different foods. Above each was a single-word description: *Microwave Convection Dehydration Combination*. Below each picture was a description of what happens when you press a button. Press one button; it's a microwave oven. Press a second button; it's a convection oven. Press a third; it's a combination of microwave and convection oven. Press a fourth; it's a dehydration oven. Wow!

The copy below each picture described the results in terms to make everyone's tongue hang out, emphasizing the golden brown for cooked meats or baked rolls. In every way possible, I related the browning and crisping of food, to let them know this was not an ordinary microwave oven, it was the Ultimate. It was, and still is today.

Now come closer. A work of art, if I may say so. False

modesty doesn't become me, as I've said before. Read this and laugh. More than that, plagiarize at will, for in similar circumstances, you will find these words are worth their weight in gold.

> Phone orders will be listed and numbered in the order received. No deposit is required. You will be contacted when the shipment arrives and your reserved unit is available. In the beginning and for some time to come in early 1981, this magnificent equipment will be on strict allocation and in short supply. If you decline acceptance, there is no obligation. The next name on the list will move up.

Can you believe that? I can't. I can't believe I wrote that. My confidence level was so high I could have flapped my arms and flown. And we know that only happens in our dreams.

One or two more lines to nail them down. Open your mouth, here comes the price, followed by the medicine man with a pain reliever. You'll hardly feel the pain.

> The special introductory price on the incomparable RMC-20 is $795, which is considerably below mainland suggested retail prices due to our warehouse-to-you operation, and which represents real value in today's world.

Hawaiians are accustomed to paying more than mainland prices because the cost for three thousand miles of ocean freight is added to everything they buy. But because we were the distributor, selling direct, we could easily absorb the freight and still be below the suggested mainland price. In this instance it was true, honest.

Lastly I had to appeal to the affluent in Hawaii and point out the attractive social consequences of being among the first to show off their purchase. So the last lines in large type read

**To be one of the first and few in Hawaii
to own the Ultimate by Amana, reserve now!**

Oh, yes, on the bottom left-hand corner it said "SALES AND SERVICE SINCE 1961." Very important. Hawaiians on average won't buy from newcomers until they've been in business for at least ten years.

Well, there you have it. This all-powerful advertisement appeared in the Sunday edition. I could hardly sleep that Saturday night, wondering what in hell would be the outcome.

I was up at 6 a.m., rushed to the door, dived for the newspaper, and flipped through the pages to find the ad. There it was, in the first section, for once beautifully placed. It could not be missed. I made myself a cup of coffee and sat down to read and reread it, word by word. If that S.O.B. doesn't work, I'll be an S.O.B.

Shortly after 7 a.m., my manager, Brick Tortora, picked me up. We drove through the light Sunday morning traffic toward the office. On the way, we stopped at one of the old cafés on Kapiolani Boulevard that serves hearty breakfasts to all Hawaiians. But we were too excited and uptight to eat. So we were in and out in ten minutes, arriving at 7:45. On the way I considered taking the phones off the hook, creating a busy signal and hopefully an illusion that our phones were swamped. I decided to do so. What the hell. It couldn't hurt the outcome one way or another.

The minutes ticked off: 7:50, 7:51, oh, so slowly. Was I missing early bird calls? Tick, tick, tick. 7:56, tick, tick. Call 911! I'm gonna need a medic. I can't take it. Put the phones back on the hook! I gotta know, I can't wait.

Bingo! At exactly 8 a.m., the first ring of the telephone had barely finished its tone when I grabbed it.

"Good morning. International Industries, Hawaii. May I help you?"

"Yes," came the reply, "I want to place my name on your list for the Ultimate."

"Yes, ma'am. May I have your name, address, and telephone number?" I asked. "Thank you. You're number 20 on the list. We'll call you as soon as the shipments arrive." (Well, they start your new checkbook at number 101, so why can't I start at 20?)

People must go by the numbers in Hawaii. When the ad said 8 a.m. it meant 8 a.m. From then on it was wildly exciting, totally fantastic, call after call, waiting on hold. The phones rang nonstop until about three o'clock in the afternoon. We had written up one hundred and seventy-two orders at $795 each, or the equivalent of $136,000 worth of business! And our gross profit was almost half of that! How high is high? Only the sky was higher than we were at day's end. That's not all, orders continued to come in, for word-of-mouth gets around quickly in Hawaii. The next day it started all over again. We ended up with almost two hundred and twenty orders. Everyone, including the Amana factory, was in shock. Hawaii broke all sales records for a consumer response to a retail advertisement, especially with a heretofore unknown product selling for over $800 with sales tax. Absolutely unprecedented.

Yes, there are other examples of tremendous response to a newspaper advertisement. In the boom days of the condominiums, people would line up in an empty lot to purchase from nothing more than a billboard or brochure, and one-day sellouts were not uncommon. A famous showbiz personality can achieve standing-room-only conditions a month or more before performing. But selling a ton of merchandise from one advertisement—well, that's something else. Nobody, but nobody, has done that before or since in Hawaii. If I'm wrong, please inform and correct me. It was one helluva ballsy shot, and it worked—one of the few that have, as this narrative has so clearly and sadly related.

I have a nagging thought that has lingered to this day. What would the total sales have been if the advertisement had run in New York City with eight million people as opposed to Hawaii, where—after subtracting the military and tourists, you have a population of a few hundred thousand. If that were the only measuring stick, sales might have been in the vicinity of five thousand units. Hmmm . . . five thousand times $795 equals $4 million! I don't want to dwell on that, for it diminishes my accomplishment and illustrates a pattern of similar minor-league victories which depicts my career to that time. I take solace in the fact, as I have mentioned previously, that there are thousands of creative salespeople, entrepreneurs, and businessmen who have accomplished so much more than I in every way you can evaluate their success; but, by the same token, there are hundreds of thousands who haven't even come close. I suggest you make out your own scorecard; just to be a bit above average earns you the right to be proud of yourself.

You might say, hey, just a minute Mr. Success, High Lama of Advertising and Merchandising, all you've done is write up paper orders. What happened when the Ultimate shipments arrived two months later? How many canceled when you phoned? The answer is less than ten percent. And those units were needed to fill the additional orders as they continued to come in, and even more when the first users began to spread the word. A note of caution here; it doesn't always work out that way. Cancellations can go higher than fifty percent. I think this case was a testimony to the product; it made good on every promise.

As the song goes, 1980 was a very good year. So was 1981. I presented the Ultimate to the military, and they automatically accepted it. My God, when I think back to the old days of the Munich introduction, the ensuing weeks and months of onesy sales, the overall lack of vision or merchandising intuitiveness on the part of the buyers in the exchange system, the apathy and very mild support, the uneasy road to acceptance and success, I have to wonder if there is such a thing as an easy road. I kinda doubt it. And if there is, is it the best way to go?

All of a sudden it seemed our children had grown into adulthood, in their own eyes as well as those of everyone else, except, of course, for Jane and myself. Perfect they are not, but above average and, to a point, exceptional they are—not to everyone (who is?), but to us most definitely. I brought Ann, Marc, and Amy into the company during high school and later during college breaks. Marc started off as a teenager sweeping the floors in our Hawaii office. Ann, after her year in France, went to Katherine Gibbs in Boston, came into our office, and later went out into the field to give her excellent cooking school presentations. Amy joined the office staff and acquired experience in this rather unique business that has held her in good stead. Pandora, the youngest, escaped the office, but with this one adorable exception we were truly a family operation.

If I had it all to do again, I would have sent them out into the world of strangers, to unknown employers where they would have been entirely on their own—a number, a clock puncher—subject to the disciplines of any business that runs by rules and regulations, which are totally unheard of in my company. Further, they would have encountered policies that prohibit personal telephone calls, extended lunch hours, leaving early to prepare for special personal activities, or just taking off now and then, completely ignoring vacation policies as to when and how long and how often. Yes, if I could do it over, they would begin at a major company with all of the aforementioned proper organization and operation. Beyond that knowledge and training, they would benefit by mingling with others of the same level or status, absorbing their thoughts, opinions, ideas, and—most important—being able to gauge their own ability against them as I did in my most early years with the Presto Pressure Cooker Company. Such experience is so invaluable and so educational in preparing oneself to meet the challenges in all of life's endeavors in business as well as in the everyday social world. That my children have all have made very important contributions to our company's success over the years in spite of not experiencing the real world of business amazes me. Yes, I have to say they are exceptional!

The sound of drums was becoming distant, more like a murmuring rat-tat-tat. After the explosive debut of the Ultimate, sales leveled off. The principal reason was price; although it really was the ultimate, almost everyone owned a conventional freestanding or wall oven and would reluctantly make do. But they definitely needed a microwave oven. The vast majority of sales were in straight microwave ovens and—if anything—in a decided trend toward the inexpensive models that were beginning to flood the market. For the most part they could only defrost or reheat. The Amana manufacturers sat on their asses and surrendered the hottest new cooking appliance in years to the Japanese and Koreans. Atta boy, American industry. Keep that up and pretty soon they won't bother to print the instructions; there will be only two words to translate (defrost and reheat). As a matter of fact, they may also give you the schedule. No, not the cooking schedule; I mean the schedule of when their ships leave the American ports loaded with U.S. dollars, so we can come down and watch our money go bye-bye. . . . Bon voyage. . . . Y'all come back again. They will.

The following three or four years were excellent from an income standpoint. Our sales pretty much held to the same levels, but the saturation of microwave ovens was reaching a point where we were selling new units to long-time users of the introductory models. We could see the end of the line, but it had been one hell of a ride. The time had come to find another Amana Radarange, an embryo product that had the same fire and excitement and potential. Good luck. Try finding a needle in a haystack; it's easier.

# Chapter 22

We decided to attend the National Electronics Convention in Las Vegas in January 1986, take the blinkers off, and see what the rest of the world was up to. One hundred thousand people attended this giant convention to see the latest innovations in electronics exhibited by every known name in the industry.

We had no hope of finding a major player who was not already represented by a military marketing company. It was our intention to seek out a small, start-up company with a new, innovative product to which we could apply our live demonstration technique and experience to achieve results similar to Amana's with the microwave oven.

While we wandered through the maze of exhibits, many of which must have cost the manufacturers over a hundred thousand dollars, to say nothing of the exhibit location and personnel expense, I realized we were looking at a multi-billion-dollar industry, most of which, alas, I must say again, was Japanese—at least eighty percent. Remind me to buy some stock in Wrigley's chewing gum. For some reason the Japanese haven't copied that!

My son, Marc, came back to me after visiting an acquaintance at one of the big guys' booths and told me he had received a strong suggestion that we visit an exhibit by Rabbit Systems, Inc. This led to one of the most exciting and mysterious episodes in marketing I have ever experienced, and I emphasize the "mysterious."

The Rabbit Systems booth was jammed with people, a good sign. What was it all about? It was about a VCR duplication system that relayed the picture and sound of a rented movie in the VCR from the living room to the bedroom or any other TV set in the house and to a second or third set if needed. VCRs were selling for $200 or more. The Rabbit, a perfectly named multiplier, had a retail of $79.95. It had tremendous potential. No question, we had struck a brand-new, fill-a-need product.

We patiently waited for the vice president of marketing, Ken Holmes, to finish his conversation with one person after another. As soon as he was free, we moved in.

"Ken, I'm Marc Van Buskirk, and this is my son, Marc. We are military representatives for Amana and their microwave oven, and we'd like to represent your company to the military exchange system."

The frenzied atmosphere seemed to make it imperative that I hit him hard and fast with Amana to grab his attention. It worked. Within a brief minute of questions and answers, he asked us to write him a letter giving a resume of our company history and our plans to represent his company. We thanked him and turned away through the army of people waiting to talk to him.

It all seemed a bit vague and not very encouraging, but that's about all we could expect in the circumstances. We did roam around after this main event but found nothing of consequence. There were all kinds of mickey mouse new products, and we probably could have bagged several if we so desired, but none had the sizzle of the Rabbit. Although if we had taken off our rose-colored glasses, we might have seen Mickey Mouse dressed as a Rabbit. Although that is partially revealing, events from the convention forward were a combination of slam-bang pursuit, storybook acquisition, unbelievable results in test marketing, and overwhelming success in selling the Rabbit to the military worldwide. This is how it all began and ended.

On our return to the office, I composed a hard-hitting letter detailing who we were, the companies we represented, the longevity of our connections, the marketing concepts we had employed, and references to confirm our good reputation as well as our ability to perform. The letter went off Federal Express to Ken Holmes. I waited two days for a reply before picking up the phone and placing a call to him.

"Ken, I wanted to be sure you received my letter, and thought it best to call you."

He replied cordially, "I have received it, and the letter was fine. But as you can imagine, I've been swamped and haven't had a chance to get back to you."

"That's understandable, Ken. I think the best thing I can do is meet with you in Chicago and discuss our program. If we agree on all matters, I'll fly on to Norfolk and visit the Navy's buying office there to get started."

"Hold on, Marc, not so fast. I can meet you in Chicago, but there are two other military representative companies who are inquiring about the line," he casually, if not ominously, stated.

Of course. Wouldn't you know; it happens every time. If not in actuality, it is certainly worth bringing up for negotiation purposes, especially when the discussion reaches the commissions-to-be-paid stage.

I replied by saying, "I have no doubt others would be interested. You can evaluate their proposals more clearly after you have heard mine, and I can be in Chicago tomorrow."

"Okay," he said, "tell you what, I'll meet your flight at the airport."

Now that was encouraging. I gave him my flight number and certainly had every right to expect we had an excellent chance of getting the line.

Off I went, early the next morning, and arrived in Chicago on time. But no Ken Holmes. Something had gone amiss. I called him; he wasn't in his office. I called my office; they hadn't heard from him. I waited around an hour to no avail, and no further phone calls produced any information.

I had booked my ticket on to Norfolk and decided to head out on the next flight. Bright and early the next day I was at the buying office of the Navy exchange, which at the time was in charge of all Navy exchanges from Norfolk to Boston. Fortunately, the man in charge was an old Far East hand I had known from Subic Bay in the Philippines. I presented him with the concept of the product, the fact that Rabbit was the sole manufacturer, and then opened his mind to the potential. He called in his buyer, showed her the brochures, and went on to explain the concept. His voice betrayed his enthusiasm, and of course she responded accordingly.

"Let's write up an order for a gross of them, plan an ad, and Marc will give a demonstration. It should be a hot seller."

Oh my, oh my, here we go again! What's the next flight to Jacksonville? Scoot to the airport. Jump on and off. I go to the headquarters of the Navy exchange for all stores in and around Florida. What a day! What fun! Let me get out my times-es machine. One hundred forty-four, times all other Navy exchange complexes—five of them in the United States—plus individual exchanges in Hawaii, the Philippines, and on and on—equals . . . and that's not all. That's a drop in the bucket; that's a small opening order; can't this plane go any faster?

On my arrival at Jacksonville, I phoned Ken's voice mail. I told him I'd phone back when I got to a hotel. Still no answer. I left another message: here's where I am, please phone. Next morning, I went on to the Navy exchange, met with the buyer, gave the Rabbit story, showed the Norfolk order.

"We'll duplicate that," she said. And I had my second order.

Finally, on my return to the hotel, there was a message from Ken. He was flying into Memphis and would be at the hotel. "Please call this evening."

Call? Hell, I flew to Memphis! Off I went on the first plane I could board. When I arrived in the early evening, he still hadn't checked in. I left word for him to call my room. When I returned from dinner, the note in my box said, "Let's meet in my room for breakfast." And so to bed.

I phoned first thing in the morning. He told me to come on up, and we met at last. First he apologized profusely for the Chicago affair and explained that his absence was due to being caught in a whirlwind. I could understand that and told him I had been swirling around myself. I then related what I had done and showed him the orders. His reply is still etched in my memory.

"I think that's terrific. Anyone who has done what you have deserves the line. Marc, you are now the military representative for Rabbit Systems, Inc."

Son of a gun, that's the way people—you and I—should be rewarded when we push and lift ourselves out of the crowd and make things happen. I know if you or I were Ken Holmes, we would have done exactly the same thing. Well, we sat down for breakfast and discussed our arrangements. The commission setup was most acceptable, and the territory included our world with options for the interplanetary systems as they became available. I could not help running the calculator in my mind and lost track after adding and multiplying the potential.

Okay, we both had business to do. I took off to call on the Memphis Naval Air Station, where I obtained another order before flying to Dallas and the Army Air Force Exchange Service headquarters.

My meeting in Dallas went extremely well but not perfectly. They instantly recognized the excitement the product could generate but took exception to the need for a wire between the original VCR and the second TV set in another room and possibly upstairs. I pointed out that the FCC refused to allow Rabbit to operate on a wireless basis (which it could do), citing the possibility of radio interference. However, the wire was as thin as a hair on your head and could easily be hidden under carpets as it made its way to the next room. It could even be routed outside the house to the designated room. I got over this hurdle, but just barely.

They decided to give it a one-time-buy status; in effect, test it out. That was more than I could have dared hope for. If the excitement I had seen at the electronics convention in Las Vegas, with sophisticated crowds jamming into the exhibit, was any indication of consumer reaction, I was in. Back to La Jolla I flew, still working on my out-of-sight sales projections and related earnings.

No sooner than I had somehow made the sun come up faster, Marc and I drove down to Miramar Naval Air Station on the outskirts of La Jolla. We met with the merchandise manager, gave him the pitch, and showed him copies of our orders from back east. Then before he placed his order, we proposed conducting a dry-run demonstration so that he would be in a better position to decide how many to order. He agreed.

The following Saturday, without any advance publicity or advertising, we set up two TV sets and a VCR at the entrance of the exchange and began the demonstration. Now if that isn't shades of the first Radarange demonstration at Ramey Air Force Base, I'll eat my hat!

It wasn't a shade, it was exactly the same color. We started to sell the Rabbit as fast as we could demonstrate it, and that was continuously. We had the same sign-up sheet: "PRIORITY SPECIAL ORDER. YOU WILL BE PHONED WHEN SHIPMENT ARRIVES." By noon we had over fifty people on the list and by day's end, well over a hundred. If they were fish, the water would be churning in a feeding frenzy. It's indescribable when you find something new that seems to obviously fill a need. More than that, it gives you immediate pleasure, you throw caution and close investigation to the wind, wanting it now. It's nothing less than a strong desire to own it and be turned on. Find a product that does all that and you turn into an automatic order taker, and so we did. Just fantastic.

To bring us to the brink of believing we had struck gold, the actual shipment arrived at the base about two weeks later. The customers were notified that their units were available, and in they came, one after another, to lay their money down, pick up their Rabbits, and carry them away. I still can't believe it, but it's true. That's exactly what happened.

The Navy exchange reported its experience to headquarters, and the buying stampede was on. One Navy exchange after another placed orders, and this was duplicated by AAFES. But before AAFES joined the fray, we had to give them a taste of the action. To do so, we went to Hawaii, where they were planning a major electronics tent fair. Like a hot knife going through butter, we obtained a large order and had it flown down in time for the fair's demonstration. We had a pyramid of Rabbits twenty feet high. We made up flyers for all to see, set up the demonstration . . . and blasted off. It seemed we sold to everyone who came close to us, another riot of customers buying within seconds of seeing the product demonstrated. The pyramid disappeared.

Now we were in high gear. AAFES placed an order for warehouse stock, and several thousand units went to Oakland, Waco, and Virginia warehouses. Our next job was to set up demonstrations, and this required people. We were long on experience in this regard. Pretty soon we had a slew of them. Next we had to train them. We thought the fastest way to do that would be to create a short TV movie of the demonstration.

So we hired a commercial TV film company to come into our office and shoot the demonstration, complete with script and TV performances by yours truly and Marc. I took the part of the presidential executive behind the impressive desk, hands folded, welcoming them to the company, informing them we had been successfully doing business with the military exchange system for over twenty years, etc., establishing the fact that we were a solid company. After that I informed them that they were going to witness the demonstration just as they would be required to give it for this amazing new electronic invention by Rabbit Systems, Inc.

I then introduced Marc, who went through the actual demonstration, following which he asked and answered the most common questions regarding the product. The camera then switched back to me, and I gave them the "go for it" speech: how much fun they were going to have on the job, how the experience would hold them in good stead for years to come. Good luck . . . fade out . . . the end. Not bad, and we briefly considered changing careers.

We sent fifty copies of these demo tapes posthaste to our fledgling reps. Within a month we had just about the whole country covered with trained representatives. The shipments arrived, our reps started the program, and the orders poured in. We obtained orders from all branches of the military, totalling thirty thousand units. The annual electronics fair on Oahu purchased fifteen hundred, and people lined up to buy; sellouts of initial shipments were the rule after the first weekend's demonstration. My God, we were dizzy with the fabulous returns. I had to tell the factory I estimated that sales in the first year would total over a hundred thousand units. I mean we sold damn near the thirty thousand on the first round of orders. Was I out of my mind or what? The number of households with two or more TV sets was in the millions. What the hell was a hundred thousand? Less than two percent of the potential, that's what it was.

Have you ever seen a falling star illuminate the sky and disappear in an instant, without a trace? If not, then the nearest thing to that was the very brief life and death of the Rabbit. Astronomers can explain the mysteries of the falling star a helluva lot easier than I can tell you why the Rabbit became sterile, but I'll try.

I loved going to the office on Mondays and Tuesdays to read the sales reports from our demonstration force coming in from all over the U.S. and the Far East bases. (Europe was excluded because its TVs and VCRs were electronically incompatible with ours, although I had the factory working on a European version.) The reports all indicated sales typical of what we had experienced with our own demonstrations. At least they did over the first two reports, separated by payday weekends—the only time our people were scheduled to work. No one is poorer than our military during the week before payday.

By this time you must know what's coming. You know I'm not going to make a million; you know something is going to happen to pull the rug out and pop me on my ass again. How could you possibly think otherwise? How could anyone?

It started with the third demonstration: the reports came in showing next to no sales. Then they hit bottom, zero. It wasn't a matter of some good, some bad. Every market dropped dead with a suddenness I have never experienced in my life. Why? What went wrong?

We frantically called our reps, and the unanimous answer was "It's the wire." The customers didn't like stringing the wire from one room to another, up a stairway, around the outside of the house, or wherever the hell they had to take it to connect with the second TV set. For chrissakes, they knew it came with a wire when they bought the damn thing. What do you mean they don't like the wire? What the hell is going on?

That's it, fellas. It was all over. We'd been done in by the damn wire. There's no other explanation. That's it. Except to ask why did they buy the goddamn thing in the first place? We didn't hide the wire during the demonstration; we told them exactly where and how to set up the system with the wire connections. There was absolutely no deception. They had a clear understanding of its hook-up and operation when they happily made their purchase. Do you think they tripped over the damn wire when walking around the house and began the famous, totally communicated, military word-of-mouth program that can easily mean life or the kiss of death to a product or service sold at the exchange? I do. I believe they became so pissed off in handling the wire that they started a verbal saturation bombing attack that told everyone on base the negative news about the Rabbit within, I must believe, hours, not days.

Now I can understand why the FDA takes so long to approve a new drug or why major companies test-market a product before mass production and distribution. We shot out without a moment's hesitation, with that treacherous overconfidence; we can't miss, it's a sure thing, nothing can go wrong, it's unsinkable, just look at those sales, Wow!

Well, I have never seen anything come to an end faster than the Rabbit. But come to think about it, it was better that way if it had to happen. If sales had just slowed down, we would have spent more money for demonstrations and probably also for advertising to boost sales.

The debacle had an ironic aftermath. A year or two later, another company purchased the rights to the Rabbit, changed the name, and came out with the same product minus the wire. Would you believe they had a winner? Well, they didn't. Consumers remembered the Rabbit. That negative, combined with the fact that the cost of buying a second VCR had gone down and the fact that the Rabbit's best signal to the second set was slightly fuzzy, did them in. We had been all set to start up again. But this time, a bit of research and pretesting gave us the above mentioned facts, so we backed away.

# Chapter 23

Sometimes it takes a while for a good idea to come to fruition. (Remember that I said a good idea at the wrong time is as bad as a bad idea anytime?) Back in the early 1970s, I had picked up the phone and called the Schwinn Bicycle Company in Chicago. During my many visits to the military exchanges I noticed that they carried only one line of bicycles—an inexpensive brand by the name of Huffy. It seemed to me they should offer a finer line than that. Schwinn was the best-known bicycle name in the country. My God, almost everyone had had a Schwinn as a kid.

"Hello, Schwinn, I'd like to speak with your vice president of marketing."

I gave my name, rank, and company affiliations and was pleased to be connected with the executive in charge of sales. I told him that the purpose of my call was to have my company represent Schwinn to the military exchange system.

Before I could go any further, he interrupted, "I appreciate your call, but we have no interest in doing business with the military. For one thing, we have orders on hand for three years' worth of production going three shifts a day. We're on strict allocation and certainly have no desire to do business with the military."

He turned us down fast and cold. At least it wasn't a matter of taking it under advisement and letting us hang.

If you can't get a yes, you should always appreciate a clear-cut no.

Well in 1987, about fifteen years later, I decided to try again. Certainly a new management team should be in place. There's nothing wrong with being persistent. This time I had trouble making my way to the top. First I spoke to a middle-management person who, after hearing me out, decided I should phone another middle person in charge of one of Schwinn's distribution centers. Again I cited my name, etc., and again I was advised that, based on sales predictions, their inventory would not be adequate, for it appeared they were going to have a bigger season than they had planned. I commiserated with him but said that our program was futuristic, and because of the international character of the business, it was important for me to speak with the supreme boss. Somehow this made a dent, and he put me in contact with Gerry O'Keefe, the vice president of sales and marketing.

Boing! I hit the bell! Instead of "He's out of the office," "He's on the phone," "May I take a message and have him return your call?" "May I ask what this is regarding?" "I'm sorry, he is unavailable at this time," "He's tied up indefinitely," the man himself answered the phone. An unbelievable event.

I said, "Mr. O'Keefe, I'm . . . and our company . . . blah blah . . . with our military . . . and we want . . . the volume . . . depression-proof . . . very profitable, etc., etc." And do you know what he said?

He said, "That's very interesting. Years ago, I used to be with Wilson Sporting Goods, and we sold to the exchanges. It was a very good business. Yes, we would be interested in talking with you. Why don't you send me a letter outlining your company's operations, and we'll take it from there."

Holy cow! We were going to go to bat with the opportunity to hit for a major win.

I dashed off my tried-and-true letter and followed up with another call. This time he was even more receptive and friendly, if possible. He said, "I've read your letter, Marc, and I'm impressed with your activity with the military."

I had included in my letter our creative marketing approach with the microwave oven and indicated that we would offer the same approach to Schwinn bicycles.

"I want to get together with you as soon as possible, but I'm leaving for the Far East and will return the latter part of the month," O'Keefe continued. "Please call me then, and we'll set something up."

"Yes, sir. I'll do that. Have a good trip," I said. "I'll look forward to calling you on your return."

I hung up feeling positive, but, not being the most patient man, slightly vexed at the delay. Still, that's the way it is most of the time.

Three weeks later we spoke again, and it was all very encouraging. He suggested that since it was almost Christmas, we should wait to meet in January at the National Bicycle Convention, which would be held in southern California. Schwinn would have a large exhibit, and our meeting there could be most productive. To nail it down he gave me the dates of the convention and suggested a late-morning appointment on the second day of the event.

All of this had started in late October; with many phone calls, finally getting through to Gerry, the ensuing correspondence, the follow-up, his being away from Chicago, two months had slipped away since my original call. Well, it takes time, dammit, and there's little you can do to hurry things along.

Finally, the convention. I had Brick Tortora, our manager in Hawaii, fly in so that he, Marc, and I could give the impression we were a pretty big outfit. On the appointed hour, we appeared, all dressed in executive attire—blazers, button-downs, striped ties, and shined shoes. Marc, my son, and Brick were handsome young men, and I looked somewhat distinguished. It's imperative to make an excellent first impression; from then on, you automatically have a more receptive audience.

Gerry greeted us warmly and guided us away from the Schwinn booth for a discussion in an isolated area of an adjacent hotel. We hit it off from the start, and after a good hour, we received the happy words from Gerry.

"Okay, fellas, I see no problem with the European and the Far Eastern military bases. But here in the United States we have a problem. The Schwinn dealers' reaction to our selling to the military would be horrendous. Competition would point out our policy all over the country, so we can't at this time approve Schwinn for stateside. When I return to Chicago, I'll get together with our people, have our legal department draw up an agreement, and we'll be under way."

It was out of this world! We had received approval to represent one of the most well-known companies in the United States. They were among the first ten manufacturers whose identification was so profound all you had to do was talk generic and a person would name the brand. For example, soft drink equals Coca-Cola, cereal . . . Kellogg's, bicycles . . . Schwinn. Wow! What a fantastic opportunity. True, it didn't include the United States, but one step at a time.

The second step was to call AAFES headquarters in Dallas and inform the military we had Schwinn. Here we go again.

"Hello. Jerry Hodges? The buyer for bicycles at AAFES? My name is Marc Van Buskirk of International Marketing Corporation. We have been doing business with AAFES for over twenty years. We represent Amana Refrigeration, Inc. and have been responsible for the successful introduction and growth of the Amana Radarange. The reason for my call is that we have been appointed as military representatives for the Schwinn Bicycle Company. I wanted you to be the first to hear about this appointment."

"Marc," said Hodges, "we would be very interested."

This reaction wasn't surprising. They carried only the inexpensive line of Huffy—a first-time-buyer's bike. Bringing in an outstanding name such as Schwinn would be a matter of instant acceptance. I can tell you that including a product in their assortment is not easy. For one thing, they are not as large as department stores as we know them (or knew them). They have fewer square feet than Home Depots or Targets or Sears. As a consequence, they are very selective about how many lines of a product they can bring in. You really have to have a number one product combined with a rock-bottom price to receive any consideration.

Well, that's what I had—the best name in the industry. And as for rock-bottom pricing, the prices were the same for all Schwinn dealers; there was absolutely no deviation from the one-fits-all price list.

Dallas made only one attempt to say "We'll give it every consideration before saying yes." Bill Sullivan, head of the sporting goods department, came on the phone and said, "Unless Schwinn sells to us in the United States, we are not interested."

Quick, find a book on the art of negotiating! What can you say at that exact moment? Do you say, "Sorry that's the only way Schwinn will sell to you," and then hold your breath until you hear him come back with, "In those circumstances we will pass, thank you." No, that's not the way. Well, what is?

I must have had divine verbal support for I came back instantaneously with, "Bill, that's the long-range plan. But Schwinn has to carefully blend in the fact that it is selling to the military exchanges to avoid negative reaction in the civilian dealer organization. Given some time, we will eventually be able to sell CONUS [meaning the continental United States]. In the meantime we will both be able to find out how Schwinn is accepted in Europe and the Far East."

That's pretty much how it was pitched, and it was understood and approved. This conversation proved that AAFES is no pushover in any circumstances, and almost discarded a sure-shot program.

With the approval of AAFES, I followed up by contacting and obtaining a fast yes from the Navy and Marine Corps exchanges; all I had to do was make the calls once AAFES fell in line. How fabulous was that? Absolutely wonderful. A rebirth of our company with a brand-new market for a product that was as high in consumer acceptance as anything in the world. Furthermore, that market would never experience saturation. The newcomers joining the armed services more than made up the volume, for they need and want everything the retirees have obtained. As we saw it, we were as close to owning a Coca-Cola bottling plant in hot weather as we could be.

In early February of 1987, we flew back to Schwinn's Chicago headquarters, to go through basic training. We learned all about the product, the service department, administration, and all the field operations. Then we were ready to go.

We flew on to Dallas and received a cordial reception from Jerry Hodges. There was no question that AAFES would purchase Schwinn. But because the CONUS market was not available, we would have to go to Europe and meet the buyer at Munich headquarters to obtain orders for the exchanges in England and the continent. Jerry went on to say, "I think you may be too late for this year's program. AAFES Europe placed orders in October and November for their projected requirements. They may not be able to act on Schwinn this year due to production and shipping times. However, that's not the case in the Far East and the Pacific bases."

With the confidence of having a gigantic sure shot in our bag, we thanked him for the meeting and said we thought it would be best to give AAFES Europe a presentation even though our chances of coming in that spring were very doubtful. We assured him we would begin immediately to contact all other overseas operations.

Within a few days of returning to La Jolla, we boarded a plane for Munich for our meeting with a buyer by the name of Ray Downs. Once again, we arrived on a blustery, snow-in-the-air day at the McGraw Kaserne, the same building I had visited many years before when I presented the first microwave oven.

Ray, it turned out, was a dynamic buyer who knew bicycles from the nuts and bolts on up. There was no point in telling him about componentry, construction, features; all we said was Schwinn. That was enough.

In Europe they carried other well-known bicycles—Peugeot, Cannondale, Bianchi—so it wasn't a matter of offering them the first opportunity to bring in a high-quality line. Obviously this negated their need to act at once to order for the coming spring season. We were disappointed, even though we had anticipated this possibility. Ray assured us that he wanted Schwinn for the next year, and spoke in terms of the thousands of bicycles he would order. This got us jumping up and down again.

Our territory had no boundaries except that it excluded

the fifty states. The rest of the world was ours and ready for the old dealer call program. We had stopped off in New York to visit Navy headquarters, received their blessing and pledge to inform the overseas Navy exchanges about Schwinn's availability. Next stop, the AAFES regional headquarters of the Far East exchange network. Once again, when you're hot, you're hot. Yes, they would advise all exchanges in the Far East appropriately. That was reward enough for us to go to Japan and around to Korea; Okinawa; the Philippines, covering Clark Air Base and Subic; and finally Guam, picking up orders. It's long flying time, tough traveling, and hot or monsoon weather. In other words, it's not easy territory to cover, but at least we had gained plenty of experience with it over the years. Our reception everywhere was nothing less than all-out acceptance.

Naturally we couldn't just take the orders. No, not us. We had to put together a sell-through program with a payday Saturday representative and a promotion. We decided on a base biathlon. Marc, having participated in several biathlons as part of his own fitness program, knew how to put one on, and within a short time all was scheduled for Okinawa, Clark AFB, and Guam. The events were programmed to coincide with the arrival of the first Schwinn orders and the appearance at each base of Marc and Brick to conduct the event.

Our first biathlon, in Okinawa, was a tremendous success. All exchange officials got behind the program with advertising and publicity. They also arranged for maps to block off the route, and provided security. They even recruited Burger King employees to line the route and pass out water. To top it off, they held a participants' dinner the night before the biathlon, offering high-carbohydrate spaghetti and other pasta dishes, and bananas for dessert.

At dinner, people passed out race numbers and course information along with T-shirts.

It was a first-class effort, and it paid off. We put up a big banner proclaiming Schwinn's sponsorship and largesse in giving prize bicycles, clothing, and accessories to the winners. This was a big-top show and included divisions for women and children. Everyone on the base wanted to participate. Hundreds of people showed up to purchase bicycles right off the starting line.

I'm telling you, it was dramatic. The base newspaper was on hand to take pictures and write up the story, ditto Armed Services TV and radio reporters, who focused on the commanding officer of the base awarding the trophies and prizes we had furnished. I can also tell you everyone on base knew that Schwinn had arrived. Sales zoomed.

We had the same results at Clark AFB and on Guam. In one outstanding, low-cost, creative program we had locked up the presence of Schwinn at all major bases in the Far East.

Shortly thereafter we covered and secured opening orders from every U.S. offshore military base around the world—Panama, Puerto Rico, Guantanamo Bay. By the time September rolled around we were ready to tackle Europe for the next year's orders.

It all sounds too good to be true, considering our record of the damn rug being pulled from under us time after time. This was no exception. I know you are saying, "Not again!" Yes, my friends, again.

The spring and summer of 1988 in Europe were the coldest and wettest in twenty years, according to all reports. Naturally that was not good for bicycle sales. As a consequence, AAFES Europe had tremendous inventories of unsold bicycles at season's end.

The blame for this situation fell on the buyer, Ray

Downs, as if he were a mad rainmaker who had caused the flooding of Europe. It should come as no surprise that he was relieved of his duties and transferred out to a Siberian post. It doesn't matter if you are a super manager of anything. If you don't win, you're out. The same applies to AAFES buyers. The reason is not important.

On the other hand, there must be medals for a buyer who won't buy, and the new one, Jack MacDonald, probably received the merchandising medal of honor for having an unused order book. He lectured us on the principles of maintaining a modest inventory to preclude the negative results of bad weather, and demonstrated that principle by ordering less than half of what should have been sold in an average season. Shows you the difference between being a hero and a bum. If the weather had been super good, Ray Downs's inventory would have disappeared, and he would have been looked upon as the greatest merchandise buyer in the annals of AAFES.

The problem with doing business with AAFES in Europe is that you can't obtain good reorders even if you have a good selling season. It's too late to manufacture and ship to Europe before the cold rain starts in Germany. So it's one big all-or-nothing shot. We accepted the orders MacDonald finally decided on—a few thousand instead of many thousands—and decided to be happy and do the best we could in the circumstances.

The best was not too shabby. We learned that Schwinn's promotional team included the world-champion freestyle trick rider. What's that? It's a kid who is a great athlete, in top condition, who can ride a BMX bike (one with small wheels instead of regular wheels) and do anything. He would ride with his feet and legs over his head, do twists, handstands, ride backwards, glide in a wide circle standing on the handlebars. Any trick you could think of, this kid,

Robert Peterson, could do. It was pure show business. In addition, we found out the Schwinn/Wheaties racing team was going to compete in the Tour-de-France and other races throughout Europe in that spring of 1988. We asked and received an okay to have them appear at various military bases to ride around, sign autographs, etc., in front of the exchanges, where large displays of bicycles would be gathered for sale.

Both programs executed beautifully. We made up flyers for each event, had TV and radio inform everyone on their news programs, and in every instance large crowds of people attended. The shows went on to great applause and autograph signing when they were over. Schwinn bicycles were right out in front, and sales were excellent.

We put Robert Peterson on tour, and he presented his exhibition on over thirty bases. Later we took him over to the Far East. He was a smash hit, becoming the Pied Piper of the Pacific. The kids went bananas—so much so that on Guam, after his show and a frenzy of autograph signing, a large number showed up at the airport to bid him farewell. Schwinn was in, for a long time after the Peterson tour was over.

It's ironic. Years later, due to the nature of the industry, bicycle manufacturers still operate on the basis of just placing bicycles in a store, advertising their brand and features, and waiting for the customers to come in and make a selection. The manufacturers conduct their business the same way they have for the last fifty years or more. And as a result, not any one of them has drawn away from the pack.

# Chapter 24

While attending the National Bicycle Convention a year later we encountered another opportunity of major proportions, which would eventually give us millions of dollars in gross sales. We were walking quite smugly around the vast auditorium housing the industry's convention, aware of the fact that we had been most successful in our first year with Schwinn. All of our promotional activity and anticipation of the coming season would double our volume of sales. Then Marc pulled me over and said, "Dad, there's a line we absolutely must have!"

I looked up and saw a small booth, the smallest at the convention. In the center was a bridge table covered with a cloth and an array of sunglasses. A good-looking, well-built young man seated on a metal chair behind the table was talking to someone. I figured my son had temporarily lost his mind and his senses of direction, taste, and smell.

"You've got to be kidding. Sunglasses? Everyone and his mother makes sunglasses. Why that line?" I asked as we stood nearby, watching what seemed to be one of those off-the-main-aisle booths of accessories, minor products, and unknown products that complete a major convention after the displays of the big guys.

"You don't understand, Dad. That line is totally cool."

"Cool? Does that mean it cools your face if you wear them? What does cool have to do with anything? What's so cool about them?" I asked, realizing that the first crack of age, or becoming out-of-touch with the next generation, had begun to show.

"They're hot, and I mean they're going to become red hot. The kids are wearing them, the surfers, the biathlon runners, the bicycle guys. Believe me, you're looking at another Hula-Hoop in the making," he said with such sincerity and confidence that I had to give in. After all, blessed are those who believe and do not see. I assumed this also included such things as a crazy line of sunglasses.

"Let's go over, tell him who we are, and ask for the line. All he can do to us is say no. If they don't have a representative firm for the military market, I'm pretty sure we'll have a new line."

The young man seated behind the table was Mike Parnell. He courteously stood to shake hands with us as we introduced ourselves.

"Mike, my son, Marc, tells me we positively must have your line for the military exchange system," I said with a smile that evoked a similar one in return. He turned to Marc and asked how and why he became interested in Oakley, which was the name of the product and the company.

Marc replied by saying he was into running and biathlons, and he knew that Oakley was on its way to capturing the youth market.

My God, if he had sat down for a week to come up with a better answer he could never have produced a more positive reply than that one. Mike then asked the sixty-four-million dollar question: "What lines do you represent?"

"We have been extremely successful with the Schwinn Bicycle Company and Amana Refrigeration, Incorporated, a division of the Raytheon Company, the only lines we represent."

That did it. When I said Schwinn, I said the magic word, because anyone who represented Schwinn, the foremost bicycle company in the United States, must be pretty good. He then asked for references at each company, told us he appreciated our visit, and asked us to contact him at his office within a week. We left feeling confident we would have a win. Somehow, sometimes, you just know.

We informed Gerry O'Keefe of Schwinn and Eldon Pugh of Amana about our desire for the Oakley line. We asked if they could say a few nice words about our results with their companies. As it turned out, Mike called both of them, and whatever they said was more than enough to help us become the new military representative for Oakley.

Shortly thereafter we met again with Mike, received a warm welcome, a tour of the factory, a meeting with their people. It was all quite strange to me, as a matter of fact—extremely different from what I considered normal. It was a fun factory made up of happy, energetic young people all pumping away at their jobs. They showed us a shortened indoor basketball court used during break time, and a soundproofed audio room where the designers worked while earsplitting music blared. This company was totally crazy, but boy, oh boy, did it ever have a formula for success.

Oakley was working to bring in every outstanding athlete and sports champion—surfing, volleyball, running, cycling, you name it—to wear and endorse Oakley. As a result, every kid who read the various sport magazines or watched TV saw the same glasses on all the champions, and had to succumb: if he wanted to be a somebody, he had to have a pair of Oakleys. That's how it started and that's how it is today.

On top of that, the entire sales force is made up of young men who, if they're not selling Oakley, are out surfing. You have heard of doing business on the golf course; well, now it's while waiting for the seventh wave. Their advertising is limited to a few sports magazines, and uses bizarre-looking young models and copy that reads along the lines of a message from one outer space station to another. To me it's all spaced out. But it sells!

We received our sample bag and went to work. If you think it was easy, think again. What has ever been easy with us? No, we have to go the hard way. First to Dallas, where we were turned down flat. "We have enough sunglasses, we're over inventoried. Sorry. Try on an individual store basis with a one-time-buy if you can get it approved." Thanks a lot. We know the hard road. It's the only one we know. Off we go.

Marc found out about a marathon at Fort Campbell, Kentucky. He picked up the phone and asked if the base would like a sponsor. Of course they would. All it would cost us would be a few glasses as prizes and a large Oakley banner for the starting line. We would obtain a relatively small order for our participation. Of course, Marc would fly back there for the event. It was a start. We made the most of it. Think about it. If we had just gone in to sell Oakley sunglasses, we would have been blocked out like Oakley blocks out the sun. Instead, we sold the sizzle, sponsoring an event, and it worked. It worked beautifully. They sold out every pair of glasses they ordered, and they ordered more.

Now we had the formula for opening the gates for Oakley. Marc contacted Luke AFB in Arizona, where they were also holding a running event and gave them the Fort Campbell story. We had a repeat win on our hands. After that, still another marathon, and the word went to the manager of the entire Western region of AAFES, so we got our one-time-buy order for all exchanges under his control. Armed with that, we gobbled up the Midwest and East

Coast. On similar programs, the Navy and Marine Corps followed suit. Pretty soon we were sponsoring marathons all over the country.

About a year later (it always takes about a year on the proving ground before being accepted into the hallowed halls) we were presented with contracts for the military world. Marc worked his tail off and it paid. And with the marvelous talent of my daughter Ann, our number one girl in the organization, we acquired representatives at all major bases through the United States, over eighty-five of them, whose job it is to take inventory and write up monthly orders and maintain communication with us. In addition to the reps, we have subreps in hub areas—Europe, the Far East—so that we can point with pride to the strong field organization that is one of the best in our industry. To describe this in crystal-clear terms, we went from a volume of four hundred thousand dollars the first year of our struggle to a point where six years later we are doing over four million dollars in gross sales. Incredible!

# Chapter 25

Time marches on. If you believe the expression "The more things change, the more they stay the same," I'd like to be the first to tell you that's not true. I'll agree that time changes things and people, but no way will I accept that they remain the same. Things and people come on new, fresh, growing, attractive, exciting, bright, and beautiful; then with time they fade away, lose color, age, wear, become average and replaceable, making way for the new people and new models, all of whom or which should be an improvement over the past. Should be, but aren't always.

As I've related, ever since we acquired the Schwinn line for Europe, we had been after them to let us cover the United States, a market five times the size of the rest of the military world. The company's main reason for opposition was the negative effect exchange sales would have on their civilian dealer organization. First thoughts might bring you to that opinion. But if you make decisions without having all the facts, you usually make the wrong one. . . . That's a fair statement.

I have to prepare you for another of the great American marketing disasters of all time, or at least my time. My carefully rock-solid presentation to overcome Schwinn's objection follows. Please understand, the stateside military exchanges sold only one or two inexpensive lines of bicycles and had a volume of over twenty million dollars yearly. They estimated they lost thirty percent of the business to higher-priced bicycles with more features. They wanted that business.

Only military people are allowed in the exchanges and they will not go off base to buy anything if it's available at the exchange. They can buy it for less and deserve to, for they make less money than their civilian counterparts. They do not have to pay sales tax. Lastly, they know that all profits made by the exchanges are earmarked, after military expenses, for their Morale and Welfare Fund to benefit all military personnel and their families.

Other companies, offering just about every recognizable brand name in the world (for example, G.E., Whirlpool, Sony, IBM, Apple, RCA, and similar giants in personal care, etc.) sell at the exchanges without negative effect.

It's a privilege to sell to the military, and the rewards make it a joy to do business with them. They pay their invoices on time; they're not going bankrupt. They ask for so little, and they offer a market that is depression-proof. Their people are paid twice a month, and when they retire or leave the service, they are replaced by newcomers who need and buy all that their predecessors have previously purchased. Quite a unique and fantastic market, as those who serve them can attest.

I might add, if you don't sell your product to them, someone else will sell another product. Your civilian dealers will not be able to sell to the military because military people will have purchased a competitive model on base.

This was my pitch, year after year. It was supported by the yearly increase we achieved with Schwinn in Europe. But I made no headway until 1990, when a combination of events occurred. The bicycle business was going gangbusters. No company could manufacture enough bikes to satisfy the demand. Therefore, those companies had no interest in selling to the military. They were all on allocation, having a nice time and a nice year; how fun.

Of course, toward the fall of the year they all individually and collectively decided they should increase their production by at least twenty percent to meet the ever-growing demand for the new year. And doesn't everyone project growth? They certainly did.

No one could imagine that the economy and their business would do anything but continue to soar, or they might have at least held their production at the existing level. Of course, they never considered a reduction. But everything started to go to hell. The first to pack up and reserve space was the bicycle industry. Business was lousy—off twenty percent from the year before. But because the companies had increased their inventory by twenty percent, I calculate they had forty percent more in their warehouses than they could sell. Very sad.

Under those conditions, I believed we had a chance to change their minds about selling to the military. I was right. Schwinn's export manager, a fine guy by the name of Mike Martinsen, informed me our year-in-and-out endeavor was finally going to be tested. Ed Schwinn, the president and supreme boss, had agreed to sell to the military exchange system on a test, using the West Coast exchanges. If all proceeded without a major negative reaction, they would quickly approve the rest of the country. Do you have any idea what that represented? Well, I'll tell you. If we sold eight thousand bicycles a year in twenty-five exchanges in Europe (one-fifth of the U.S., in comparison), where we had three major competitors, how many would we sell in over a hundred exchanges in the United States, where we would have no competition and where the southern markets plus Hawaii have a climate for year-round selling? Okay,

I'll tell you. I estimated a minimum of forty thousand bicycles at an average cost of $250, or ten million dollars of business at cost. And this was conservative, for the plans that I rapidly put together, including, of course, our demonstration program, made another five million dollars. Oh, my! What a fantastic opportunity.

The first thing to do was pick up the phone and tell Dallas. John Akridge, the new buyer, was absolutely delighted. He was a bicycle enthusiast and knew componentry, features, etc., as well as a mechanic but also recognized the power of the Schwinn name and its potential at military exchanges. I suggested that Mike Martinsen and I fly to Dallas to present the program and prices, etc., and have them prepare orders for immediate shipment. He agreed, and we set an arrival date within the week.

It's so rare to plan a meeting where the buyer wants your product or service just as much as you want him to order. That's a salesman's heaven.

When we arrived we were met by John and Bill Sullivan, the merchandise manager of the sporting goods department. We probably could have met with the director of all merchandising if we so desired. We quickly outlined our program, said that we planned to place a representative on base with a supply of parts to provide warranty service and customer assistance in explaining the features of Schwinn bicycles. In addition, we were going to offer a free, thirty-day tune-up after purchase, plus signs displaying our toll-free 800 number, brochures with the specs of each bike, and a sales meeting with the employees of the department. In every way it was a self-contained program that precluded any need for a customer to go to an off-base Schwinn dealer for service.

I then told them about Schwinn's concern regarding its civilian organization and said that our program, aided by whatever the exchange could do, would be appreciated and certainly work to our mutual benefit.

Bill Sullivan hardly needed to be told about the sensitivity of the situation, but he did come out with the following.

"Marc, as you know, AAFES carries just about every brand name in every category of retail merchandise and has for many years. In the entire history of AAFES only one manufacturer has ever sold to us and then informed us they would no longer do so and asked that any inventory in our warehouse be returned to the factory. That company was Toro, which makes lawnmowers. The only explanation was that the lawnmowers had been purchased by people who lived off base and took them to their local Toro dealer when they needed service. Normally a military man can fix anything up to a broken-down atom bomb. But those lawnmower motors went back to the dealer. Of course the dealer complained to Toro, and Toro decided to stop military sales. That is the only company, as I have said, to have done so."

"Well, our program pretty much prevents that, and the military have been repairing their own bicycles since they were kids," I replied, adding, "We're ready to go and make this program and Schwinn a matter of pride to all concerned."

"Very good, Marc. You'll have our complete cooperation."

Have you ever heard that sweet music before? How sweet is that? Very.

They informed us they would be placing orders for the West Coast distribution center without delay. Our meeting was over. As a salesman, or if you are an attorney who has just won a big case, a doctor who has cured a patient, an engineer whose calculations turned out to be perfect, or just a person who has experienced a happy event, you can understand our feelings. The tingle stayed with us as we drove to the airport for the flight home. We were totally happy. My company and Schwinn's would reap tremendous rewards.

Each of us would be recognized as the person who brought in a ten-million-dollar volume of business. Mike would be rewarded because corporations acknowledge good work with raises, perks, and titles. And me, I owned the company, and the consensus was that the volume was going to be substantial. Schwinn combined with Oakley was going to bring us back to the good ol' glory days of Amana and the microwave oven. Hot diggity damn. It's a wonderful world and I love everybody. After a toast at the bar to our good work and fortune, we said good-bye at the airport, Mike to return to Chicago, Marc and I to La Jolla.

Homecoming after a major victory always meant a gathering of the clan—all the kids, the best dinner Jane could put on, which was the best of the best, laughter, happy talk, dog's tail wagging, the good life.

Now you know I'm going to get kicked in the ass again, just as sure as God made those little green apples. How could it be any other way? Not again! Yes. But you don't know how, and how is a most extraordinary climax to all the downers I've related.

You may find it hard to believe this, for it really is unbelievable. Furthermore, there is no way I can soften the shock of what I'm about to say. But at least you're now battle-scarred veterans of my many salesman's wars, so you'll live through another.

The next morning I was barely seated in my office when the phone rang. Mike Martinsen calling. Before I could say "Good morning" or even "Hi," Mike asked,

"Who do you think is the new CEO of Schwinn?"

"I thought Ed Schwinn was. Is he all right? What's going on?" I replied.

"He's okay. But again, who do you think is the new CEO?"

"Damned if I know. Did they bring Gerry O'Keefe out of retirement? How 'bout Byron Smith; he's a brainy VP? . . . I give up. Who is it?"

"The new CEO of Schwinn Bicycle Company is a guy by the name of Ralph Murray."

"I haven't heard about him. Where did he come from?" I asked, not particularly interested or concerned; my world was another world.

"Marc," Mike said, "Ralph Murray is the former president of Toro, and he has been brought in by Ed Schwinn to take over the CEO spot. How does that grab you? I know how it grabbed me!"

"Oh no! You've got to be kidding! That's the worst possible news!"

"I'm not kidding. I'll keep you informed. G'bye."

I sat there in shock. My mind borrowing big trouble, reducing me to only one conclusion, we had had it.

The very next day, Mike called again and told me that Ralph had stopped by his office to ask about the arrangements we had made with Dallas, further wanting to know if we could put them on hold. Mike went on to say he had told Ralph it was too late. They were in the process of computerized ordering, and they had informed all of the exchanges involved that they would soon have Schwinn. It was all on schedule. Mike said Ralph walked away saying nothing, leaving him with the thought we might be okay after all.

Fat chance. The next day, Ralph walked into Mike's office and told him flat out that Schwinn was canceling our arrangements with AAFES, effective immediately.

Mike told me to phone John Akridge, the buyer in Dallas, and advise him accordingly. No need in this case to worry about the messenger being shot. The messenger was quite willing to kill himself.

Can you imagine the impact of this devastating turn of events? One day before, I had been counting commissions in the hundreds of thousands; multiplied by five years, that pops into the millions. And the very next day—totally wiped out, zero. Not only that, but the fun of winning was lost, of building a representative force to work at the major exchanges, of the exciting reports coming in from the field about the number of sales, the reactions of exchange management and customers to the introduction and excellent sales of Schwinn, and the sheer fun of receiving phone calls asking for additional shipments. Damn it, there's more. The putting together of Schwinn-sponsored biathlons, triathlons; having the likes of Robert Peterson touring the United States bases to give his exhibition and convert thousands of kids to the Schwinn bicycle, which would undoubtedly lead to their buying Schwinns when they became teenagers and on through the ages of their lives.

My telephone call to AAFES was one of the two they have ever received to tell them, "Sorry, but we have decided not to sell to the military." My God, just about every company on planet Earth that is not selling to them would do so if it only had the chance.

It was my unhappy task to explain that the new CEO of Schwinn was the former top executive of Toro, the only company that had ever pulled out of military sales after it had taken and shipped their orders.

This new CEO of Schwinn, Ralph Murray, was absolutely adamant, and since he had been personally appointed by Ed Schwinn, the owner and president of the company, he received unswerving support. Don't they all in the beginning? And in the end, they were as wrong as they could be. It reminds me of my old boss, Lewis Phillips of Presto, who refused to go along with the new concept in the supermarket industry—offering appliances at a discount—because it would have a negative effect on the regular dealer organization. At that time selling to stores other than straight appliance stores or hardware stores was debatable. But come on, in the 1990s you have to be kidding. For one thing, the mom-and-pop stores have disappeared in all but the small crossroads towns. The world of merchandising revolves around the big discount chains and mass merchants. For a bicycle company to refuse to sell to the military seems incredibly stupid to me.

Oh yes, I did put up a fight. A few days later we met with Ed Schwinn, Ralph Murray, and the other VPs who were kowtowing to the party line. Step by step, I went over our intended safeguards to preclude the military from going to civilian dealers. For chrissakes, we planned to put Schwinn servicing dealers on base, with our own Schwinn representative to offer sales assistance, a thirty-day free tune-up, bike stands, all necessary parts and tools, plus an 800 telephone hot-line service number. I then launched into my "the world is changing" pitch and told them they needed to change if they wanted to survive.

The dealers had already changed. At one time they carried only Schwinn in their stores and displayed the famous Schwinn logo on a sign outside the door. Now they have three or four competitive lines on display. They'll promote and sell any bicycle that gives the best profit and fastest turnover. I pointed this out and ended by telling them they were trying to make a virgin out of a whore if they believed they could convert, or even hoped to convert, their dealer organization back to a single-line dealership.

In the end the Schwinn executives thanked me, told me they respected my effort, but that they were going in new directions that did not include the military. What the hell are new directions? I subsequently found out. They went bankrupt within a year, taking all their creditors to the accounts-not-payable window.

But at the time, as I walked away, I muttered aloud my own take-off on a scene from *Casablanca*. Of all the companies in all the world looking for a CEO, and of all the guys looking for a CEO position, why among all the fates in life did Schwinn and Ralph Murray find each other? Utterly incredible. But doesn't it now strike you as a pattern in my life?

# Part Four

---

# How to Become a Millionaire in Fifty Easy Years

# Chapter 26

Lest you now have only vague recollections, allow me to remind you of my numerous if onlys, maybes, could haves, should have beens. Let's go way back to my Presto days, without a shadow of a doubt the foundation of my selling, marketing, and managing acumen. At the time, that foundation didn't give me pleasure, brains, or money. If it had, I would have bought stock at $1.25 a share when I first joined Presto. Ten thousand shares could have sold for nine hundred thousand dollars just a few years later, while I was still a salesman. Let me tell you, in the 1950s, nine hundred thousand was pure, fuck-you money. One would have had to be an idiot not to easily turn it into millions. So that has to be one of my runaway leaders among the if onlys.

Next we go on to the StaPut paper plate story. One rotten run of bad applications for my StaPut plates, and the whole brilliant marketing introduction was blown away. Another could have been that wasn't.

How about my coin-operated pressing machine program for the military that fell apart because the machines fell apart? Those machines would still be coining money, for the need still exists within the military rank and file. Another should have been. Certainly if I had been more selective in choosing military bases for contract, untold thousands of dollars would not have been wasted in supplying equipment and servicing it when even in the best of circumstances that equipment could not have been profitable. Expanding volume without adequate profit or capital can be a disaster for any company. The only warm sensation involved is to say you had more contracts and more machines on military bases than any other competitor. Wouldn't that make you feel good?

The greatest business achievement of my life was with the Amana microwave oven, wherein we earned several hundreds of thousands of dollars in commission. But whatever the total, it could have been far more than doubled if its potential had been clearly perceived in the beginning. All the if onlys, couldas, wouldas, and shouldas are wrapped in this one, and there's no maybe about it.

The undue delays and lack of vision came about in the very beginning. If Amana, which advertised the greatest invention since fire for cooking food, had invested money in winning over the military market with a heavy advertising and promotion campaign; if Herman Eisencraft, a name indelibly imprinted on my mind, had not said, "Special order, Marc!"; and if, as a result, I had not spent a year and a half in that restrictive mode of selling, rather than their bringing in warehouse quantities to be dispersed for immediate sales throughout Europe, the start-up could have been dramatic and the volume of business tremendous, keeping in mind that the happy owners spread the word of the microwave's wonders and advantages faster than the best advertising campaign. Together, word of mouth and advertising should have created a multimillion-dollar business from the very beginning instead of trench warfare for almost two years. In spite of all of this, we conquered the market. All of Europe was exclusively ours; orders came in by the carload; and I was seriously considering opening my own bank. Of course something happened. It wouldn't be life if it hadn't.

Just when I was spending most of my time counting money, the general of the AAFES exchange system in Europe made an inspection tour of the bases in the United Kingdom. Of course he visited Lakenheath Air Force Base, the largest in England. While there, he toured the service and repair facility. Lo and behold, he found an extremely large inventory of what the civilian service people said were malfunctioning Amana microwave ovens. Good-bye to being the exclusive microwave in AAFES. Hello, here come the Japanese. It didn't matter that the units he inspected, for the most part, needed only to be converted from 50- to 60-cycle configuration for the owners' return to the States. No, all that mattered was that it looked like we were selling a poor-quality product, as portrayed and emphasized by the service personnel in the repair facility.

Just as fast as possible the general ordered his merchandising people to bring in competitors' models. The Japanese invasion was awesome; several manufacturers had two or more models, an inundating advertising campaign, plus a copy of our demonstration program. I mean they swamped us. At one time, you could open up the customer ordering book kept at each exchange and see Amana after Amana covering pages of the book. After the invasion, you would turn the page over and see one Amana for every twenty Japanese. It was nothing less than heartbreaking. Saddest of all was to learn that the service men in England were apprehended for falsifying repairs to keep the units in their service depot and then selling perfectly good units on the black market. That they were imprisoned where I hope they rot did very little to make me feel better or correct the situation. The Japanese were in, and they spent millions of dollars in the European military market to ensure their sales of a wide range of electronics products in addition to the microwave oven.

The Japanese have employed this program in the civilian market worldwide. When you drive in from any airport throughout the entire Far East, Middle East, South America, or Central America you see billboards and neon signs atop most buildings along the way, all advertising Japanese products until you can easily believe you are in Japan instead of Manila, Bangkok, or one of the many other cities they have economically captured. No question, they have achieved more as a result of losing World War II than they ever would have obtained had they won by armed force.

Although it appears I'm conjuring up all the elements possible to explain why my struggles have been so intense, why my success has been tempered and delayed and hard won over many years, the truth in great part lies with my own mistakes—missing opportunities so obvious a child could have seen them, and in some cases not having the courage to engage those opportunities when I did see them. Here I primarily refer to investing money to make money, and using that to enhance and strengthen my position with additional people, advertising, and promotional programs. All of this would have been possible if I had invested our earnings in the very companies I was working for at the time, since I had such a fierce belief in and dedication to the ultimate success of the products and the companies. I should have known that all would be reflected in their stock on the New York Exchange. Hell, they all went to the sky and beyond. In addition to Presto, Raytheon was at about twenty-eight dollars a share when they introduced the microwave oven. It went to sixty dollars and then split two for one, and thereafter split four more times after reaching the sixty-dollar level. It makes a mockery out of the need for busting your ass, flying all over the world, putting up with endless days away from home, missing the fun and love of being with the family and all things beautiful that make for a wonderful life.

There's only one other way to make it. Work hard, ring those bells until you find the truth in your endeavors. Once you have found that truth, and all systems are go, then reach for it. The important opportunities of life are few and far between. By all means reach for them when you are young; the worst that can happen is that you will lose and have to start over again. No big deal. I'm not trying to moralize about the need to work the project before investing, I'm simply pointing out that to do otherwise, you may as well go to Las Vegas and play roulette.

# Chapter 27

Well, my friends, the time has finally come to begin to realize and accept that we're coming to the end of the line. Better check the overhead racks containing memories and look around to see what we have to clear up before closing the attaché case and leaving the territory. No doubt a few important matters have to be sorted out. But the memories are there to be brought up at will: I can still see myself on that first Greyhound bus, going down the hills to Wilkes-Barre, so young, so excited.

The water splashing down from the man's hat into my face as I looked up while demonstrating the pants presser.

Saying to Mr. Haney, as I applied for a job at the World's Fair, "You have a wonderful product, Mr. Haney. I can work the World's Fair at night when the others become tired."

Buying my first car in Kansas City and sliding off into the farmer's field.

Driving the two-lane blacktop to and from the quiet, slow, river towns along the Mississippi.

Enjoying the colorful events in New York City, and becoming the number one salesman of the company.

Introducing the new Presto products, having the whole city run advertisements on the same day.

Holding a meeting of the New York dealers at Toots Shor's and having them all write up orders.

Being in the office when the man with the heavy German accent asked the sales manager, "Who are you to tell me I can't do the job? I was a good man in Germany before the war." And hearing the sales manager instantly reply, "You're hired!"

Sitting next to Jane in the restaurant, telling her I had been offered a promotion to regional sales manager but at a lower salary than I was earning as a salesman, and hearing her tell me with woman's intuition to accept, for I would surely do the same good work for the region that I had done in New York.

Flying in small DC-3s and DC-4s up and down the turbulent East Coast.

The triple payoff: marrying Jane at the big Waldorf Astoria wedding, being promoted to national sales manager, and moving to Eau Claire, Wisconsin.

Renting our second-floor apartment for all of eighty dollars a month.

Buying a house for all of fifteen thousand dollars but waiting a long three weeks before they approved my loan.

Jane, planting turnips upside down in the garden.

Patches, our dog, peeing on the pigeon at the field trials.

Taking leave of Presto and finding a new job in the paper plate industry. The excitement of creating the StaPut paper plate and the agony of its disaster. But not before the hilarious food brokers' convention in Chicago.

Moving afterwards to Michigan and an ill-fated association with the wrong company.

The very gloomy days of being out of a job in the middle of nowheresville.

Going to California with a temporary job as a consultant and turning it into my own company.

Building the vending business in the hard, start-up days without financial support.

Finding a house on the ocean after the destructive warehouse fire burned up everything we had in the world.

Meeting with the attorney who had placed liens on our house and everything we owned.

Making the decision to represent companies, and selling my vending equipment.

Opening a distributorship in Hawaii.

Introducing the first microwave oven on a military base in Puerto Rico.

Jane's selling the first Amana Radarange in Stuttgart, Germany, and the cold rainy days of demonstrating in one exchange after another.

The beginning of a new era with the first warehouse order for Europe.

Introducing the Radarange to the Far East, selling to every one of the bases, and then going all the way back to sell what I had sold them, demonstrating until, when the smoke had cleared, we owned the market worldwide. Just to be certain, the trips to Alaska, Panama, Guantanamo, Kwajalein, and God knows where else. The sun never set without an Amana Radarange demonstration going on some place on this earth. In effect, we picked up where the British Empire left off.

Those memories are only the short list. However, combined with the long list, they permit me to say, like an old-time peddler on the road, "That reminds me of the time . . ." For it seems to me, one way or another, I've had the experiences of a full life, especially those of a salesman.

It is now 1994, and I am on the leading edge of being called an old man. Somehow I don't exactly feel that way. Yes, quite a few grunts and a light groan, a weak link or two within the chain are showing up. My tennis is about the same, perhaps four steps slower. My zest for selling something that has never been on the market before and has the potential for overwhelming acceptance, as in the case of the pressure cooker and the microwave oven, is just as strong as ever. The problem is finding an invention or product of this kind, one that needs a live demonstration to get it started, and away we go. It has been and always will be a sure-shot formula for a successful introduction and establishing the foundation for future rewarding advertising and promotional programs. It's tough to find such a product. They are few and far between.

Now there a few things to tidy up. First, the family. The loss of Jane was, and is, the most devastating of my life. There is a lack of meaning in what is important from the day she passed on. Without a doubt, the best years of our lives were ahead of us. This is so sad, but so true. For many years in the 1970s and 1980s I was, when the money was real, earning over a hundred thousand a year. Unfortunately, bringing up a family of four wonderful kids in a town like La Jolla was not inexpensive. Sending all of them from the very beginning to every type and kind of medical, mental, physical, educational, social, cultural, and athletic improvement program conceived by man and woman and God to get them ready to enter the real world outside the home required just about all that we earned. We spent the money happily. It has been immensely rewarding, for they have all turned out to be wonderful adults who have appreciated and loved us all of our days. I believe Jane and I could always say we were and are one of the many fine families of our town, all the more so in spite of the radical social, moral, and economic changes of the last twenty-five years.

There is a time for all things, as the Bible says. The time came to sell our home on the ocean. The time to know this is when your kids reach an age when they begin to rant and rage about leaving the house for a place of their own, even though they don't have the money to pay the rent and don't hesitate to ask for contributions.

Of course college sent them away for several years. They became semiaccustomed to living many hundreds or thousands of miles away. I can safely tell you, however, next to the pull of gravity, the most certain and powerful force in their being drew them back most willingly and sealed them in La Jolla. For all its change, it is still one of the loveliest places on earth to raise children and live out your life.

Somewhere in the early 1980s, when the business was going full blast, we received an offer of about a million dollars for the old barn on the ocean. It came from two very nice people by the name of Peggy and Sam Goldwyn, Jr., he the son of *the* Sam Goldwyn. A million was a figure, if you remember, that I had been striving for all my life. Of course I was tempted. Until I rolled the offer by my long time C.P.A., John Pfuhl, who was with the firm I'd gone to when I had first formed my business back in 1961. That was when I counted coins on the center table at the bank, watched with a he-won't-last stare by my friendly banker. John told me I could not at that time afford to sell because of the tremendous capital gains tax I'd have to pay. If you remember, I had purchased the house for under seventy-five thousand dollars. The tax, combined with the tax on my income, made the sale not as attractive as it appeared. Thank God for John, who said the timing would be better when my business income slowed down. Did he know something I wasn't aware of? Why, my business would go on forever, just pouring money over me year after year.

Well C.P.A.'s are an extremely conservative, negative, doubtful, suspicious group about everything except the truth of their figures and accounting. And so it came to pass that I passed on the most exciting offer presented to me to that time.

A few years later, at the peak of the totally prosperous 1980s, another very interested buyer came on the scene, coinciding with the decided downward turn of our Amana microwave business. The timing for a sale was as perfect as it had been when I was in the umbrella escort business just when a sudden downpour threatened the crowd coming up from the subway station to walk home.

Because this turned out to be one of the most momentous events of our lives, it deserves a certain amount of behind-the-scenes detail on how to buy and sell a house that you might find educational. If not educational, then amazing, or just plain unbelievably fantastic.

In those days in La Jolla, shacks with an outhouse would sell for over a hundred thousand dollars. People would camp out overnight to bid on or to be among the first in line to buy a house in the new developments that were opening one after another eastward toward the Rocky Mountains. Countless families would take advantage of the housing shortage and easy-money times to sell their houses at marvelous prices. Then they'd turn right around and buy another one to fix up and sell, repeating the action over and over again. It was a wild period in real estate, exceeded only by the feverish speculation of land sales in Florida in the 1920s before the big hurricane destroyed all, or by the big boom in Hawaii after the jets and later on the Japanese visitors arrived to make their yen-against-the-dollar advantage known to all locals who owned valuable, well-located property, especially along the waterfront.

During the lunatic days of La Jolla real estate pricing (I did not say sales), I joined the frenzy of the mob and priced my property at a comfortable price: comfortable in that I had absolutely no concern that anyone would buy it at that price—$6.3 million.

We were hardly disturbed by people wanting to view the house, let alone make an offer. So we continued to let it be listed at that level. (After all, we could always say "Sale!" and drop off a couple of million. Not a bad thought.) After about six months, we decided it was time to become a bit more serious, so we lowered the price to $4.8 million. They say your first markdown should be your best one. Hmmm. Nothing happened for a couple of months. Then by chance a realtor was showing a house nearby to a couple who asked if "that house," pointing to ours, was for sale. The realtor, being typical of the majority, said, "Yes, but it's much higher priced than you indicated was in your range." How dumb.

The clients responded by saying, "We'd like to see that one. Please arrange a visit."

And so, to the astonishment of the realtor, they made an offer of $3 million.

It floored us as well. But this was only the opening round. To the consternation of the family, I declined the offer and countered by reducing the price to $4.3 million. The game was on. The next move was his. He played it with an unusual twist. He asked the realtor to have me quote my "bottom line." Thinking this was the last and final play, I decided I'd drop it down to rock bottom and quoted $3.8 million. I dutifully lined up with the dummies who are pretty new when it comes to selling a home. For instead of respecting and honoring my "bottom line," he came back with an offer of $3.1 million. I'd been had!

You might give this tactic some consideration when negotiating on a home or whatever high-priced purchase you have in mind. If you live long enough, my guess is you'll experience opportunities for all life has to offer. So you might as well be prepared to pay for those material matters that are for sale at the lowest possible price.

By now the pressure from the family to close the sale was very intense. Just as I finished wrestling with my thoughts of a further reduction, I was informed he was not proceeding with the negotiations due to newly developed business problems, and everything came to a standstill. Ye gads; I blew it. The game was called off because of darkness, and I mean it was pitch black.

There was, however, one tiny bit of light over the next three months. My daughter Ann saw the couple walking down the beach and around the property on one or two occasions, stopping and pointing out to one another something about the area.

Shortly thereafter we received a call from the realtor. The buyers were back and ready to go. And I might add, so were we. Within a day their offer came in, splitting the difference between 3.8 and 3.1, as they quote million-dollar properties —all cash, no contingencies. The entire family agreed this was a wonderful offer and without further ado we signed our name to the bill of sale. Considering what I had paid for the house, this certainly has to go down as one of the best home sales in all of California.

So, we were truly millionaires, several times over, but it had taken almost a total lifetime. It wasn't as if we were entering a new world, as we might have been if we had won a lottery while working at the gas station. No, we had had more than a taste of what the world had to offer, having been around it several times, including the grand tours with the children, the *QE2*, the Concorde, the grand hotels, the Rolls Royce, the cruise ships, the jewelry, furs, parties, balls, practically all that one can do no matter how wealthy one may be. Perhaps best of all, we had won financial peace of mind—not only for Jane and me, but for all of our kids' lifetimes as well.

The happy days we looked forward to for the rest of our

lives were completely shattered by Jane's sudden demise barely a year after we sold the house. No one in the family has totally recovered from our loss. It's the saddest event of our lives. Everyone has or will experience such a loss to various degrees. Ours was one of the deepest because Jane was a wonderful person, wife, mother, and friend. Damn, damn, damn.

We took leave of our home, which was torn down the day after escrow closed. At least we didn't go through the emotional tear of seeing new people living where we had been for twenty-five years. We had purchased a very unusual townhouse in the heart of the village. It came complete with a private elevator for all three floors, a garden patio in the back, and a sun and garden deck on the roof. So very pleasant. For the first time in our lives, all we had to do was lock the door and fly away whenever we desired. We were so free, so rich in so many ways until. . . .

For three months after Jane's death, living in that townhouse was close to unbearable; every niche of the house brought on the pain of missing her. I was depressed and despondent and knew I had to move on and out quickly.

Before I could make the necessary arrangements to place the house on the market, I was approached by a long-time realtor friend who told me his ex-wife would dearly love to purchase the place. It seemed that her new husband was unable to drive, or whatever, and she was having eye trouble. They definitely wanted to be in the center of the village. The old expression "It only takes one special buyer" held true. They bought it at a price that was profitable, without contingencies, and I was out of there. I began to believe that real estate was my game.

The next problems to solve were, Where would I go? What should I do? The first was solved when I found a house on the ocean just two doors up from our old one. It is so beautiful, absolutely stunning. Its outside deck has a sweeping view of the ocean, and the finely shaped lower lawn leads to the seawall. On the other side is a twenty-yard lap pool and jacuzzi hidden by lovely, rare, Torrey pines and landscaping. On the whole, it is rather small, two bedrooms really, and a quasi-den/bedroom. It has high ceilings with cove lighting and a kitchen so sublime it begs one to start cooking. Above all is the location on the ocean, where at night one can immediately go to sleep to the sound of the waves, breathing the cool sea air under a featherdown comforter, and awaken in the morning to see the sun shining through the turquoise waves. Truly as close to heaven on earth as one can be. I bought it for over, way over, two million dollars, all cash on the barrelhead. It's nice to be able to do it that way without haggling over a mortgage, points, closing costs, all that they put you through, don't you think?

Now I'm back in the office. At first, things were quiet. No more exciting activity with Amana microwave ovens, no more Schwinn bicycles. The only thing we had going was Oakley sunglasses, which I told you about. However, that business was going pretty well, up a million dollars a year in volume over each of the preceding years. That's okay. But I was sitting on my tail wondering what we could do to reignite or rebuild.

Just about the time I was starting to doze off, the phone went "briinnnggg!" My secretary informed me the president of Peugeot North America was on the phone. I picked it up. The man came on to say, "Marc, we are aware of the fine job you have done with the military exchange service and Schwinn. How would you like to represent Peugeot bicycles?"

How would a curled up old firehouse dalmatian named Spot respond to a fire alarm? Well, I can tell you. Put on your helmet, grab your attaché case, slide down the pole, start the engines, turn on the siren, and hit the street and the road. You're going to make a call again, with all the anticipation and eagerness that Spot had back when he was a pup, oh, so many years ago. Here we go again!

As we come to the present it seems to me that all I have aspired to has been achieved and experienced. That it has taken a lifetime is perhaps one of my many imperfections. I have certainly related the hard way of arriving at a millionaire's status. If that is your goal in life, it is possible your road will be made easier by having read about mine. I certainly hope so.

Perhaps a bit of going-away music, so to speak, to cheer you on your way, in the form a chuckle, possibly a laugh, a shake of your head, but certainly a warm feeling all over as when you hear someone say "only in America." Let your favorite song run through your mind, possibly Frank Sinatra's "My Way"; hum along as I offer my farewell thoughts about how you can become more successful in whatever endeavors you undertake so that you too may say in review, "It's been a wonderful life."

First, good health is most precious. With it, you can enjoy the time of your life. Be serious in applying every minute to learning and to worthwhile pursuits. The world is growing smaller; learn languages, gain knowledge, formalize your education and widen its scope by trying to personally experience all that you have seen from the magic carpet. You will then possess the courage, strength, and vision to seize opportunities when they arise. The buying of my new house on the ocean was a combination of all three of these.

It's possible my life's work would have been better devoted to real estate. You will get your best laugh now. Mine is the last one, for a month ago I leased my house for a year for well over a quarter of a million dollars. No doubt this is one of the largest sums ever paid to rent a home in La Jolla, or almost anywhere, certainly for what is described as a two-bedroom house.

Whatever possessed me? I still wonder. Perhaps it was the huge amount of money, although I certainly had no need of it. Was it an ego trip? Look what I have done? Yes, in the past years I've rented it in the summer for about twenty-five thousand a month. But not for a whole year. Well, I'll try it. Especially since these fabulously wealthy people spent more than a hundred thousand dollars to have the house perfectly suited to them—new this, new that, on and on. That certainly is unbelievable, incredible, but that's what happened.

What is flabbergasting is how hard I've worked all my life to reach my present financial level. And here people come along and pay me, plus putting into my home more money in one year than I made in the first twenty years of my working life. Let's all shake our heads together. Life isn't fair; it's really as cruel and as beautiful as the sea.

Now I've just returned from my first visit to Russia. Ye gads. What a country. They need and want everything we have in the West. Makes you want to pack your bag and cover the territory. I'm ready. My company is ready. I'm a salesman. That's all I've ever been. That's all I want to be. I'm free.

La Jolla, California
April 12, 1995

If you have enjoyed *The Life of a Salesman* and wish to share your thoughts or comments with the author, you may do so at the address listed below.

Should you wish to order additional copies for friends, family, or perhaps your business sales staff, you may do so by phone or mail. The cost is $23 per book, plus $3 for postage and handling. We accept Visa, Mastercard, and American Express.

Phone: 1-800-975-7355

You may also send your check or money order to:

IMC
Post Office Box 1436
La Jolla, CA  92038

———

P.S.  To order a copy of *The Kids First Microwave Cookbook*, please send $7 (inclusive of postage and handling) to the address above.